ESSENTIAL ENGLISH
BOOK FOUR

KING'S COLLEGE CHAPEL, CAMBRIDGE (see p. 220)

ESSENTIAL ENGLISH

for
Foreign Students

BOOK FOUR

revised edition

by

C. È. ECKERSLEY

LONGMAN

LONGMAN GROUP LIMITED
Longman House, Burnt Mill,
Harlow, Essex CM20 2JE, England
and Associated Companies throughout the World.

First Published 1942
Third edition 1963
*Twelfth impression *1984*

ISBN 0 582 52020 7

Illustrations by
James Moss and John Barber

> **ESSENTIAL ENGLISH**
> **BOOK FOUR**
> **TEACHER'S BOOK**
> with
> Teaching notes, additional lesson
> material, Dictation Exercises and
> a Key to the Exercises

Printed in Hong Kong by
Commonwealth Printing Press Ltd

PREFACE

REVISED EDITIONS of Books I, II and III of *Essential English* have already been produced; this present edition brings Book IV into line with its three companion volumes. The book has been completely overhauled; those parts that the experience of teachers and students had proved to be of interest and value have been retained, the rest has been replaced by newer and, it is hoped, more interesting, material. In this task I have had most generous and valuable assistance from teachers and students in all parts of the world, both in conversations that I have had with them and in letters they have written to me. One thing that particularly impressed me in these letters and conversations was the lively interest that was shown in the "characters" of the book—especially in Hob! I have therefore tried to tell something more about them in this book; to reveal the mystery of Hob that has aroused so much curiosity; to follow Jan's romance; to see Olaf and Pedro and Lucille leaving Mr. Priestley's class and starting out in life. The scene, too, has widened. Thanks to Hob's somewhat unusual relatives we get something of the atmosphere of the industrial north; with the aid of Olaf we visit Scotland, from Pedro we hear about Cambridge and (a completely new departure) there is a leap across the Atlantic. In "The American Scene" Lucille records her lively impressions of life in America, and Mr. Priestley, in addition to his talks on some of the more picturesque events and outstanding figures in English history and literature, touches also on the history and literature of America.

On the linguistic side, attention is paid to some of the points of formal grammar not previously dealt with, e.g. the infinitive, participles, gerunds, the complement, word order, etc. There is, too, a full treatment of prepositions, and particular stress has been laid on the usage of the chief phrasal verbs.

In this book, as in previous ones, copious exercises have been provided with each lesson. Some of these, e.g. the "Comprehension Exercises", have been modelled on the type of question

v

set in the Cambridge Lower Certificate examination and are at about the same level of difficulty, so that the student who has worked through this volume should find this work of assistance in preparing for that examination.

C.E.E.

ACKNOWLEDGMENTS

For permission to use copyright material I am indebted to Mr. John Murray for "A Message to the Public" from *Scott's Last Expedition*; to Messrs. Samuel French Ltd. for the play *Wanted—Mr. Stuart* by Arthur Watkyn; and to the University of Cambridge Local Examinations Syndicate for the use of a past *English Composition and Language* paper of the Lower Certificate in English examination.

CONTENTS

Each lesson is followed by exercises based on it

LESSON 1

Readers of the earlier books of *Essential English* I, II, and III will remember that the lessons are built round a little group of characters, the teacher, Mr. Priestley and his wife, the students, Lucille, Frieda, Olaf, Jan, Pedro and Hob. Book IV completes the story of the students, and when this book closes we shall have seen them all leaving Mr. Priestley and going out into the world. At the end of Book III we saw that Frieda and Jan had fallen in love with each other; so, naturally, Book IV opens with the announcement of their engagement.

Frieda and Jan Break the News

SCENE: MR. PRIESTLEY'S *living-room*

Characters—MR. PRIESTLEY, MRS. PRIESTLEY, FRIEDA, JAN

JAN: Mr. Priestley, Mrs. Priestley, there's something I—we—want to tell you. Frieda and I are engaged to be married.

MRS. PRIESTLEY: Oh, how nice!

MR. PRIESTLEY: Congratulations and best wishes!

FRIEDA and JAN: Thank you both very much.

FRIEDA: You are the first people we have told—except for my parents.

JAN: Yes, I wrote to Frieda's father a week ago, telling him we wanted to get married and asking for his permission.

I

FRIEDA: And we had replies this morning; it's all right and they are very happy about it.

MRS. PRIESTLEY: Oh! I'm so glad.

JAN: You don't look very surprised at the news.

MRS. PRIESTLEY: I'm not surprised—I'd expected it for months[1]—but I'm very pleased indeed.

MR. PRIESTLEY: I might as well admit that it's a complete surprise to me—I never notice things even when they are right under my nose—but I'm really delighted at the news. I think you are very lucky, Jan, to get such a girl as Frieda.

MRS. PRIESTLEY: And I think you are very fortunate, Frieda, to get such a fine fellow as Jan. I hope you will be very happy together.

MR. PRIESTLEY: Are you thinking of getting married soon?

FRIEDA: Well, that's one of the things we are not agreed on. As you know, Jan is starting at London University in October to study to become a doctor. He wants us to get married at once. I would rather wait for a year or two—at any rate until Jan has taken his first examination.

JAN: But what's the point of waiting?

FRIEDA: So that you can really work hard. Don't you think, Mr. Priestley, that he would think about his work more if I wasn't there?

JAN: But don't you see that if we were not married I should be thinking about you all the time and wanting to be with you instead of working. Whereas if we were married——

[1] You will probably remember her remarks to Mr. Priestley, *Essential English*, Book III, p. 301.

FRIEDA: Do you hear that? Once we are married he won't think about me any more. That's a fine thing to hear from a man you have just become engaged to.

JAN: Oh, Frieda, you know I didn't mean that. I only meant——

FRIEDA: But that's not the only thing we don't agree on.

MR. PRIESTLEY (*smiling*): Dear me, this sounds terrible. What is the further cause of disagreement?

FRIEDA: Well, I want to live in a house; Jan thinks we ought to have a flat or rooms in a house.

JAN: A friend told me of a small flat in the centre of London overlooking King's Cross station that will be vacant in October.

FRIEDA: But I don't want to live in a small flat in the centre of London. I'd much rather have a little house in the country looking out on fields, where I can breathe fresh air and see trees and hear birds singing.

JAN: But a flat is so much more convenient. We could get some labour-saving devices that would save you a lot of housework, and there are lots of little restaurants near King's Cross where we could go out for something to eat in the evening so you wouldn't need to cook meals.

FRIEDA: But I *want* to cook meals. I'm really quite a good cook, and I don't mind doing housework. I like it. Besides, I looked at the flat you are talking about and I didn't like the look of it at all.

JAN: I agree it wasn't very attractive-looking, but the rent was low.

FRIEDA: You know, I don't like the idea of paying rent. My parents have paid rent on our house for thirty years. I wish I had all the money they have paid in rent. They've paid enough to buy the house twice over and yet they don't own a single brick of it.

JAN: Yes, I agree. I should like to buy a house, but we haven't the money, at least not now; in four or five years' time it may be different. You see, Mr. Priestley, it's like this. My grandfather, my mother's father—he was a Scotsman—left me a sum of money in his will, and some useless property, a factory; but the money is in trust until I am twenty-five. I get the income from it, and that has been enough to keep me and pay for my classes; with a bit of a struggle, it will just about keep us both—at least I hope so. But we've no hope of buying a house—at least not for a time. So if we *must* pay rent, let's pay the least we can and have a flat.

FRIEDA: Oh dear, I do wish I could have a house all to myself, with a garden where I can grow flowers and lettuces and cabbages. I was so looking forward to it. Isn't there any way we could buy one?

MR. PRIESTLEY: I don't want to look as if I was poking my nose into what isn't my business, but——

FRIEDA: Oh, we don't mind; we'd welcome your ideas, wouldn't we, Jan?

JAN: Yes, rather! But don't you agree with me, Mr. Priestley, that it would be much better to be married soon and live in a flat and not wait a year or two as Frieda says.

FRIEDA: Don't you think it would be better to wait until we can get a house and not live in a flat? Isn't that what we ought to do?

MR. PRIESTLEY: Well, I'm not going to say what you *ought* to do.

MRS. PRIESTLEY: Neither am I.

MR. PRIESTLEY: But I know what you *will* do.

MRS. PRIESTLEY: And so do I.

MR. PRIESTLEY: You'll get married soon and not wait.

JAN: Very good!

MRS. PRIESTLEY: And you'll have a house and not a flat or rooms.

FRIEDA: Hurrah! That's what I say.

MR. PRIESTLEY: Well, if that's what's going to happen I should like to make a suggestion if I may.

JAN and FRIEDA: Oh yes; please do.

MR. PRIESTLEY: Well, you know you could buy a house through a Building Society. You look round, choose the house you want to buy and then approach the Building Society. You put down a proportion of the money—say ten per cent—and pay off the rest at so much a month. The monthly payments will not be much more than a rent would be, and you will have the satisfaction of knowing that your payments go towards buying the house.

JAN: Well, there's probably something in that, but——

FRIEDA: Oh, Jan, it would be lovely. As a matter of fact I've been looking round and I've already seen the house I want.

JAN: What!

FRIEDA: Yes. You know that little cottage, Mrs. Priestley, that you see from the back of your garden?

MR. PRIESTLEY: What, the one in Darvell Lane, "Rose Cottage" I think it is called?

FRIEDA: That's the one. I heard it was for sale so I went round there at once. It has a comfortable little sitting-room, a tiny but very nice dining-room, a kitchen, three bedrooms and a bathroom. There are roses round the front door and an apple-tree in the garden.

MRS. PRIESTLEY: Frieda, it sounds perfect.

FRIEDA: It is. But what's the use of it? Jan would prefer to live in London overlooking King's Cross with millions of people all round us.

JAN: Well, if it would make Frieda happy I don't mind living in a house in the country, and I'm quite willing to dig the garden for her.

FRIEDA: That's the way to talk, darling. I certainly *would* like it. I've saved a bit of money and that would help towards buying the furniture. We shouldn't need very much for a start. I don't mind how simply we live. I would do all my own work and clean the house and cook the meals. Oh, it would be lovely!

JAN: Yes, it certainly sounds very nice when you put it like that, but all the money I have in the world will only just keep us and pay for my studies at the University. How much do they want for this house of yours?

FRIEDA: They are asking £3,800, but we might get it for £3,600 or £3,650. We would have to put down about £360 to £370.

JAN: Sorry, Frieda. I wish I could do it but it just can't be done.

MR. PRIESTLEY: Look here, Jan; as I said, I don't want to poke my nose into your affairs but I have a bit of capital, £300 or £400 in the bank doing nothing, and I'd much rather lend it to you if that would help you than have it there doing nothing.

JAN: Oh, Mr. Priestley, that's very kind of you, but I couldn't accept that from you.

MR. PRIESTLEY: Nonsense. You can pay me back easily when you become a successful doctor—as I am sure you will. So that's settled. We'll say no more about it now, but come to my study afterwards and we'll talk it over together. . . . Bless my soul, Frieda! What are you crying for?

FRIEDA: I'm—'m—not crying. I'm just happy, that's all.

VERB STUDY (I): **look**

In this book we shall consider a number of verbs each of which can have a variety of meanings. This is particularly the case when the verb is used with a preposition or an adverb, e.g. *go on* working, *give up* smoking, *burst out* crying, *keep on* trying, etc. Verbs like this are sometimes called "phrasal verbs". One of the aims of Lesson 1 was to illustrate the uses of *look*.[1] You will find these examples there:

> I *looked at* the flat. I was *looking forward* to having a house. I don't want to *look as if* I was poking my nose into what isn't my business. *Look here*, Jan. A house *looking out on* fields. I don't want to live in the centre of London and *look over* King's Cross. A part of London *overlooking* King's Cross. It has a small but *pleasant-looking* dining-room. You *look round* and choose the house you want.

EXERCISES

I. *Word Study: Use the following words, taken from Lesson 1, in sentences of your own:*

> engaged (use also *engagement*. What is an engagement ring?) Make sentences using *engaged to*, *engaged in*, *engaged with*; congratulations (and the verb *congratulate*), admit (note two meanings; use also *admission*), whereas, agreement (What is the opposite?), flat (two meanings), breathe (also *breath*; note the difference in pronunciation), rent, brick, lettuce (give the names of three other vegetables), suggestion (also *suggest*), approach, proportion, dig, furniture (mention four different articles of furniture), capital (make three sentences using one of these phrases in each, "a capital letter", "the capital of England", "capital in the bank").

II. *Use the following in sentences of your own:*

> look at; look for; look forward to; look after; look as if; look like; look as though; look down on; look into; look someone up; look on; onlooker; look something up; the look of; have a look at.

III. *Show the difference between* look out *and* outlook; *to* look over *and* to overlook.

[1] Further examples and explanations of this verb and all the other verbs discussed are given in the *Teacher's Book* IV.

IV. Make sentences of your own, using want; should like; would rather; it would be better; prefer; I don't mind; wish; I'm quite willing.

V. Use each of the following idioms in a sentence of your own:

to lead a person by the nose; to pay through the nose; as plain as the nose on your face; to keep one's nose to the grindstone; to poke one's nose into other people's business; can't see beyond his own nose; to turn one's nose up at.

VI. Explain:
1. "Look before you leap."
2. "Lookers-on see most of the game."
3. "Don't look a gift horse in the mouth."

VII. Write a short story to illustrate one of the proverbs in Exercise VI.

VIII. Describe:
1. "Frieda's house."
2. How to buy a house through a Building Society.

IX. Composition Exercises

1. Your ideal house.
2. "Life in the country or life in the town." Which do you prefer?
3. Would you rather live in a house or a flat? Discuss the advantages and disadvantages of each

X. Study the pictures on p. 10 and rewrite the story they tell.

GOOD DOG!

LESSON 2

Some Personal Letters

I

JAN TO FRIEDA'S PARENTS

This was the letter that Jan wrote:

DEAR PROFESSOR and MRS. LANG,

I don't know whether this letter will come as a surprise to you, for I think you must have seen during the happy time I spent in your home last Christmas, how very fond I was of Frieda. We have worked together every day at Mr. Priestley's, and for some time now I have realised that the friendship and affection that I have always had for her had turned to love. I hardly dared to hope that Frieda felt the same way towards me, but last night I told her of my love and asked her to marry me, and to my great joy she said Yes. I hope you will feel that she and I have known each other long enough to be quite sure in our own minds that we love each other and want, more than anything else in the world, to be married. It would make us both very happy to know that our engagement would have your approval and blessing, and so I am writing formally to ask for your consent.

I realise that there is very little that I can offer
Frieda materially. I have only a small private income
on which to live until I qualify as a doctor, but Frieda
is quite confident that under her careful management
we can have a comfortable little home on it. For my
part, I will devote my life to ensuring that she will
be as happy as all my love can make her.

My best wishes to you both.

Yours sincerely,
JAN SOLSKI.

II

PROFESSOR LANG TO JAN

MY DEAR JAN,

My wife and I are both very happy at the thought
that you and Frieda want to be married. Thank you
for writing to us as you did. Let me say at once that
we both gladly give our consent and blessing to your
engagement. Though we have only met you once
when you came here for a short time last Christmas,
we all grew very fond of you during that time, and
Frieda s letters home have been so full of you that
we both feel as if we had known you for years. The
dearest wish of us all is for Frieda's happiness, and
her letter to her mother today leaves us in no doubt
about that or the cause of her happiness.

Thank you, too, for being so frank about your
financial position. I have no doubt that life will not
be easy at first for Frieda and you and it may be
difficult at times to make ends meet on your small

income. But when love is there, the struggle will only draw you closer together. I believe the English have a saying, "When poverty comes in at the door, love flies out at the window." Don't believe it! When my wife and I were married, my income was probably smaller than yours and we have never been rich, but I know, beyond any doubt, that that English saying is not true, and I am sure you will find the same. We are all longing to see you both soon—and that may be earlier than you think, but I'm leaving that news to my wife who is writing today to Frieda, so I will merely say now, "Congratulations and bless you both."

Yours sincerely,
JOHANN LANG.

III

MRS. LANG TO FRIEDA

MY DARLING FRIEDA,

Your letter to me and Jan's to your father have made us both very happy. There is no one we would rather have for a son-in-law than Jan and we are both delighted to welcome to our family someone of whom we are both so fond, and I am sure this is one occasion when the old saying about "not losing a daughter but gaining a son" is the simple truth. Our hope and prayer is that you may both continue through life always as happy as you are now. We are all longing to see you both again soon—and now comes my great news. Today your father received an invitation to come to Oxbridge University for a year to give a

course of lectures on Philosophy. He is going to accept
the offer, and we shall all of us be coming to stay in
England. A house will be provided for us in Oxbridge
and we are hoping you will be married from there
and that we shall meet your friends Mr. and Mrs.
Priestley, Lucille, Olaf, Pedro and Hob. Need I tell
you that Hob is the one that Hans and Peter are most
wanting to meet. Gretchen and Ruth are hoping that
you will want them to be bridesmaids at your wedding and are already planning the dresses that they
will wear.

You must take me to
Harridges and help me to
choose my dress and hat for
the wedding, and Jan and
Pedro must take your father
firmly in hand and get him to
go with them to that place
in London where you can
hire clothes and arrange for
him to be fitted for a
morning coat and top-hat,
otherwise he will turn up at
the wedding to give you

MORNING COAT AND TOP-HAT

away in his old tweed jacket and gardening
trousers! Isn't everything wonderful! I can hardly
wait for the day when we shall all be together again.

God bless you both, my dear.

All my love,
MOTHER.

VERB STUDY (2): **come**

In this lesson there are several sentences with *come*, e.g., "This letter will *come* as a surprise"; "You *came* here last Christmas"; "When poverty *comes in* . . ."; "Now *comes* my great news"; ". . . an invitation to *come* to Oxbridge"; "We shall *be coming* to stay in England". There are many phrasal verbs formed with *come*. Here are some examples:

I *came across* (= met accidentally) Joe Smith yesterday; I hadn't seen him for ten years.

"How did you *come by* (= obtain) this book?" "I *came across* (= found) it in a second-hand bookshop.

I knocked at the door and he cried, "*Come in.*"

Don't throw those small pieces of cloth away; they'll probably *come in useful* (= be of use) some day.

"What day does that magazine *come out*?" "It *comes out* (= is published) every Wednesday."

When does he *come of age*? (= reach the age of twenty-one).

Come away from that machine or you may get hurt.

Hob didn't *come down* (= come downstairs) for breakfast until 10 o'clock.

My shoe-lace has *come undone*.

PREPOSITIONS (1)

Prepositions are used with nouns or pronouns to make a phrase. This phrase (a PREPOSITIONAL PHRASE) sometimes does the work of an adverb, e.g.

He stood *behind me* (Place).
I saw him *at six o'clock* (Time).
He came *on foot* (Manner).
She died *of a fever* (Cause).

Or it may do the work of an adjective, i.e. by telling more about a noun, e.g.

> He bought a coat *with a fur collar*.
> The girl *with fair hair* is Frieda's sister.
> She wore a dress *of silk*.

Many prepositions are also used as adverbs, e.g.

> She put the books *in* the bookcase (Preposition).
> Come *in* and rest (Adverb).
>
> The garage is *behind* the house (Preposition).
> The carriage approached; there were motor cyclists in front and cars *behind* (Adverb).
>
> She walked *round* the garden (Preposition).
> Go in and look *round* (Adverb).
>
> The kitten ran *up* the ladder (Preposition).
> The price of butter has gone *up*.

Where the word is a preposition it is used with, and followed by, a noun or pronoun and makes a phrase ("in the bookcase"; "behind the house"; "round the garden"; "up the ladder"). When it is an adverb it is used with a verb and is not followed by a noun ("Come in"; "were behind"; "look round"; "gone up"). In the exercise on p. 181 and the exercises in the *Teacher's Book*, pp. 95–6, where you are asked to put in the prepositions, the word "preposition" stands for "preposition or adverb".

Prepositions mainly express TIME (e.g. *after, before, since, till*, etc.) or PLACE (e.g. *above, across, over, towards, under*, etc.), but they express many other ideas, and though an attempt has been made in the lessons that follow, it is almost impossible to give their "meanings"; and though I state that *in*, for example, expresses "position" in such a sentence as, "He lives *in* London", that *by* expresses "time" in "He travelled *by* night", or that *from* expresses "cause" in "She is suffering *from* a bad headache", these ideas are expressed not really by the preposition but by the PREPOSITIONAL PHRASES in which they are used, *in London*; *by night*; *from a bad headache*. So the simplest and by far the best way is to learn them by examples. In the lessons that follow (and in the "Further Examples and Exercises" in the *Teacher's Book*) examples of the various uses of the most usual prepositions will be given.

EXERCISES

I. *Word Study: Use the following in sentences:*

whether (also *weather*), fond, hardly (How does this differ from *hard*?), approval (What is the corresponding verb?), formally, confident (use also *confidence* and *confidential*), devote (also *devotion*), ensure (also *insure, assure, insurance, assurance*), frank (Is this the same as *Frank*?), congratulations, invitation (use also *invite*), a *course* of lectures (use also *of course, in the course of, a racecourse*), bridesmaid (also *bride, bridegroom*), hire (What is *hire purchase*?), tweed (What is it? How did it get its name?), to *turn up* (idiomatic).

II. *Give the opposites of the following and use each opposite in a sentence:*

approval; blessing; consent; income; doubt (*noun*); poverty; comfortable; careful; sincere; formal; close together; friendship.

III. *Explain or express in another way:*

1. I hardly dared to hope. 2. There is very little that I can offer Frieda materially. 3. Her letter leaves us in no doubt. 4. We know beyond all doubt. 5. Thank you for being so frank about your financial position. 6. It may be difficult to make ends meet. 7. We are all longing to see you. 8. "When poverty comes in at the door, love flies out at the window." 9. You must take your father firmly in hand. 10. To my great joy.

IV. *Use in sentences of your own:*

come down; come up ; come in; come out; come by; come away; come in useful; come of age.

V. *Composition Exercises*

Write a composition or short story having for its title one of the following:

It will come in useful.
The coming-of-age party.
All things come to him who waits (*Proverb*).

If you are a girl, write (*a*) the letter that Frieda might have written to her mother; (*b*) a letter to Frieda from a girl friend who has just heard about her engagement.

If you are a man, write (*a*) the letter that Frieda's father might have written to her; (*b*) a letter from a man friend congratulating Jan on his engagement.

LESSON 3

Invitations and Requests

Some general information about letter-writing—
the writing of an address, the greeting and the
ending—has already been given you,[1] but some other
matters about letter-writing can now be considered;
first of all the sending out of formal invitations, etc.

Now that Jan and Frieda are engaged, Jan has
had a notice put in *The Times*.

FORTHCOMING MARRIAGES

Mr. J. Solski and Miss F. Lang

The engagement is announced, and the marriage will take
place shortly, between Jan, only son of the late Dr. and Mrs.
Solski of Poland, and Frieda, eldest daughter of Professor
and Mrs. Lang of Oakwood, 25 The Parks, Oxbridge.

Then about a fortnight before the wedding Professor
and Mrs. Lang will send out invitations to the wedding. The one that Mr. and Mrs. Priestley received is
shown on the next page. Notice that the invitation
is not in the first person, i.e., not "We should like
you to come...", but in the third person, "Professor
and Mrs. Lang request the company of...". So it will
read something like this:

[1] *Essential English* II, pp. 98–100.

Professor and Mrs. Lang
request the pleasure of the company of

Mr & Mrs Priestley

on the occasion of the marriage of their daughter

Frieda

to

Mr. Jan Solski

at St. Peter's Church, Oxbridge,
on Saturday, 2nd September, at 2.30 p.m.

and to the reception afterwards at the Royal Hotel.

25 *The Parks,*   R.S.V.P.
Oxbridge.

A formal invitation requires a formal reply also in the third person. Mr. and Mrs. Priestley's reply was:

> Mr. and Mrs. Priestley have much pleasure in accepting Professor and Mrs. Lang's invitation to the wedding of their daughter on 2nd September.

There is, as you see, no greeting ("Dear Professor and Mrs. Lang") and no "Complimentary close" ("Yours sincerely", etc.).

If the persons invited are not able to attend the wedding they may send a formal refusal, e.g.

> Dr. Theophilus Hobdell thanks Professor and Mrs. Lang for their invitation to their daughter's wedding, but much regrets that as he has to conduct an examination of Third-Year students at his College on that date,[1] he is unable to accept.

[1] Other reasons given might be "owing to a previous engagement . . .", "as business matters necessitate his absence from the district", "as he will be away on holiday . . ." etc.

If an invitation from a friend or acquaintance is being refused, a reason should always be given. With a completely impersonal invitation a reason is unnecessary, e.g.

Invitation (Formal)

[ER]

The Lord Chamberlain is commanded by

Her Majesty to invite

Mr & Mrs Priestley

to an afternoon Party in the Garden of Buckingham Palace on Thursday, the 14th July 19— from 4 to 6 o'clock p.m.

Morning Dress or Uniform or Lounge Suit.

Acceptance

Mr. and Mrs. Priestley have much pleasure in accepting the invitation to the afternoon party in the Garden of Buckingham Palace on Thursday, the 14th July 19—

Refusal

Mr. and Mrs. Priestley regret that they will not be able to be present at the afternoon party in the Garden of Buckingham Palace on Thursday, the 14th July 19—

If the invitation is from a close friend, and you are refusing it, it would be preferable to write a personal letter (i.e. not in the third person).

You will note, by the way, that the order of names in the invitation, on a letter and on the envelope, is:

"Mr. and Mrs. Priestley" *or* "Mr. and Mrs. Charles Priestley",
"Dr. and Mrs. W. G. C. Kennedy" etc.

This is one of the occasions when the rule "ladies first" does not apply. Note, too, that before titles like *Professor*, *Dr.*, *Captain*, etc., we do not write *Mr.*

Formal invitations are generally used only for the larger, more elaborate social happenings, a wedding, a banquet, an important reception. A formal invitation should always include husband and wife in the case of married couples; you never invite the husband without the wife or *vice versa*[1] unless it is a purely male function or an afternoon tea-party for women only.

It may happen that the arrangements that you have planned have to be cancelled. In that case a newspaper announcement will be made or a formal letter sent (or, if time does not allow that, a telegram), e.g.

Mr. and Mrs. Forbes beg to announce that the marriage of their daughter Rosamund Joan and Captain George Osborne arranged for September 15th will not take place.

*   *   *

Mr. and Mrs. Kenneth Harris regret that owing to the severe illness of their son it is necessary to cancel the party planned for February 12th.

---

[1] *vice versa* ['vaisi 'və:sə] (Latin) = put the other way round; in this case = ". . . or the wife without the husband".

There are, of course, other ways of giving invitations besides the formal ones, e.g.

DEAR MRS. BROWN,

Richard and I would be very pleased if you and your husband could join us for dinner on Thursday, Jan. 9th at 7.30 p.m. A friend of ours, Mr. John Chapman, will be with us. He is going out to Uganda shortly and would very much like to hear of your experiences there.

Yours sincerely,
MARY RIDGEWELL.

Acceptance

DEAR MRS. RIDGEWELL,

Thank you very much for your kind invitation to dinner on Thursday, Jan. 9th. Both my husband and I accept with great pleasure, and Jack will bring along some colour photographs which he took in Uganda. We look forward to meeting Mr. Chapman.

Yours sincerely,
ELIZABETH BROWN.

Refusal

DEAR MRS. RIDGEWELL,

Thank you so much for your kind invitation to dinner on Thursday, Jan. 9th. Unfortunately, Jack is away on business in Edinburgh and will not be returning until Saturday and so we are unable to accept. I am sure he will be as sorry as I am to miss the pleasure of dining with you and meeting Mr. Chapman.

Yours sincerely,
ELIZABETH BROWN.

With close friends the letters would be even more informal, e.g.

MY DEAR JACK,

We are having a bit of a party next Wednesday, the 6th, and I hope you and Ann are free on that evening and can come and join us, say about eight o'clock. There'll be about a dozen of us—all people that you know. I do hope you can manage it.

Yours always,
BILL.

Acceptance

MY DEAR BILL,

Thank you for the invitation to your party on the 6th. Ann and I will be delighted to come. It seems ages since I saw you and I'm looking forward to a good old chat with you.

All the best,
JACK.

Refusal

MY DEAR BILL,

Thank you for the invitation to your party on the 6th. We'd have loved to come but Ann's mother is staying with us just now and I have booked three seats for *My Fair Lady* for the 6th. Isn't it bad luck ? I was saying to Ann only a day or two ago what a time it was since we saw Angela and you. I'll give you a ring sometime next week and we must fix up to have dinner together.

Give our kindest regards to Angela.

Yours as ever,
JACK.

Invitation to stay the week-end

DEAR PETER,

I wonder if you are free to come and spend the week-end, June 7th to 9th, with us here. It is so long since we saw you and we are dying to hear about your experiences abroad. There will be no one here except Roger and you and me so we can have a real good talk together, and hear some Chopin on the piano again. I do hope you can come. Roger can meet the 12.45 from Victoria, which arrives here at 3.20: that's your best train.

Looking forward very much to seeing you,

Yours sincerely,
MARY CLARKE.

Acceptance

Dear Mary,

Thank you very much indeed for your kind invitation to stay the week-end June 7–9 at your home. I shall be delighted to come. I'll get the 12.45 from Victoria as you suggest and am looking forward with the greatest pleasure to seeing you and Roger again.

All good wishes,

Yours sincerely,

PETER.

Refusal

Dear Mary,

Thank you very much for your kind invitation to spend the week-end at your home, but I'm afraid I can't accept it. I'm very sorry indeed for I have the most happy memories of the last week-end I spent with you and Roger. You may remember I was keen on hiking. Well, I am now secretary of a hiking club and one of our walks is fixed for that very week-end. As I am leading it, I feel I must go, but I am most terribly disappointed; I only hope you will ask me again for some other week-end and that I shall have better luck that time.

Kindest regards to Roger and you,

Yours very sincerely,

PETER.

VERBAL INVITATIONS

There are several ways of giving, accepting or refusing verbal invitations, for example:

On the tennis court

Invitation: Would you care to make up a four at tennis with us ?
Acceptance: Thanks, I should be very pleased to. OR:
Delighted. Thank you. OR:
With pleasure. Thanks. OR:
Yes, I don't mind.

Refusal: Sorry, I'm not playing at present, I've sprained my wrist. OR:

Sorry. I've already fixed up with Jack and Tom and Fred; they'll be here any minute now.

At tea

Hostess: Will you have another cup of tea? OR:

Can I give you another cup of tea? OR:

Try a piece of this cake; it's home made.

Won't you have another scone?

Acceptance: Yes, please. OR:

Thank you, I will.

Refusal: No, thank you. OR:

I'm sure the cake is $\Big\}$ delicious, but I'm afraid I
The scones are $\quad$ couldn't. Thank you.

Note, too, the use of the imperative in invitations, e.g. *Have* a cigarette. *Come* and meet my wife.

Very Informal Invitations

Joe: "Let's go to the cinema, shall we?"
Susan: "I'd love to. Let's."

*   *   *   *   *

Jack: $\left\{ \begin{array}{l} \text{Who's for} \\ \text{Who says} \end{array} \right\}$ a game of tennis?
George, Alice, Mary: Me![1]

*   *   *   *   *

Jim: $\left\{ \begin{array}{l} \text{Who's for} \\ \text{Who says} \end{array} \right\}$ a dip in the sea?
Mary: Not me! It's too cold.

*   *   *   *   *

Bill: $\left\{ \begin{array}{l} \text{How} \\ \text{What} \end{array} \right\}$ about a drink, Tom?
Tom: A good idea!

[1] No one—not even a teacher—would use the more grammatical "I".

Bill: What'll you have?
Tom: I'll have a dry sherry, thanks.
Both together: Cheers![1]

"WHAT'S IT TO BE?"

(*A little later*)
Tom: Now, Bill, { you must have one with me. / this one's on me. } What's it to be?
Bill: Thanks, I'll have the same again—dry sherry.

JAN: Talking about accepting invitations reminds me of a little poem I once saw. It's called:

The Perfect Guest

She answered by return of post
The invitation of her host.
She caught the train she said she would
And changed at Taunton as she should.
She brought a small and lightish box
And keys belonging to the locks.

.   .   .   .

She left no little things behind,
Excepting loving thoughts and kind.

[1] Sometimes "Good Health!", "Here's to you!" (*to* stressed), "All the best!"

VERB STUDY (3): **take**

The essential meanings of *take* are:

1. *grasp, seize, receive*, e.g.

    He *took my hand* and shook it in a friendly manner.
    I can't *take money* from you.
    He was *taken prisoner*.
    Pedro *took the first prize* for English.

2. *carry, have with one*, e.g.

    Will you *take* this letter to the post for me?
    If you are going to Scotland *take* your overcoat; you'll need it.
    I'm going to *take the dog for a walk*.

3. The general meaning of *have, get, make use of, need*, e.g.

    Do you *take* sugar in your tea?
    I'll *take* a pound of sugar and half a pound of butter.
    I *took* the train from Oslo to Stockholm, and then I *took* a taxi to Olaf's house.
    To make this cake, *take* a pound of flour, two eggs, etc.
    It *takes* five hours to go from London to Manchester by train.
    "It *takes* two to make a quarrel." (*Proverb.*)
    "*Take care of* the pennies and the pounds will *take care of* themselves." (*Proverb.*)

4. *remove*, e.g.

    Someone has *taken* my book.
    Take that knife away from baby.
    If you *take* 8½d. from 1s. you have 3½d. left.
    Take your shoes *off*; they are wet through.

EXERCISES

I. *You have received the following invitation:*
Dr. and Mrs. Wallis request the pleasure of the company of Mr. and Mrs. Smith (*yourself and wife*) to dinner on Thursday, 10th October at 7 p.m.
Write two replies, one accepting, the other refusing.

II. *You intend to hold a cocktail party. Write a formal invitation to Mr. and Mrs. John Ledger and their 21-year-old daughter. Show also how you would address the envelope.*

III. *Write* (a) *an invitation to a friend and his wife to spend Christmas at your home;* (b) *an acceptance;* (c) *a refusal.*

IV. *You have advertised your car for sale. Write to a prospective buyer who has enquired about it asking him to call and see the car and discuss its purchase with you.*

V. *Without looking at your book, fit in Bill's remarks in this conversation that appeared on pp. 26–7:*
 Bill: " . . . . ?"
 Tom: A good idea!
 Bill: " . . . . ?"
 Tom: I'll have a dry sherry, thanks.
 Both together: . . . . !
 and, a little later, Tom's return invitation, and Bill's reply.

VI. *Use in sentences of your own:*
take in; take into one's head; take off; take charge of; take time; take down; take up; take a fancy to; take advantage of; take a pride in.

LESSON 4

Football

SCENE: MR. PRIESTLEY'S *room*. MR. PRIESTLEY *and* HOB *at work. Enter* FRIEDA

FRIEDA: Oh, Mr. Priestley, are you very busy?

MR. PRIESTLEY: Well, I was just going to give Hob a private lesson, but what's the matter? You look very excited.

FRIEDA: I must tell you my news. Jan has been chosen to play football for London against Oxford University.

MR. PRIESTLEY: That's splendid! He must be very pleased about it, isn't he?

FRIEDA: Yes, he is, although he doesn't say much. The match is next Thursday at three o'clock.

HOB: I say, couldn't we all go and see it and shout for Jan's team?

MR. PRIESTLEY: We mustn't neglect our work, Hob. If you want to learn English you have to work, not go watching football.

HOB: But sir, you needn't sit in a classroom to learn English. Why, I went to see a football match last Saturday and I learned a lot of words I had never heard in this classroom.

MR. PRIESTLEY: I can quite believe it!

HOB: And besides, sir, you know, a fellow mustn't work *too* much. As the proverb says, "All work and no play makes Jack a dull boy."

MR. PRIESTLEY: You needn't worry, Hob. You will never be made dull by too much work.

HOB: But football, sir, is very important. You know the saying, "The battle of Waterloo was won on the playing-fields of Eton."[1]

MR. PRIESTLEY: Yes, I've heard it—though I'm doubtful how many of the soldiers who fought at Waterloo had ever been to Eton.

HOB: You know, sir, I think sport must be in an Englishman's blood, they just have to play football.

MR. PRIESTLEY: There's probably something in that. Henry VIII[2] passed a law to say that men mustn't play football because it took them away from archery. But it didn't stop football in England.

HOB: That reminds me of my young cousin Ted— Uncle Ben's son. He's only a lad of nine, but he's mad on football. I was staying at Uncle Ben's house in Lancashire a week or two ago, and on Saturday young Ted didn't come home for dinner. However, he turned up about three o'clock and I said, "Hello, Ted, what have you been doing?"

TED: I was playing football in the street and a policeman came up and said, "Here, young

[1] Eton = famous English school near Windsor about 20 miles from London.

[2] Henry VIII reigned 1509–47.

man, you mustn't play football in the street."
Well, as soon as he went away I started playing
again. He came back and said, "Didn't I say
you mustn't play football in the street? Go on,
run off home." Well, I just waited till he turned
the corner and I started playing again—and then
he came again and caught me.

HOB: Oh, what did he do?

TED: He said, "Now you'll have to come to the police-
station to see the sergeant."

HOB: He said you were to go the police-station, did
he, and what did the sergeant say?

TED: He pretended to be angry, but he's a friend of
Uncle Albert's and he used to play football for
Manchester City himself when he was younger,
and after he'd talked to me he asked me if I'd
had any dinner, and when I said I hadn't he
said, "You must be hungry," and he gave me a
good dinner—meat and potatoes and cabbage
and a roll. After I'd finished the plate of meat
and potatoes, I said, "Must I eat the roll,
Sergeant?" He said, "You don't have to if you
don't want it."

HOB: So what did you do then?

TED: I put it in my pocket till I got outside, and then
I played football with it.

HOB: One of these days, Mr. Priestley, that lad will
be playing football for England.

MR. PRIESTLEY: I can quite believe it, Hob, but he
must be rather a trial to his parents and his
teachers.

*   *   *   *   *

(Reproduced by permission of the Proprietors of "Punch")

THE HUMAN TOUCH

"Hi! Come down off there! Half a mo'[1]—who scored?"

FRIEDA: I don't like missing lessons, Mr. Priestley,
but Jan is hoping we can go and watch the match.
He has sent me six tickets. Do you think——?

MR. PRIESTLEY: Well, perhaps we could manage it.

HOB: Hurrah!

MR. PRIESTLEY: I quite agree that you mustn't miss
the lesson, but we needn't have it on Thursday.
Just for once, we could have it on Saturday. I
can see Hob looks rather disappointed because
he's got to come here on a holiday. But what
about the others?

FRIEDA: They won't mind coming on Saturday. I
know they all want to go to the match.

[1] Half a mo' (*slang*) = Wait half a moment.

MR. PRIESTLEY: Well, then, we'll all go to the match
    on Thursday and shout for Jan's team.

FRIEDA: Oh, thank you very much, Mr. Priestley. I
    must tell the others the news as soon as I see
    them this afternoon.

MR. PRIESTLEY: You needn't wait until this afternoon.
    All of them are in the library at the moment
    doing some private study. Go there now and
    tell them. But tell them they are not to stop work
    just now to talk about football—well, not for
    more than ten minutes.

FRIEDA: Very well, Mr. Priestley.

MR. PRIESTLEY: And now, Hob, we must get down to
    some grammar, the grammar of the verb *must*.

HOB: Oh, Mr. Priestley, *must* we?

MR. PRIESTLEY: Yes, Hob, we *must*.

EXERCISES

I. *Word Study: Use the following:*

excited (use also *excitement*, *exciting*), shout, team, neglect
(use also *neglectful*, *negligence*, *negligible*), archery (use also
archer, *arch*), remind (how does *remind* differ from *remember*?), cousin, policeman (use also *the police*, *police-station*),
corner, sergeant (note the pronunciation ['saːdʒənt]; you
have the same vowel sound in clerk [klɑːk], Derby ['dɑːbi],
Berkshire ['bɑːkʃə]),[1] pretend (and *pretence*), roll (*noun*) (use
it also, with a different meaning, as a *verb*), pocket (use also
pocket-book, *pocket-knife*, *pocket-money*, *to be in pocket*, *to be
out of pocket*), parents, ticket, disappoint (also *disappoint-
ment*), library (also *librarian*; what's the difference between
a *library* and a *bookshop*, a *librarian* and a *bookseller*?).

[1] But Americans pronounce the words [kləːk] ['dəːbi] ['bəːkʃə].

II. *Explain briefly what you understand by the follow-ing phrases in this lesson:*

1. a private lesson. 2. *I'm doubtful how many* of the soldiers who fought at Waterloo had ever been to Eton. 3. sport must *be in an Englishman's blood.* 4. he's *mad on* football. 5. he *turned up* about three o'clock. 6. *Run off* home! 7. he must be *rather a trial* to his parents. 8. I don't like *missing* lessons. 9. perhaps we could *manage it.* 10. *What about* the others? 11. we must *get down to* some grammar.

Use each of these phrases in sentences of your own.

PROVERBS

III. *Hob mentions two proverbs or sayings:*

1. "All work and no play makes Jack a dull boy."
2. "The battle of Waterloo was won on the playing-fields of Eton."

Explain these.

And here are five more proverbs for you to explain:

3. "Take care of the pennies and the pounds will take care of themselves."
4. "Better late than never."
5. "He laughs best who laughs last."
6. "A little learning is a dangerous thing."
7. "It's the early bird that catches the worm."

IV. *Composition Exercises*

1. Tell Hob's story about Cousin Ted.

2. Sport in your country, *or* Your favourite sport.

3. Write an essay on one of the proverbs in Question 3.

4. How would you (1) set and light a fire, (2) put up a tent, (3) make marmalade.

5. Tell the story of the picture on p. 33 and ex-plain the title.

LESSON 5

The Special Finite **must, have (got) to, am to**

MR. PRIESTLEY: The verb *must* is one of the "special" verbs that I told you about earlier,[1] but I didn't deal with it fully then, so let us have a look at it now.

1. Like the other special verbs it forms its interrogative by inversion, e.g.

Affirmative	*Interrogative*
I *must* go.	*Must* I go ?

and its negative by adding *not*,[2] e.g.

Affirmative	*Negative*
You *must* go.	You *must not* (*mustn't*) go.

2. In meaning, or at least in one of its meanings, it has an imperative quality, i.e., it suggests a command or an obligation, and in the negative a prohibition. There are several examples of this use of *must* on pp. 30 to 34 e.g.

> Henry VIII passed a law to say that men *mustn't* play football.
> The policeman said, "You *mustn't* play football in the street."

[1] See Book III, Lessons 18, 20, 23, 25, 26, 28, 30 and 32.
[2] But see later, p. 37–8.

Must I eat the roll, Sergeant?
I *must* tell the others the news.
We *must* get down to some grammar.

Note that *must* (*mustn't*) is used only with a *present* or *future* meaning, not with a *past* meaning.

3. There is a second meaning (you have had this in Book I, p. 203):

Eggs *must* be very scarce here (= surely eggs are very scarce here; that is the only explanation I can think of in the circumstances).

Must here expresses not compulsion, not what someone is obliged to do, but rather what seems to be the only reasonable explanation, the thing that one would naturally think. There are four examples of this usage in Lesson Four.

Jan *must* be pleased about it (= I am sure that, naturally, he is pleased).
I think sport *must* be in an Englishman's blood (= that seems to be the explanation).
He said, "You *must* be hungry" (naturally, if you haven't had any dinner).
He *must* be rather a trial to his parents (= that's what I should think in the circumstances).

Or in such a sentence as:

If he left here at four o'clock he *must* be home by now (it is only reasonable to think that).

4. But sometimes the negative of *must* is not *must not* but *need not* (*needn't*) or *don't* (*doesn't*) *need*. It depends on the meaning

to be expressed. *Mustn't* is a prohibition, an obligation *not* to do something; *needn't* implies no compulsion; with *needn't* there is a freedom of choice. There are four examples of this in Lesson Four, e.g.

You *mustn't* miss the lesson, but we *needn't* (*don't need to*) have it on Thursday (i.e. it is not absolutely necessary to have it on Thursday).

You *needn't* (*don't need to*) wait until this afternoon.

You *needn't* (*don't need to*) worry, Hob (= there is no necessity for worrying). You will never be made dull by too much work.

One *needn't* (*doesn't need to*) sit in a classroom to learn English.

Other examples :

"*Must* I be at the party by seven o'clock ?" "No, you *needn't* (*don't need to*) be there by seven, but don't be much later."

"*Must* I answer all the questions ?" "No, you *needn't* (*don't need to*) answer them all; it will be sufficient if you do four of them.

You *needn't* go home yet but I *must*.

5. When the meaning of *must* is "a reasonable explanation" (para. 3) the negative is *can't*, e.g.

Affirmative: You *must* be hungry if you have had no dinner.

Negative: You *can't* be hungry yet; you had a big dinner only an hour ago.

Affirmative: If Fred left here at 4 o'clock he *must* be home by now.

Negative: If Fred only left here at 5 o'clock he *can't* be home yet.

Affirmative: If he said that, he *must* be mistaken.

Negative: If he said that, he *can't* be telling the truth.

6. Instead of *must* we sometimes use *have to* or *have got to*. This form can be used to express the present, past, future or conditional.[1] (You will remember *must* cannot be used to express the past.) Here are five examples from pp. 30 to 34:

> If you want to learn English you *have to* work.
> Sport must be in an Englishman's blood; they just *have to* play football.
> He said, "Now you'll *have to* come to the police-station."
> "*Must* I eat the roll?" "You don't *have to* if you don't want it."
> Hob looks disappointed because he's (=he *has*) *got to* come here on a holiday.

Here are some further examples:

PRESENT

I *have to go* (or *I've* to go or *I've got* to go) to the dentist today about my bad tooth.

PAST

I *had* (or *I'd got*) *to go* to the dentist yesterday about my bad tooth.

FUTURE

I shall *have to go* to the dentist about my bad tooth.

CONDITIONAL

The dentist said that if my tooth went worse *I should have to* have it out.

All these sentences express something that is necessary. The opposite of *have to* is *needn't*, *don't need*, or *don't have to*, e.g.

> They *needn't* play football (they *don't have to* play football).

[1] *have to* is used in the conditional and future, but *have got to* is not.

You *needn't* eat the roll (you *don't have to* eat the roll).

Hob *needn't* come here on a holiday (Hob *doesn't have to* come here on a holiday).

I *needn't* (I *don't have to*) go to the dentist.

I *didn't need to* (*didn't have to*) go to the dentist yesterday.

I *wouldn't need to* (I *wouldn't have to*) have my tooth out.

7. Another form that can be used instead of *must* is *am* (*is, was, were,* etc.) *to.* You get this particularly in indirect speech, e.g.

He says *I am not to* ask silly questions.

He said *you were to go* to the police-station, did he?

Here are one or two further examples:

Mr. Priestley told us *we were not to* waste time.

I told him *he was not to* make that mistake again.

.   .   .   .   .

A: "He's treated you very badly; I'll go and tell him what I think about him."

B: "You *are not to* do that."

A: "I certainly will; *you are not* to try to stop me.'

MR. PRIESTLEY: Well, that's nearly everything about *must.* You might like to read Lesson Four through again now and note the various uses, and you will find some further examples in Lesson Six.

OLAF: If you say *we are* to remember all this, I'll *have to* write it down.

MR. PRIESTLEY: You *needn't* write all of it down but you *must* try to remember the main points.

Summary of usage with *must*

Compulsion	Prohibition	No Compulsion
I must	I must not (mustn't)	I need not (needn't)
I have to	I have not (haven't) to	I do not (don't) need to
I am to	I am (I'm) not to	I do not (don't) have to

EXERCISES

I. *In the following sentences use the* have to *form instead of* must *or* need:

   1. We must work hard to learn English.
   2. Hob must come to the class on Saturday.
   3. I must go home now.
   4. You needn't sit in a classroom to learn English.
   5. You needn't eat the roll if you don't want it.
   6. The students needn't come for a lesson every day.
   7. Hob must go to the dentist's tomorrow.
   8. Hob needn't go to the dentist's tomorrow.
   9. You needn't wait until this afternoon for the money.
  10. We must get down to some grammar tomorrow.

II. *In the following sentences use the* am to *form instead of* must *or* have to:

   1. I must go to the dentist's tomorrow.
   2. You must come to the class on Saturday.
   3. Must I understand that you are not coming tomorrow?
   4. I told him he must not make that mistake again.

5. He says that I have not to ask silly questions.
6. He said that I have not to ask silly questions.
7. Mr. Priestley says we mustn't be late tomorrow.
8. He said we have to be here at nine o'clock.
9. I said, "You mustn't do that.'"

III. *Give the opposite of the following, implying that there is no necessity:*

1. They must come to the class tomorrow.
2. You must sit in a classroom to learn English.
3. The sergeant said that Ted must eat the roll.
4. I have to finish this work by Thursday.
5. You must go at once.
6. You must put on your best clothes to visit my friend.
7. He must look for the book at once.
8. We must learn all this grammar in one lesson.
9. He must sell the house this year.
10. I must go to my lesson tomorrow.
11. They must answer all the questions.
12. You must cook the ripe apples.

IV. *Note the use of* must *and its variants on pp. 30–4 and 43–6. Now give the opposite of the following:* (a) *implying prohibition* (*three forms*), (b) *implying no compulsion* (*three forms*):

1. Jan must give up his studies.
2. He must stay in London.
3. You must shout for that team.
4. They must pay me for the work I have done.
5. You must tell everyone that Mr. Priestley played football a long time ago.
6. I must answer that letter today.
7. We must begin our lesson before nine o'clock.
8. Tell Hob he must eat all the chocolates.
9. You must answer all the questions.
10. He said I had to write something. (Be careful with "something".)

LESSON 6

The Football Match

must, need, have to (*continued*)

Characters—MR. PRIESTLEY, LUCILLE, FRIEDA,
PEDRO, OLAF, HOB

PEDRO: I say, what a crowd! There must be 20,000 people here. The ground's absolutely full.

MR. PRIESTLEY: Yes, this is one of the most popular sporting events in England.

FRIEDA: It's lucky for us we have reserved seats.

MR. PRIESTLEY: Yes, if you haven't tickets you've got to be here an hour before the match starts to get a good seat.

OLAF: Whereabouts are our seats?

MR. PRIESTLEY: Row A, numbers 16 to 21. That's right in the front. We'll have to push through the crowd to get to them. . . . Excuse me. . . . Excuse me. . . . Do you mind. . . . Sorry. . . . Excuse me. . . . Well, here we are at last.

LUCILLE: What splendid seats! We'll be able to see everything from here.

PEDRO: Yes, Jan has certainly looked after us well. We'll have to take him out to dinner after the match.

THE OTHERS: Good idea, Pedro, we certainly must.

HOB: And we must shout for his team. I hope Jan is on form today.

MR. PRIESTLEY: I hope he is. I hear they are to choose the players tomorrow for the international match, and if he plays well today Jan may be chosen.

PEDRO: Yes, I heard that the Selection Committee[1] would be at the match and I told Jan he was to play his best today because they were watching him.

HOB: I told him he must play his best because Frieda was watching him.

FRIEDA: You mustn't talk nonsense like that, Hob!

HOB: You needn't blush like that, Frieda!

OLAF: It must be exciting to play in an international match. You played for England, didn't you, Mr. Priestley?

MR. PRIESTLEY: Oh, that was a long time ago—there's no need to talk about that now. It must be nearly time for the match to start.

PEDRO: It is, and here are the teams coming out. Jan is leading the London team. He must be the captain.

FRIEDA: Yes, he is.

HOB: Jan must be a good player.

OLAF: He is; you have to be a good player to be captain of London team.

LUCILLE: If Jan is chosen for the international match

[1] i.e. The Committee that *selects* (= chooses) the team for a future match.

will he have to give up his studies and go into training?

FRIEDA: He mustn't do that. He must go on with his studies. They are more important than football.

MR. PRIESTLEY: He needn't give up his studies. He has been playing football regularly and is in good form.

OLAF: You needn't worry about Jan, Frieda. He knows he has to work to make his living—and he'll do it.

MR. PRIESTLEY: I'm sure he will.

HOB: Jan's lost the toss and the Oxford captain has decided to play with the wind.

OLAF: Oh well, they'll have to play against the wind in the second half. I see Jan is playing centre-forward. He's just getting ready to kick off. There they go.

HOB: Come on, London!

About an hour and a half later

MR. PRIESTLEY: This has been a grand game. I hardly remember ever seeing a better one. Jan has played the game of his life.

LUCILLE: I've nearly lost my voice with shouting " Come on, London." Oh, I wish London could win.

MR. PRIESTLEY: I don't think they can. It must be nearly time now. It's one goal each and the Oxford defence is magnificent.

OLAF: Yes, if my watch is right, they have three minutes to go.

FRIEDA: Look! Jan has got the ball. He's going like lightning towards the Oxford goal. Oh, go on, Jan!

PEDRO: That Oxford centre-half is trying to stop him.

LUCILLE: Go on, Jan. You mustn't let him stop you.

MR. PRIESTLEY: Jan has passed the ball to the inside-right, a wonderful pass.

LUCILLE: Oh! The inside-right is down, he's had to part with the ball.

OLAF: Look, Jan's got it again, he's beaten the full-back and is racing towards the goal.

HOB: Shoot, Jan, shoot! *IT'S A GOAL!*

PEDRO: Oh, what a shot! The goal-keeper hadn't a chance.

MR. PRIESTLEY: And there's the whistle for full time, and London have won. Well, they'll have to choose Jan for the international match now.

VERB STUDY (4): **do, make**

LUCILLE: One of my difficulties is with *do* and *make*. It's the same verb, of course, in French. Could you give me any help with it?

MR. PRIESTLEY: That certainly is a difficult point and the various idiomatic uses can only be learned by experience. The broad distinction is that "do" implies generally *action* and "make" implies *construction*. The verbs have gone away from these meanings in many cases, but you will see the distinction here.

> What are you going to *do* this afternoon?
> I'm going to *make* a book-case.

Doing is naturally a more general word, you can *do* without *making* but you can't *make* without *doing*. So we say,

What does the baker *do* ? He *makes* bread.
What does the dressmaker *do* ? She *makes* dresses.

You see, *do* is a substitute for practically any verb of action, e.g.

What are you *doing*, Pedro ?   I'm writing.
What are you *doing*, Frieda ?   I'm reading this book.
What are you *doing*, Jan ?   I'm taking notes.
What are you *doing*, Olaf ?   I'm studying this lesson.
What are you *doing*, Lucille ?   I'm copying this down.
What is Hob *doing* ?   He's sleeping!
Now you know what they are all *doing*.

The patterns with *do* as a full verb are:

(1)

Subject	*Verb*	*Object*
He	did Do	his work what I tell you

(2)

Subject	*Verb*	*Indirect Object*	*Direct Object*
He	did	me	a favour
This medicine	will do	you	good
He	has done	me	wrong
Hard work	doesn't do	anyone	harm

Here are further examples of the use of *do*:

You must always *do your best*.
Some hard work wouldn't *do him* any *harm*.
Uncle Albert will *do a good turn to*
  (=help) anyone if he can.
What does your car *do* (=travel) to the
  gallon? About 30 miles.
What you say *has nothing to do with*
  (=doesn't concern) the matter.
Your work is very unsatisfactory, Hob.
  This *won't do*.
I hear you have won a scholarship. *Well done!*

The most usual patterns with *make* are:

(1)

Subject	Verb	Object
Mrs. Priestley	made	a cake
Hob	makes	many mistakes
"Many hands	make	light work" (*Proverb*)

(2)

Subject	Verb	Indirect Object	Direct Object
Mrs. Priestley	made	me	a cake
Frieda	made	herself	a new dress
Jan	made	the boy	a toy aeroplane

(3)

Subject	Verb	Object	Infinitive (*without* to) *etc.*
Hob	made	everybody	laugh
I	can't make	my radio	work
What	made	you	do that ?
The heavy rain	made	the rivers	overflow their banks
The frost	made	the pipes	freeze

(4)

Subject	Verb	Object	Adjective or Past Participle
Bad work	makes	Mr. Priestley	angry
All this food	is making	me	fat
Grammar	makes	Hob	tired
He	couldn't make	himself	understood

Here are examples of the use of *make*:

He has to work hard to *make a living*

Frieda will *make an excellent wife* for Jan.

What *time do you make it* ? (= what time do you say it is).

I don't like that photograph; it *makes me look* an old man.

Don't *make a fool* of yourself. *Poduvice*

I can't *make out* (= understand) what you are saying.

Try these cakes; they are *home-made*.

The strong wine *made him drunk*.

T̶w̶e̶n̶t̶y̶ ̶s̶h̶i̶l̶l̶i̶n̶g̶s̶ *make* a pound.

100   *Pence*

Hob has *made a joke*; I'll *make a cup of tea.*
Come on, Hob, *make yourself useful.*

And here are six proverbs with *make* or *do*:

"*Make* hay while the sun shines."
"Two wrongs don't *make* a right."
"One swallow doesn't *make* a summer."
"You have *made* your bed; you must lie
   on it."
"Well begun is half *done.*"
"*Do* to others as you would have them
   (=like them to) *do* to you."

SWALLOWS

EXERCISES

I. *Word Study: Use the following:*

crowd, popular (use also *unpopular*, *popularity*), event,
reserved, row (*noun*) (use also, with a different meaning, the
verb *row* and *rower*), push, international (use also *national*,
nation, *nationalise*), nonsense, blush (*noun and verb*), lead
(*verb*), captain, train (*verb*) (use also *training*, *trainer* and,
with quite a different meaning, *train* as a noun), form (*noun*)
(there are several meanings; use also *form* (*verb*), toss (*noun*
and *verb*), goal, lightning, pass (*noun and verb*), part (*verb*;
and, with a different meaning, use *part* as a noun), race
(*verb*) (use also as a noun (two different meanings); use also
race-horse, *race-course*), shoot (also *shot*), whistle (*noun and
verb*).

II. *Explain the following phrases:*

1. *what a* crowd! 2. *reserved seats*. 3. Jan has *looked after us*
well. 4. *take him out* to dinner. 5. I hope he is *on form* today.
6. he has to *play his best*. 7. will Jan have to *give up his
studies*. 8. *go into training*. 9. he is *in good form*. 10. to play
with the wind. 11. *to kick off*. 12. Jan has *played the game of
his life*. 13. I've nearly *lost my voice* with shouting. 14. they
have three minutes *to go*. 15. The goal-keeper *hadn't a
chance*.

III. *Make sentences using the following idioms:*

do one's best; well done!; done for; done with; do wonders;
do without; to do with; done up; won't do; do a good turn;
do you good.

IV. *Make sentences of your own using:*

make a point of; make room; make up your mind; make up
one's face; make up for lost time; make oneself useful; self-
made; made-up story; make fun of; make someone laugh;
make a fortune; home-made; make a mistake.

V. *Use in sentences the proverbs on page 50 so as to
bring out their meaning.*

Composition Exercises

1. Write an account (in about 300 words) of a
football match or any other sporting event.

2. Write the conversation that led up to this
remark.

(Reproduced by permission of "Woman's Journal")

"SEE WHAT I MEAN?"

LESSON 7

WORD STUDY: **already, yet, still**

These three words cause a great deal of difficulty.

dussagesöbe

already *schon*

Already means *before now, up to now, by this time, so far*, e.g.

> I have *already* explained this.
> Hob has *already* eaten six cakes and is starting on the seventh.

By the way, don't confuse *already* and *all ready*. You have examples of both these forms in the following sentences:

> Susan has *already* set the table for dinner.
> It's *all ready* now.
> At last *all is ready*.

noch yet =
noch nicht

schon bei Fragesätze

yet

Yet has the meanings, *up to now, so far, at this moment*, e.g.

> He hasn't *yet* replied to my letter.
> I haven't finished my work *yet*; I can't come out just *yet*.
> Has the postman come *yet*?
> Have you heard from your brother *yet*?

schon

The difference in usage between *already* and *yet* is:
  already is used in affirmative statements,
    yet is used in negative and interrogative
      sentences.
But *already* can be used in interrogative sentences
where you expect an answer "yes", e.g.

> "Here's my work, Mr. Priestley." "What! Have you finished
> it *already*?"

Already and *yet* are generally used with the Perfect
Tenses of a verb, but can be used with a Continuous
Tense, e.g.

> "The girls are *already* planning the dresses they will wear"
> (p. 14).
> You are not going *yet*, are you?

still

Still has the meaning "*right up to the present
moment*", e.g.

> The doctor is *still* there.
> It is eleven o'clock but Jan is *still* hard at work.

In some cases *still* and *yet* may have the same meaning, e.g.

> I've *still* a few pages to read (I've a few pages to read *yet*).
> Are all the students here? No, Hob hasn't come *yet*. (No,
> there's *still* Hob to come.)

Still is often contrasted with *not yet*, e.g.

> He is *still* busy; he has *not yet* finished his work (he *has not*
> finished his work *yet*).

When *still* is used in questions it often suggests feeling of some sort, e.g. surprise or annoyance.

> What, are you *still* working? I thought you had gone home.
> Is that fellow *still* here? I wish he'd go away.

Notice another construction with *still* and *yet*, viz., with comparatives, e.g.

> You must work harder *yet* (You must work *still* harder).
> We have exported a lot of goods but we must export *still* more.
> (We must export more *yet*.)

VERB STUDY (5): **give**

"He will have to *give up* his studies." *Give up* = abandon, stop. There are two usual patterns with *give*:

(1)

Subject + give	(Pro)noun	to	(Pro)noun
He gave	food	to	the hungry man

(2)

Subject + give	Indirect Object	Direct Object
Mr. Priestley gave	his class	an English lesson

Other idiomatic usage with *give*:

The teacher will *give out* (= distribute) the books.
Henry says he is going to *give up* (= stop) smoking.

The railing on which he was leaning *gave way* (= broke) and he fell from the cliff.   *Mead geben*

He pretended to be English but his foreign accent *gave him away* (= betrayed him).   *Liess ihn verraten*

PREPOSITIONS (2)

About

About has the meaning (*a*) "concerning", e.g.

I want you to tell me *about* your work.
I shall be thinking *about* you all the time you are away.
That is all right for you but what *about* me ?

(*b*) "approximately", e.g.

I'll see you at *about* six o'clock.
There is *about* £120 difference between this car and that one.

(*c*) "in various directions or places", e.g.

I go *about* the country a good deal.
You will be warm enough if you move *about*.
This is not screwed down firmly, it moves *about* when you touch it.

(*d*) (with *come*) "happen", e.g.

I hear that George has broken his leg; how did that *come about* ?

Above   *über, höher als*

Above (*a*) has often the same meaning as *over* and can be contrasted with *below*, e.g.

In Mr. Priestley's room there is a clock *above* (*over*) the fireplace.[1]
We flew *above* the clouds.

(*b*) "mentioned earlier", e.g.

In the *above*[2] examples (in the examples *above*).

---

[1] See picture *Essential English* I, p. 93.
[2] *Above* in this case is an adjective.

(*c*) "most important of", e.g.

Think about what I have told you; but *above* all, don't breathe a word of it to Henry.

Idiomatic expression: Brown's business is not doing well; he is finding it difficult to *keep his head above water* (= to pay his way).

Across   *überqueren*

Across means "from one side to the other", e.g.

The child ran *across* the road.
You cross a cheque by drawing two lines *across* it and writing "& Co."

Run *across* can also mean "meet unexpectedly", e.g.

I *ran across* our friend Smith yesterday.

After

After is generally used to denote time or order, e.g.

I'll see you *after* dinner.
He goes on working day *after* day, week *after* week without any change.

"To look *after*" = to care for, e.g.

If my wife goes away for a week, who's going to *look after* me and the children?

After all = "in spite of what you thought", e.g.

You can see I was right *after all*.

Against

Against expresses the idea of:
(*a*) "opposition," e.g.

He who is not for us is *against* us.

(*b*) "support", e.g.

He rested his bicycle *against* the wall.

(*c*) "to avoid the danger from", e.g.

My house is insured *against* fire.

Among (Amongst)

Among (*amongst*) expresses:

(*a*) "position in the midst of", e.g.

You can see my house *among* the trees.

(*b*) "included in", e.g.

Shelley is *among* (= one of) the world's greatest poets.

(*c*) "sharing", e.g.

The sweets are to be shared *among* the five children.

With this last meaning *between* is generally used for two, *among* for more than two, e.g. "The sweets were divided *between* the two children". But this distinction is not always strictly observed.

At

At is used mainly to denote a place or point of time, e.g.

I'll see you *at* the station *at* four o'clock.
He lives *at* Torquay in Devonshire; I live *in* London.

At is generally used for small towns, *in* for large cities, counties, or countries, but it depends on how we are thinking about a place. We could say "I live *in* the village of Newton" because I am thinking of the place and its surroundings, but "Does this train stop *at* Crewe" (a big town) because we are thinking

3

of Crewe merely as a point on the railway. But there
are many other meanings of *at*, e.g.

> The apples were sold *at* 6d. a pound, but that was really *at*
>   a loss not *at* a profit.
> He is good *at* football/English/his work.
> Shakespeare died *at* the age of fifty-two.

(Many further examples of all prepositions are
given in the Teacher's Book IV.)

EXERCISES

I. *In the following sentences put in the word* yet *or*
already *or* still. (*In some cases more than one of the
words may be correct.*)

1. Pedro is going to leave London; the others have *already* gone.
2. Hob hadn't arrived when the lesson started.
3. I had learned some English before I came to England.
4. I have studied English for some years but I am learning.
5. What, are you here? I thought you had gone home.
6. Hasn't that letter come?
7. Are you going to see the picture at the Cinema? No, I
   have seen it.
8. You have worked hard but you must work harder.
9. Have you read that book? I thought it would take you
   longer.
10. I told you to take all that wood away and it is there.

II. *Write six sentences each containing an example of*
give *as a phrasal verb.*

III. *Study the pictures on p. 59 and then tell the story
of "The Reading of the Will".*

THE READING OF THE WILL

LESSON 8

Great Britons (1): **Charles Dickens** (i)

PEDRO: I've been trying my hand at making a little play out of a scene from Dickens's *David Copperfield* turned into Essential English. Would you mind reading it?

MR. PRIESTLEY: I should be delighted. When will it be ready?

PEDRO: Tomorrow, I think. I don't know what you will think of it, but I've often thought how naturally Dickens's novels could be made into plays. They seem more like a collection of separate scenes than a single novel.

MR. PRIESTLEY: That is what they are, especially the earlier books. Later, when he got to know Wilkie Collins,[1] another popular writer of the times, he tried to construct a plot, but it is never for the plot but for the characters in his books that we remember Dickens. This lack of construction is largely due to the circumstances in which they were written. *Pickwick Papers* and many of the other novels came out in fortnightly parts and the story developed as it went along. Dickens himself often didn't know how it was going to

---

[1] Wilkie Collins (1824–1889). Wrote *The Moonstone*, *The Woman in White*, etc.

end, he just went ahead and let the story go wherever his imagination led him.

OLAF: I don't know anything at all about Dickens. Before we read Pedro's play could you tell us something about his life?

MR. PRIESTLEY: Certainly, and perhaps the best place to begin is at the beginning. Charles Dickens was born in 1812 at Portsmouth, where his father was a clerk in the Navy Pay Office. But Dickens didn't live long in Portsmouth. When he was about four years of age his family moved to Chatham, and the five years he spent there were the happiest of all his boyhood. Just as young Shakespeare resolved that some day he would return to Stratford and buy the big house, New Place, there, so little Charles dreamed that some day, perhaps, he might live in a big house that he loved, Gadshill Place, at Rochester. And one day the dreams of both of them came true. But at the time there seemed little chance of it for Dickens. He was the oldest of a large family, eight in all, and his father, a happy-go-lucky, irresponsible man (the original of Mr. Micawber in *David Copperfield*), was, like Mr. Micawber, always "waiting for something to turn up". What schooling Dickens had, he got at Chatham at a small day-school, and from his mother, who was a well-educated woman.

Then one day, in a room upstairs, he found a pile of books, *Robinson Crusoe*,[1] *Roderick Random*,[2] *Tom Jones*,[3] *The Vicar of Wakefield*[4]

[1] By Daniel Defoe (1661–1731).   [2] By Tobias Smollett (1721–71).
[3] By Henry Fielding (1707–54).   [4] By Oliver Goldsmith (1728–74).

—rather strong meat for a boy of nine, but Dickens was delighted; the key to the treasure-house of English literature had been put in his hand and his own imagination was wakened.

In 1821 the Dickens family moved to Camden Town, London, into " a mean, small house ". Mr. Dickens was heavily in debt and didn't know which way to turn for money. The few possessions that they had were sold one by one, but things got no better, and finally Mr. Dickens was taken to the Marshalsea Prison, London, for debt. You will find the Marshalsea fully described in *Little Dorrit*. Dickens knew it only too well from bitter experience, for when all the goods had been sold, Mrs. Dickens and the younger children went to the prison, too, to join the father.

Meanwhile, Charles had got a job in an under-ground cellar at a blacking[1] factory at Old Hungerford Stairs in the East End of London. This was the most unhappy time of all his life. He was lonely and hungry (though later he got his breakfast and supper in the prison and so was better fed). He hated the coarse, rough boys with whom he had to work and who cared for none of the things that he loved. " No words," he wrote, " can express the secret agony of my soul as I sank into this companionship and compared these people with those of my happier childhood and felt my early hope of growing

---

[1] *Blacking* was stuff for giving a polish to black shoes. Now we use *shoe-polish*.

up to be a learned and famous man crushed in my heart."

But his fortunes took a turn for the better. He was able to leave the blacking factory and he entered a lawyer's office in Lincoln's Inn. He learned shorthand and was able to do some reporting in the House of Commons for newspapers. Finally, in 1834, he was taken on the staff of a newspaper, the *Morning Chronicle*, and his life-work of writing had really begun. He went all over the

CHARLES DICKENS

country getting news, writing up stories, meeting people and using his eyes.

I have said rather a lot about Dickens's early days but they are important, for they made a very deep impression on his mind, and all these stored-up impressions are poured out later in his books *Little Dorrit*, *Nicholas Nickleby*, *Oliver Twist*, and above all, *David Copperfield*.

(*Continued on p.* 71)

VERB STUDY (6): **turn**

Note the three uses of *turn* in Lesson 8:

His father was, like Mr. Micawber, always waiting for something to *turn up* (= some good fortune to come).

Mr. Dickens was heavily in debt and *didn't know which way to turn for* (= what to do to get) money.

His fortunes *took a turn* (= changed) for the better.

Here are some further examples of the uses, idiomatic and otherwise, of *turn*:

The wheels of the cart *turn round*.

When he became rich he *turned his back on* (= refused to recognise) his old friends.

She could not be *turned aside* (see p. 205).

Thundery weather often *turns milk* (= makes it go) sour.

The pretty girl got so much flattery it quite *turned her head* (= made her foolishly conceited).

Even a worm will *turn* (= there is a point where even the most gentle and humble person will get angry).

The weather has suddenly *turned* (= become) colder.

I have been very lazy but I am going to *turn over a new leaf* (= make a new start, behave better) and work hard.

I will *turn the matter over in my mind* (= consider it) and tell you tomorrow what I have decided.

When he is in trouble he always *turns to* (= applies to, trusts to) his mother for help.

Hob isn't here yet; he probably won't *turn up* (= come) at all. "Ted *turned up* at 3 o'clock" (page 31).

IDIOMATIC ENGLISH (1): **hand**

In Lesson 8 you have the expression "I've been *trying my hand* (= making an attempt) at making a play", and in Lesson 2, "Pedro must *take* your father *in hand*". There are many more idiomatic expressions with *hand*. Here are some of them:

My house is *close at hand* (= near).

The poet was starving and lived from *hand to mouth* (= in great poverty, unable to save anything).

The two little children went to school *hand-in-hand*.

The thief pointed a gun at the man and said "*Hands up!*"

I thought the book was on my shelves but I can't just *lay hands on* (= find) it.

A teacher who tries to teach a class of fifty children like Ted *has her hands full* (= is very fully occupied).

"A bird *in the hand* is worth two in the bush." (*Proverb*.)

He gave me some real *first-hand* information.

I don't like wearing *second-hand* clothes.

"Many *hands* make light work." (*Proverb*.)

PREPOSITIONS (3)
Before

Before generally expresses:

(1) time (contrasted with *after*), e.g.

> Come and see me tomorrow any time *before* five o'clock.
> *Before* long you will find this work quite simple.
> That happened in 400 B.C. (*Before* Christ).

(2) position, order, e.g.

> She sang *before* a large audience.
> My appointment is not until 10-15; you go in *before* me.

Behind

Behind expresses position:

(1) in space, e.g.

> The garage is *behind* the house.
> He stood just *behind* me.

(2) in time, e.g.

> The train is *behind* time (= late).
> He is *behind the times* (= old-fashioned).

And here's a little joke to illustrate the two meanings of *behind* and *before* as preposition and as adverbial particle.

WIFE (to husband trying, clumsily, to fasten her dress): "Hurry up; have you never hooked up a dress *behind before*?"

HUSBAND: "No; you never had a dress *before* that hooked *behind*."

Below

Below generally has the meaning "under", e.g.

The temperature is *below* freezing point.
Write your name in the space *below*.

It is contrasted with *above*, e.g.

To keep warm you need blankets *above* and *below* you.
Jan's work is *above* average; Hob's is very much *below* it.

Beside

Beside = "by the side of", "near", e.g.

Go and sit *beside* Richard.
The church at Stratford is *beside* the river.

Note the idiomatic phrases,

He was *beside himself* (= almost mad) with anger.
What you have said is quite *beside the point* (= not connected with the subject).

Besides

Besides = "in addition to", e.g.

There are many others *besides* me who disagree with what you say.

Besides (as an adverb) can also have the meaning "moreover", e.g.

I don't want to go for a walk; I'm tired, and *besides*, it's beginning to rain.

There is an old comic song with the lines:

"I do like to be *beside* the sea . . .
And there's lots of girls, *besides*,
I should like to be *beside*, *beside* the sea."

Beyond

Beyond has the meanings "on the other, further, side", "further on", "more than", e.g.

The woods go for about two miles *beyond* the river.
He lives in a small castle, about four miles *beyond* Oxford.
He loves her *beyond* measure.

Note the idiomatic expressions:

The explanation you give is quite *beyond* me (= I can't understand it).
He is living *beyond his means* (= spending more than he earns).
The prisoner's guilt was proved *beyond* doubt (= there was no doubt about it).

By

By is used with a great many meanings. It expresses :

(*a*) nearness, e.g.

Come and sit *by* me.

(*b*) direction or movement, e.g.

We came to Oxford *by* way of Warwick and Banbury.

(*c*) agency, e.g.

The book was written *by* Dickens.

(*d*) time, e.g.

We travelled *by* night.

(*e*) measurement, e.g.

These goods are sold *by* weight.

He is older than I am *by* ten years.

Idiomatic phrases:

I will see him *by* and *by* (= before long). Learn this *by heart*. I mention this *by way* of illustration.

Hob isn't a fool *by any means* (= he is a long way from being a fool).

EXERCISES

I. *Word Study: Use each of the following:*

scene (also *seen*), delight, novel (note two meanings: (*a*) as a noun, (*b*) as an adjective), plot (here = plan of a story; compare with *plot* (= secret plan)), lack, clerk (give the pronunciation, in English and in American), resolve, happy-go-lucky, responsible (also *irresponsible*, *responsibility*), treasure, mean (*adjective* and *verb*; note also *means*, and use the phrases "by all means", "by means of", "to live beyond one's means"), later (compare with *latter*), coarse (compare with *course*), agony, shorthand, impression.

II. *Make each set of simple sentences into a complex sentence by means of relative pronouns or conjunctions:*

1. Dickens become friendly with Wilkie Collins. Collins was another popular writer. Dickens then tried to construct a plot.

2. Dickens wrote many novels. He was born at Portsmouth. His father was a clerk there.

3. He spent five years in Chatham. He was then a boy. These were the happiest years of his youth.

4. Dickens dreamed. Some day he would live at Gadshill Place. He would be rich then.

5. The early experiences of Dickens are important. They made a deep impression on his mind.

COMPREHENSION EXERCISE

III. *From this lesson answer the following:*

1. What other novelist was writing at the same time as Dickens?

2. Why are most of Dickens's novels "more like a collection of separate scenes than a single novel"?

3. What house did (*a*) Shakespeare, (*b*) Dickens buy?

4. Who was the original of Mr. Micawber?

5. Mention three novels that Dickens wrote.

6. How was "the key to the treasure-house of English literature" put into Dickens's hand?

7. In which of Dickens's novels will you find a description of the Marshalsea prison?

8. Why was Dickens unhappy in his job at the blacking factory?

9. What other work did he do in his early days before writing his novels?

10. Why is a knowledge of Dickens's early life important for the understanding of his novels?

IV. *Explain what is meant by each of the following phrases as it is used in the passage:*

1. he just *went ahead*. 2. his father was *happy-go-lucky*. 3. waiting for something *to turn up*. 4. *What schooling he had* he got at Chatham. 5. *strong meat* for a boy of nine. 6. The *key to the treasure-house of English literature*. 7. from *bitter experience*. 8. these *stored-up* impressions.

V. *Show that you understand these idioms by using each in a sentence:*

1. to turn one's back on.
2. to turn a deaf ear to.
3. didn't turn a hair.
4. to turn an honest penny.
5. to turn someone round one's finger.
6. to turn a girl's head.
7. to turn out.
8. to turn against.
9. the worm will turn.
10. to turn over a new leaf.
11. to turn one's nose up at something.
12. take a turn.
13. a good turn.
14. wait one's turn.
15. done to a turn.

VI. *Use the following idioms in sentences:*

at hand; put in hand; from hand to mouth; hand and foot; he has his hands full; second-hand; give a hand; hands wanted; time hangs heavy on my hands; to keep one's hand in.

VII.   *Composition Exercises*

1. Write a summary of the passage from "Charles Dickens was born . . ." to the end. Your summary should not exceed 150 words.

2. Write a short account of a great novelist of your country.

LESSON 9

GREAT BRITONS (1): **Charles Dickens** (ii)

MR. PRIESTLEY: In 1833 Dickens had a number of papers published under the title *Sketches by Boz*, but it was in 1836 that he rose to fame as suddenly and as unmistakably as Scott had done. The circumstances were rather strange. A firm of publishers, Chapman & Hall, had a number of pictures by a humorous artist, Seymour, and they wanted to get some short articles to illustrate them so that pictures and articles could appear together in a magazine in fortnightly parts. Someone suggested that the young newspaper reporter, Charles Dickens, might do the job. It was a job after his own heart. He accepted the offer, but asked for a rather freer hand in the writing than had been originally planned. He was allowed to have his way— and so *Pickwick Papers* came into being.

HOB: What is *Pickwick Papers* about ? Should I like it ?

MR. PRIESTLEY: You ought to get the book, I think you would like it. It is about Mr. Pickwick and his three friends, Mr. Tupman, Mr. Snodgrass, and Mr. Winkle. Mr. Pickwick is a stout, good-natured, cheerful, very simple-hearted old gentleman. He is the General Chairman of the Pickwick Club, and he and his three friends decide to travel about England and send to the Pickwick Club in London an account of their journeys and their observations on the character and manners of the people they meet on these journeys. The humour of the book consists chiefly in the absurd situations that Mr. Pickwick and his friends get themselves into—deceived by smooth-tongued rogues, put into a debtors' prison, involved in an action for breach of promise—and yet, though we laugh at Mr. Pickwick, we don't think any the worse of him for being a figure of fun—in fact we love him all the more. That's what we mean by "humour"; and next to Shakespeare's Falstaff, Mr. Pickwick is perhaps the greatest comic figure in English literature.

But to continue the story of Dickens. For the first fortnightly part of *Pickwick Papers* the publishers printed 400 copies, but such was its popularity that for Part Fifteen more than 40,000 copies had to be printed. At one stride Dickens had become the most popular living novelist (Scott died in 1832; Dickens's first book appeared in 1833) and he held that position until his death. The rest can be told in a few words. It is a story of work, and work without rest. He poured out novel after novel—*Oliver Twist*, *Nicholas Nickleby*, *The Old Curiosity Shop*, *A Christmas Carol*, *David Copperfield* (perhaps the greatest work of all), *A Tale of Two*

Cities—these are but a few of the more famous. At the same time he was editing newspapers and magazines, visiting America, Italy, Switzerland, Paris; giving readings from his books to huge crowds of people and writing constantly. It was the excitement of these readings (this excitement and the applause of his listeners was what he loved) and the strain of his continual work that brought about his sudden death in 1870. He had asked that his burial should be quite simple, but the whole nation wanted to give him the highest honour they could, and so he lies buried in Westminster Abbey, but as he wished it, with nothing on the stone except his name, "Charles Dickens".

OLAF: Thank you, Mr. Priestley, I've enjoyed your story of his life. But why is Dickens great; I mean, what is there is his books that has made him read by all, by learned and simple, rich and poor alike—for that seems to be the case?

MR. PRIESTLEY: You are quite right, it *is* the case. I don't think there is any other novelist in England who has such a hold on all classes of people. He had it in his own day, he has it in ours too (*David Copperfield* is still a "best seller"), and I believe he will keep that popularity as long as English is read.

I think the chief cause is the great-heartedness of the man himself. He, like Abou ben Adhem,[1] was one "who loved his fellow-men", and it

[1] In the poem "Abou ben Adhem", by Leigh Hunt (it appears on p. 68 of *Brighter English*, published by Longmans, Green and Co.). Leigh Hunt (1784–1859) was an essayist and poet.

was not only the good ones who came in for his love; his kindly, humorous, understanding eye looked with a wide tolerance on good and bad alike.

He was, too, so full of life himself. Leigh Hunt said of Dickens's face, "It has the life and soul of fifty human beings", and his face was a true picture of his mind. It was this tremendous vitality of Dickens that makes all his characters so memorable. He is often blamed for making his characters unreal, strange, grotesque creatures that never could have existed. There may be something in this, but though they may not be, as the critics say, "true to life", they certainly spring to life in his pages. They are more real to us than the characters of any other novelist, English or foreign—and they were real enough to Dickens. His biographer, Forster, writes:

"I remember he said to me that during the composition of his stories he could never quite get rid of the characters about whom he happened to be writing; that while *The Old Curiosity Shop* was being written, Little Nell followed him about everywhere; while he was writing *Oliver Twist*, Fagin would never let him rest; that at midnight and in the morning Tiny Tim and little Bob Cratchit[1] were ever pulling his coat as if impatient for him to get back to his desk and continue with the story of their lives. He said that when the children of his brain had once been sent into the world, free and clear of

[1] In *A Christmas Carol*.

him, they would sometimes turn up in the most
unexpected manner to look their father in the
face. Sometimes he would pull my arm as we
were walking together and whisper, 'Let us
avoid Mr. Pumblechook[1] who is crossing the
street to meet us', or 'Mr. Micawber is coming,
let us turn down here to get out of his way'.
He always seemed to enjoy the fun of his
humorous characters and had unending laughter
over Mr. Pickwick's amusing misadventures.''

And so we believe in his characters because he
believed in them himself. He shows us a great,
moving picture of everyday life and everyday
people.

We must admire, too, the noble feeling that
filled Dickens in the writing of many of his
novels—the desire to show up some wrong and
put it right. He had suffered so bitterly himself
as a child and had seen so much evil that he
burned with the longing to fight it to the
utmost. So in *Oliver Twist* he attacks the cruel
workhouse treatment of children, in *Nicholas
Nickleby* the evils of badly-run schools, in *Little
Dorrit* the tragedy of the debtors' prison, in
Bleak House the slowness of the law. No man
has done more to get these wrongs righted than
has Dickens.

In some ways, of course, he belonged to his
age and had its weaknesses. Dickens himself and
his readers cried together over the long-drawn-
out deaths of Little Nell and Paul Dombey.

[1] In *Great Expectations*.

Most of us now feel that the sentiment, and especially the pathos, is overdrawn, and wish Dickens had not let himself go so much, just as we wish sometimes that his humour was not quite so rough and forcible, or that his efforts at "fine writing" instead of clear, simple writing were not so frequent. But when all this is said there still remains the great writer and great man, the man who knew London as few men have known it and who loved its common people humorously and understandingly. And that is why the common people have taken him to their heart.

Idiomatic English (2): **heart**

In the passage on pp. 71 to 76 you have the sentences:

It was a job *after his own heart* (= of the kind he very much liked).

Mr. Pickwick is . . . a *simple-hearted* old gentleman.

The chief cause (of his popularity) is the *great-heartedness* of the man himself.

And that is why the common people have *taken him to their heart*.

Here are some further common idiomatic uses of *heart*.

He is not a man who *wears his heart on his sleeve* (= shows his feelings openly).

He may seem cold but *his heart is in the right place* (= he has true, kind feelings). He has a *heart of gold*.

When I heard that strange cry in the darkness *my heart went into my mouth* (= I was afraid).

When I think of my examination tomorrow *my heart goes into my boots* (= I feel in despair).

I didn't win the prize but I am not *downhearted* (= sad, discouraged).

I learned that piece of poetry *by heart* (= by memory).

PREPOSITIONS (4)

Down

Down expresses movement from a higher to a lower position, e.g.

They walked *down* the hill.
The sun goes *down* in the west.
Sit *down*; there is plenty of room for everyone.

There are some idiomatic usages of *down* as an adverb, e.g.

The arrangement for sending letters abroad seems to have *broken down.*
Write these notes *down* in your notebook.
He has come *down* in the world (= become poorer or less important).
The wind has died *down* (= become less strong).
The sleeve of my coat is too short; I will ask the tailor to let it *down* an inch.
He looked very *down in the mouth* (= unhappy, out of spirits).
Perhaps he was *down on his luck* (= in misfortune).

Except

Except (*for*), *excepting* means "not including", "apart from", e.g.

We have lessons every day *except* (*excepting*) Saturday and Sunday.
This essay is good *except for* the careless mistake.

Except that is used to introduce a clause, e.g.

He is a good student *except that* he is occasionally careless.

For

For has a great many meanings:

(1) space of time or distance, e.g.

I am staying here *for* a week.
The forest goes on *for* twenty miles.

(2) purpose, aim, intention, e.g.

We come here *for* English lessons.
He uses an electric razor *for* shaving.

(3) Amount, e.g.

The house was sold *for* £5,000.

(4) Direction, e.g.

Which is the train *for* Brighton.

(5) Point of time, e.g.

The meeting is arranged *for* seven o'clock.

(6) Cause, e.g.

I couldn't see anything *for* smoke.
He gained a medal *for* bravery/*for* saving a boy's life.

(7) Exchange, e.g.

I'll give you my watch *for* your camera.
He paid £50 *for* that picture.

(8) Advantage (or disadvantage), e.g.

This holiday has been good *for* you; too much work is bad *for* you.

NOTE. *For* is used when the duration of time is measured;

      Since is used when the starting point is given (see *since*, p. 144).

In negative sentences *for* is used for a period of time, *before* for a point of time, e.g.

    He will not be here *for* an hour yet.
    He will not be here *before* seven o'clock.

From

The principal meanings of *from* are:

(1) A motion away, departure, removal, e.g.

    He rose *from* his chair.
    She came *from* Scotland last week.

(2) A starting point, place of origin, e.g.

    He read *from* page 16 to page 21.
    The wool came *from* Australia.
    The roses are *from* Richard.

(3) Cause, e.g.

    She is suffering *from* a bad headache.

(4) Separation, e.g.

    He is far away *from* home and wife and children.

EXERCISES

I. *Word Study: Use the following:*
publish (also *publisher*, *publication*), circumstances, magazine, accept (compare with *except*; what is the opposite of *accept*?), plan, originally, stout (what is the opposite?), simple-hearted, absurd, smooth-spoken, humour (also *humorous good-humoured*, *to be in a bad humour*), stride (*noun* and *verb*;

what is the past tense of this verb ?), pour (not *poor*), edit (use also *editor, editorial, edition*), applause, burial (also *bury*; compare *berry*), tolerance (use also *tolerate, toleration, intolerant*), vitality, memorable (use also *memory, memorial, remember, remembrance*), grotesque, biographer (use also *biography*; what is an *autobiography* ?), composition (use also *compose, composer*), avoid, misadventures (use also *adventure, adventurous*), sentiment (also *sentimental*), pathos (and *pathetic*).

II. *Note the following rather idiomatic expressions. Express the meaning of each sentence in a different way without using the words in italics.*

1. He *rose to fame* as suddenly and unmistakably as Scott had done.
2. He asked for a rather *freer hand* in the writing.
3. He was allowed to *have his way* and so "Pickwick Papers" *came into being*.
4. The humour consists chiefly in the absurd situations that Mr. Pickwick and his friends *get themselves into*.
5. They are deceived by *smooth-spoken* rogues.
6. We don't *think any the worse of him* for being a *figure of fun*.
7. *Such* was its popularity that for Part Fifteen more than 40,000 copies had to be printed.
8. *At one stride* Dickens had become the most popular living novelist.
9. He *poured out* novel after novel.
10. The strain of his continual work *brought about* his sudden death in 1870.
11. No other novelist in England *has such a hold* on all classes of people.
12. It was not only the good ones who *came in for* his love.
13. They were impatient for him *to get back to his desk*.
14. His characters would sometimes *turn up* in the most unexpected manner.

15. Let us *turn down* here and *get out of his way*.
16. We *believe in* his characters.
17. He wrote his novels to *show up* a wrong and *put it right*.
18. He *burned with desire* to fight evil *to the utmost*.
19. No man has done more than Dickens *to get these wrongs righted*.
20. Dickens and his readers cried together over the *long-drawn-out* death of Little Nell.
21. The pathos is *overdrawn*.
22. We wish Dickens had not *let himself go so much*.

COMPREHENSION EXERCISES

III. *From this lesson answer the following:*

1. What other English novelist besides Dickens rose suddenly to fame ?
2. What work was Dickens doing when he was asked to write *Pickwick Papers* ?
3. What were the members of the "Pickwick Club" going to write about ?
4. What misadventures does Mr. Pickwick meet with ?
5. What proof is there that *Pickwick Papers* grew in popularity as it appeared ?
6. What work, other than writing novels, occupied Dickens after 1833 ?
7. Why was Dickens buried in Westminster Abbey ?
8. What is a "best seller" ?
9. Give three reasons why Dickens has such a hold on all classes of people.
10. How could you show that Dickens's characters were real people to him ?
11. What evils did he attack in his novels ?

IV. *Write a summary of the passage on p. 73 from "I think the chief cause . . ." to the end of p. 76. Your summary should not extend to more than 200 words.*

V. *Make the following groups of words into sentences. Add as many more words as you wish. You can use the words in any order you please.*

1. Publishers, pictures, humorous, articles, magazine.
2. Mr. Pickwick, chairman, travel, account, observations, character, journeys.
3. Dickens, asked, burial, simple, nation, honour, Westminster.
4. Dickens, face, life, fifty, picture, mind.
5. During, composition, rid, characters, writing.
6. Children, brain, sent, world, clear, turn up, unexpected, look, face.
7. Suffered, child, evil, desire, fight, utmost.
8. Feel, pathos, overdrawn, humour, rough, "fine writing".

VI. *Use each of the following idioms in a sentence:*

His heart is in the right place; my heart went into my mouth; in one's heart of hearts; heart and soul; take to heart; to be disheartened; heart-to-heart; to set one's heart on; by heart; downhearted.

VII. *Composition Exercises*

(*a*) Write a brief account of any book by Dickens that you have read.

(*b*) What qualities do you think a good novel ought to have ?

Write a composition or a short story on one of the following:

(*c*) "Don't wear your heart on your sleeve."

(*d*) "The man with the hand of iron but the heart of gold."

LESSON 10

David and the Waiter

(*This is the play that Pedro made out of a scene from "David Copperfield".*)

Scene: *An inn at Yarmouth. Maps on the wall. Table set for dinner; the* LANDLADY *is dusting chairs. A sound of wheels and horses outside, then* DAVID, *a boy about ten years of age, enters shyly and sits down on the edge of the chair nearest the door.*

Characters—LANDLADY, DAVID COPPERFIELD, THE WAITER.

LANDLADY: Are you the little gentleman from Blunderstone?

DAVID (*jumping up*): Yes, ma'am.

LANDLADY: What name?

DAVID: Copperfield, ma'am.

LANDLADY: That won't do. Nobody's dinner is paid for here in that name.

DAVID: Is it Murdstone, ma'am?

LANDLADY: If your name is Master Murdstone, why do you go and give another name first?

DAVID: I'm really Copperfield, David Copperfield, but my father died and my mother married Mr. Murdstone, so that's her name now.

LANDLADY: Oh, I see. Well, your dinner's ready. I'll get it sent in. (*She rings the bell.*) William! William!

(WILLIAM *the* WAITER *enters, running out of the kitchen.*)

LANDLADY: William, bring in dinner for this gentleman. (*She goes out.*)

(*The* WAITER *brings in a dish of chops, plates, glass, jug of beer, etc.*)

WAITER: Now then, six foot, come on. (*He stands looking at* DAVID, *who gets more and more shy and nervous as he tries to eat with the* WAITER's *eye on him.*) There's half a pint of beer for you; shall I get it now?

DAVID: Yes, please.

(*The* WAITER *goes to the table and pours out the glass of beer and holds it up to the light.*)

WAITER: My eye! It seems a lot, doesn't it?

DAVID: Yes, it does seem rather a lot.

WAITER (*still holding the beer*): There was a gentleman here yesterday, a rather fat gentleman by the name of Topsawyer—perhaps you know him?

DAVID: No, I don't think I do.

WAITER: Fellow with a grey coat, big hat——

DAVID: No, I'm sorry, I haven't the pleasure——

WAITER: He came in here, ordered a glass of beer, *would* order it—I told him not to—drank it and fell dead. It was too old for him. This beer ought not to be drunk, that's a fact.

DAVID: How terrible. Perhaps—do you think I had better have some water?

WAITER: Well, you see, the landlady gets annoyed if things are ordered and then left. But I'll drink it if you like. You see, I'm used to it, and use is everything. I don't think it will hurt me if I throw my head back and get it down quickly. Shall I?

DAVID: I should be much obliged if you are quite sure it won't hurt you?

WAITER: Well, we'll see. (*He drinks it at one drink without spilling a drop,* DAVID *watching him very anxiously but quite relieved when nothing serious happens. He sets down the glass and then takes up a fork and sticks it into the dish.*) Why, what have we got here? Not chops?

DAVID: Yes, chops.

WAITER: Lord bless my soul. I didn't know they were chops. Why, a chop is the very thing to get rid of the bad effects of that beer. Isn't it lucky? (*He takes up a chop and a potato.*)

DAVID: Have another chop. That beer needs two.

WAITER: I will—and a potato. If only we'd had chops and potatoes when Topsawyer drank that beer we might have saved his life.

DAVID: There's still one more chop. Won't you have that?

WAITER: Well, perhaps it would be safer; why there's another potato too—better take that and then I think I'll be quite safe.

(*The chops and potatoes being finished, the* WAITER *takes away the dishes and brings in a plum pudding.* DAVID *begins eating.*)

WAITER: How's the pie?

DAVID: It isn't a pie, it's pudding.

WAITER: Pudding! Why, bless my soul, so it is! (*Comes nearer.*) You don't mean to say it's a plum pudding?

DAVID: Yes, indeed it is.

WAITER (*taking up a large spoon*): Why, a plum pudding is my favourite pudding. Isn't that lucky. Come on, boy, let's see who gets most. (*They both eat,* DAVID *with his small spoon and rather slowly;* the WAITER *with his tablespoon and very fast.*) Come on, you're getting behind.

DAVID: Well, your spoon is so much bigger.

WAITER: There's just one little piece more. Ah! I just beat you for that. Well, it was a good pudding, wasn't it, and I like a bit of fun, don't you?

DAVID (*rather doubtfully*): Yes. (*Sound of horses and wheels outside.*) I must go now. Er—is there— do I—is there anything else to pay for besides the dinner?

WAITER: No, there's nothing except the waiter.

DAVID: What should you—what ought I—what would it be right to pay the waiter, please?

WAITER: Well, if I hadn't a family and that family wasn't all ill, I wouldn't take sixpence. If I didn't keep a poor old father and a lovely sister (*he almost bursts into tears*) I wouldn't take a farthing. If I had a good place and was treated well, I should ask you to accept something from me instead of taking it from you. But all I get to eat are dry crusts and I sleep on the coals. (*He buries his face in his hands.*)

DAVID: Well, here's a shilling.

WAITER (*his tears quite forgotten*): Thank you, sir; thank you. You are a real gentleman. Thank you. Whenever you come here again, ask for me.

(*Enter* LANDLADY.)

LANDLADY: Come on, the coach is waiting. Here, William, help him into the coach.

(*The* WAITER *takes* DAVID *out and puts him into the coach; the* LANDLADY *looks at the table*.)

LANDLADY: Bless my soul, he's eaten six chops and the whole pudding. He'll need helping into the coach. (*Puts her head through the window and shouts to the coachman.*) Take care of that child, George, or he'll burst!

(*Curtain.*)

VERB STUDY (7): **get**

There are eight examples of the use of *get* in Lesson 10, i.e.

1. Your dinner's ready. I'll *get* it sent in.
2. David *gets* more and more shy.
3. There's half a pint of beer for you. Shall I *get* it?
4. The landlady *gets annoyed* if things are left.
5. It won't hurt me if I throw my head back and *get it down* quickly.
6. A chop's the very thing to *get rid of* the bad effects of that beer.
7. Come on, *you're getting behind*.
8. All I *get* to eat are dry crusts.

Here are the meanings and some examples of other idiomatic uses:

1. "to obtain" (as in 3 and 8 above), or "become the owner of:"

    I *got* a letter this morning.
    I *got* a bad cold at the dance last night.
    He always *gets* his own way.
    What schooling Dickens had he *got* at Chatham (p. 61).

2. "become" (as in 2 and 4):

    In time everyone *gets old*.
    You will *get better* if you work harder.
    Sit by the fire and you will soon *get warm*.
    If you are not careful you will *get hurt*.

3. "to arrive", "to go":

    I didn't *get* home till 10 o'clock.
    The train was so full I couldn't *get into* it.
    This is where I *get off* the bus.
    Never *get into debt* if you can avoid it.

4. "cause to be done":

> Why don't you *get* your hair cut ?
> I must *get* the tailor to *make* me a new suit.
> I'll *get* him *to do* the work.

There are three common patterns with *get*:

(1)

besorgen

Subject, etc.	get	Indirect Object	Direct Object
Will you	*get*	me	some cigarettes, please ?
His uncle	*got*	him	a good job.

verschaffen

(2)

Subject, etc.	get	(Pro)noun	Adjective, Participle
You	have *got*	your feet	wet.
They soon	*got*	the fire	burning.
I	must *get*	that radio	mended.

(3)

Subject, etc.	get	(Pro)noun	Infinitive
They finally	*got*	him	to sign the paper.
I	will *get*	the boy	to write you a letter.

4

EXERCISES

I. *Word Study. Use the following:*

inn (compare with *in*), map, dust (*noun* and *verb*), shy, landlady (what is the masculine form ?), chop (*noun*) (*chop* is also
a verb with a different meaning; what would you use to *chop*
wood ?), pour (compare with *poor*), annoy, use (*noun* and
verb, both forms are used on p. 85; note the difference in
pronunciation), spill, drop (*noun*; use it also, with a different
meaning, as a verb), anxious (what is the corresponding
noun ?), stick (*verb*; use it also, with a different meaning, as
a noun), effect (use also *affect*), still (note the use of it in the
play; its use was explained on p. 53–4), crust, coach.

II. *What is the difference between:*

1. a teaspoon and a tablespoon. 2. a pie and a pudding.
3. dinner and lunch. 4. a landlord and a landlady. 5. a pint
of beer and a quart of beer. 6. a waiter and a waitress.
7. a shilling and a farthing.

III. *Turn the following into indirect speech:*

1. David said, "I am really Copperfield; that is my name."
2. The landlady said, "Are you the little gentleman from
   Blunderstone ?"
3. The waiter said, "There's half a pint of beer for you; will
   you have it now ?"
4. The waiter said, "I will drink it if you like. I am used to
   it. I don't think it will hurt me if I throw my head back
   and get it down quickly."
5. David said, "Have another chop. That beer needs two."
6. David said, "I must go now. Is there anything else to pay
   for besides the dinner ?"
7. The waiter said, "All I get to eat are dry crusts and I
   sleep on the coals."
8. The waiter said, "Whenever you come here again, ask
   for me."

9. The landlady said, "Come on, the coach is waiting. Here, William, help him into the coach."
10. The landlady shouted, "Take care of that child, George, or he'll burst!"

IV. *Explain carefully:*

1. How you would set a table for dinner.
2. How you would make a pie (or a pudding).

V.　COMPREHENSION EXERCISE

1. As David's name was Copperfield, why was his dinner ordered in the name of Murdstone?
2. Why does the waiter address David as "six foot"?
3. Do you think the waiter's story of Mr. Topsawyer was true? Why does he tell David that story?
4. What reason did the waiter give for drinking the beer himself?
5. Why (according to the waiter) wouldn't the beer do him any harm?
6. What excuse did he give David for eating David's chops?
7. Why did the waiter get more of the pudding than David did?
8. What tip did David give the waiter?
9. What account did the waiter give of his hard life?
10. What did the landlady shout to the coachman? Why?

VI. *Use the following in sentences of your own:*

get a cold; get better; get rid of; get annoyed; get round someone; get your own way; get warm; get off; get made; get into trouble; get into debt.

VII.　*Composition Exercises*

1. Tell the story of this play (1) as David, (2) as the waiter might have told it.

2. Take a scene from any other novel that you know and turn it into a play.

LESSON 11

Hob Tells the Life-story of
a Great Briton

HOB: You have told us about one or two great men in history but I'd like to tell you about a great man who is still living. May I ?

MR. PRIESTLEY: Certainly, Hob. Who is it ?

HOB: My Uncle Albert, Mr. Albert Hobdell.

PEDRO: Well, you've been threatening us with this for the last two years, so let's get it over.

HOB: Well, I'll tell you the story exactly as I had it from him.

THE STORY OF UNCLE ALBERT

"Fifteen years ago," said Uncle Albert, "I was a caretaker at Greyfriars Street School in Manchester. I swept the floors and cleaned the blackboard and put the desks straight after school and opened the windows in the morning and locked the doors at night, put coal on the fires and did about a hundred other odd jobs—all for five pounds a week.

"As a matter of fact I quite liked the job. The headmaster, Mr. Brown, was a nice old fellow, friendly and easy-going, and he was always very kind to me. I'd known him for years, in fact I'd been a boy at his school, though I must say I was no credit as a scholar to him, or to any other teacher for that matter. I was one of those boys who just can't learn, at least can't learn any of the things they teach in school. Now if it was making things with my hands, I was clever enough at that—I could make anything from a fishing-rod to a dining-table, but reading and writing were completely beyond me, and to this day I can't read or write—and I've never felt that I wanted to——"

FRIEDA: Do you mean to say he can't read or write anything at all?

HOB: Not a word. He can't even write his own name —for that matter, he can't even say it properly; he always calls himself Albert 'Obdell. But he's one of the cleverest and best men I know. There's nobody like him for telling a story— not even me. And as a judge of character he is one of the shrewdest I've ever met. He can weigh up anyone in the first few minutes and he is hardly ever deceived in a man.

Well, to come back to Uncle Albert's story: "... I went on quite happily at Greyfriars Street until old Mr. Brown the headmaster retired and a new young head, Mr. Johnson, came in his place. Mr. Johnson was quite different from old Mr. Brown. He was the new broom that sweeps clean. He was going to organise everything properly; he would make the school really efficient and up-to-date. The work was going to be better; the boys were going to learn twice as much in half the time and get more scholarships.

The play, too, was going to be organised; the school must win all its football matches and all its cricket matches. All day long you heard nothing but 'organisation' and 'efficiency' until you were tired to death of the words. If anyone was inefficient he had to go. 'Get on—or get out' was Mr. Johnson's motto.

"At first I got on all right. I could do my work quite well and there were never any complaints. Then Mr. Johnson had the idea that what was wanted to make the school more efficient was a 'time-book'. Every one of the staff had to sign this every morning when he came to school, putting in the exact time that he arrived, and sign it again in the evening, putting in again the exact moment that he went away. At the end of the week the headmaster looked at the book to see that no one had come at eight minutes to nine instead of ten minutes to, or had dared to go away before he himself had gone. So on Friday he picked up the book and looked at it; yes, it seemed all right—and then he noticed that my name was not there at all. He could hardly believe his eyes. I was sent for and I went, feeling rather worried, to the headmaster's room.

" 'Oh, Hobdell, I gave orders that every man had to sign the time-book. Did you know about that order?'

" 'Yes, sir.'

" 'I don't see your signature here. Did you sign the book?'

" 'No, sir.'

" 'When I give orders I expect them to be carried out, and any man who doesn't carry them out leaves. Do you understand that ?'

" 'Yes, sir.'

" 'Well, why didn't you sign ?'

"It was an awkward question but I felt the only way was to be quite truthful about it.

" 'Because I can't write.'

" 'What! Can't write! Good heavens! You'll tell me next that you can't read.'

" 'No, sir; I mean, yes, sir, I can't read.'

" 'This is terrible. I can hardly believe it. An official in an educational establishment (that sounded better to him than "school") and can't read! Well, you know I can't have inefficiency here. You must leave. Take a week's notice.'

" 'But, sir, I've done this job for over twenty years and no one has ever found any fault with my work. Why should I be dismissed now ? The rooms are always well cleaned and warmed, aren't they, and——'

" 'Oh, yes, that's all right; but the fact of the matter is I can't have a caretaker in my school who can't read and write. No, you must go.'

*　　　*　　　*

"I went home that evening feeling very worried. I wasn't married; I lived in a little house all by myself and looked after myself, cooked my own food and kept the place very clean and comfortable—at least everyone who came there always said so. I used to take my lunch (usually bread and cheese) to school with me, as I never had much time during the lunch hour to get a meal then. But I did like to have something tasty for my tea when I got home. A good strong cup of tea—with three lumps of sugar—and a kipper, a tin of salmon or a bit of bacon, but, above all, sausages. I was, and am, a great man for sausages. If ever I felt down-hearted I used to find that a good plate of fried sausages always cheered me up again. So I thought I'd get half a pound on my way home and fry them for my tea and then, perhaps, I'd feel less miserable.

"And then I remembered . . . Mrs. Wiggs who kept the little shop where I always bought sausages had died and the shop was empty now. Yes, here it was looking as cheerless and un-happy as I felt. There would be no sausages tonight, for there was no other shop anywhere near that sold sausages—at least none that were eatable—and I knew there was nothing else in my cupboard at home. That was the last straw, the straw that breaks the camel's back; just when I needed sausages most there wasn't a sausage anywhere.

" 'I can't understand why there isn't more than one good sausage shop in the whole of south Manchester,' I said, feeling really bad-tempered. And then I stopped; an idea had struck me. Why not? I'd a little bit of money saved and I'd no job now. Why shouldn't I take Mrs. Wiggs' shop and sell sausages?

" I got so excited at the idea that I forgot all about my tea and the job I had lost. I knew the landlord of the shop, and I went round that evening to see him. There was no difficulty at all; within a week the shop was open and I was behind the counter selling sausages. And then I had another idea.

Why not sell sausages ready-cooked? So I fried sausages and had them all hot just about five o'clock. It was a cold, foggy November just then and I kept the shop-door open so that the smell of fried sausages floated out into the street. Soon I was selling them as fast as I could fry them. Mind you, they were *good* sausages. I knew a good sausage when I saw one, and in my shop there was nothing but the best. I used to sell them on small sticks (I was the first man in England to think of that idea) with a piece of bread. Before the month was out I was employing two assistants in the shop and still I couldn't sell sausages fast enough.

" Then I had another idea. I engaged a boy with a bicycle to go round and sell hot sausages in the streets. I had to hire a bicycle—five shillings a week it cost me. But I soon needed two more assistants to cook sausages for the boy and then two more boys to take round the sausages. 'Hobdell's Sausages' were becoming known and I had started on Big Business. I opened two more shops and still couldn't supply all my customers. It was then, too, that I started to manufacture sausages instead of buying them wholesale.

"But summer came and I thought there would be very little business now until the winter. It was a beautiful hot summer; no one wanted hot sausages—in fact no one wanted hot food at all. Then came another idea. As no one wanted to do any cooking why not supply customers with cold food ready-cooked? And so the boys went round on bicycles with cold sausages on little sticks and we sold more in summer than we had done in winter.

"But I don't need to tell you any more about how the business has grown since then. From that first day I have never looked back. You must have seen the boys on the bicycles and 'Hobdell's Sausage Shops' in every street of London. Now they are in every street in England You have seen, I expect, the advertisements in the daily papers, 'EAT MORE SAUSAGES', 'SAUSAGES ARE BEST', 'BUY BRITISH —HOBDELL'S SAUSAGES ARE BRITISH TO THE BACKBONE'. Every cinema in England has shown the film 'The Birth of a Sausage'. Aeroplanes have written 'HOB-

DELL'S SAUSAGES' in the sky. I spent
£50,000 last year on advertising. People who
haven't heard of Shakespeare's plays have heard
of Hobdell's Sausages. There are 10,000 men
and girls frying sausages for me now. I've
extended my factories as far as I can and am
looking now for a bigger building with enough
land round it for 100,000 pigs.

"Funnily enough, up to five years ago I had
never had a banking account, but everyone told
me I ought to have one, so I went to see the
manager of the bank in the place where my
factory is and said I wanted to open an account
with him.

"He was very polite and friendly. 'Certainly,
Mr. Hobdell. How much would you like to start
with?'

"'Oh, about £200,000.'

"'Very good, Mr. Hobdell. Oh, yes, we'll
arrange all that. Now you will need a cheque
book and we shall want a copy of your signature.
Will you please sign here?'

"I laughed. 'Sorry, Mr. Parke,' I said, 'you
may hardly believe it, but the fact of the matter
is I can't even write my name—I can only make
my mark.'

"The manager was certainly surprised, but
feeling, I suppose, that to a man with such a good
balance in the bank he must say something
pleasant, he said, 'You do surprise me, Mr.
Hobdell. And yet you have made such a success
of life. You have done all this without any

education at all. What would you have been, I wonder, if only you had learned to read and write?'

"I laughed. 'Caretaker at Greyfriars Street School at five pounds a week!' I said."

VERB STUDY (8): **break**

On p. 96 you have the sentence:

"That was the last straw, the straw that *breaks* the camel's back."

Here are further examples of the use of *break*:

You can *break up* (= knock to pieces) that box for firewood.

The school *breaks up* (= begins holidays) on Friday.

The police *broke down* the door and entered the room.

The car *broke down* (= wouldn't go) when we were twenty miles from home.

When the woman heard the bad news she *broke down* (= was overcome with sorrow).

The little girl *broke into tears* (= cried) and cried as if *her heart would break*.

EXERCISES

I. *Word Study: Use the following:*

history (also *historical*; note the difference in accentuation), threaten, caretaker, odd (what are the first four *odd numbers* and the first four *even numbers*; use the phrases "four pounds odd", "odds and ends", "an odd glove", "to fight against heavy odds"), easy-going, shrewd, retire (use also *retirement*), organise (also *organiser*, *organisation*), efficient (what is the opposite?), scholarship, match (two meanings), motto, staff, sign (what is the corresponding noun?), awkward, worry, tasty, salmon (can you name three other fishes?), down-hearted, fry (what other verbs do you know connected with cooking?), cupboard (note the pronunciation), counter, ready-cooked (what is a *ready-made* suit?), fog, assist (also *assistant* and *assistance*), bicycle, hire (compare *higher*), customer, manufacture, wholesale (the opposite is *retail*), advertise (also *advertisement*; note the different accentuation), film, cheque (compare *check*), balance.

II. *Choose twenty of the following words or phrases, and give for each another word or phrase of similar meaning to that in which the word is used in the passage:*

1. Let's *get it over*.
2. reading and writing were *completely beyond me*.
3. shrewd.
4. *weigh up* someone.
5. retire.
6. broom.
7. *up-to-date* school.
8. You had to *put in* the exact time you arrived.
9. he *picked up* the book.
10. I expect orders to be *carried out*.
11. *awkward* question.
12. *an educational establishment*.
13. dismiss.
14. I felt *down-hearted*.
15. I am *a great man for* sausages.
16. The shop looked *cheerless*.
17. An idea had *struck me*.
18. The smell *floated* into the street.
19. I *engaged* a boy.
20. Manufacture.
21. Wholesale.
22. *Extended* my factories.
23. To *open* an account.
24. *As a matter of fact.*
25. a good *balance* in the bank.
26. From that first day I have never *looked back*.

III. *Choose ten of the following words and give for each another word or phrase opposite in meaning to that in which the word is used in the passage:*
clever, best, organise, efficient, up-to-date, win, truthful, clean, strong, down-hearted (there's no word *up-hearted*!), wholesale, extended, polite, success.

IV. *Make the following sentences negative:*

1. He lived in a house all by himself.
2. He used to take his lunch to school with him.
3. He had some sausages in the house.
4. I knew there was something else in the cupboard at home.
5. I forgot about my tea, I thought about the job I had lost, I went back to the school.

V. *Turn into indirect speech the following, e.g.*

Direct: Hob said, "I will tell you about my uncle."

Indirect: Hob said that he would tell them about his uncle.

1. "I will tell you the story exactly as I know it."
2. "I am a caretaker at Greyfriars Street School."
3. "I can't write my own name, but I can tell a good story."
4. Mr. Johnson said, "Get on—or get out."
5. Mr. Johnson said, "Hobdell, do you know about that order?"
6. "Why didn't you sign the book?" he said.
7. Mr. Johnson said, "This is terrible. I can hardly believe it. I can't have such inefficiency here. You must leave. Take a week's notice."

VI.   COMPREHENSION EXERCISE

1. What was Albert's work as caretaker?
2. What is your opinion of Albert (*a*) as a scholar, (*b*) as a business man?
3. What did Hob mean when he said Albert could "weigh up anyone in the first few minutes"?
4. How was Mr. Johnson different from Mr. Brown?
5. What was Mr. Johnson's aim for his school (*a*) in work, (*b*) in sport?
6. What was Johnson's motto?
7. What was the aim of the "time-book"? Do you think it was a good idea?

8. What does "Take a week's notice" mean?
9. What did Albert like to eat?
10. Why couldn't Albert buy sausages on this particular evening?
11. What sort of an evening was it when Albert opened his shop for the first time? Why did he leave the door open?
12. Why did he think there would be very little business in summer? How did he overcome this difficulty?
13. Mention some of the advertisements that Albert used.
14. What did his advertising cost him last year?
15. What is a cheque? Draw a sketch of one and fill in the details.

VII. *Make sentences of your own containing the following idioms*:

break up; break down; break into; break off; break out; break the back of; break the ice; break the news.

ūḃaṛoinḍaṛ

VIII. *Composition Exercises*

1. Tell the story up to Albert's receiving notice as if you were Mr. Johnson.

2. What would be your duties if you were (*a*) a caretaker, (*b*) a schoolmaster, (*c*) a shopkeeper.

3. Tell in about 400 words the story of Uncle Albert.

4. Write a letter congratulating someone on having suddenly made a fortune, *or* on becoming a father, *or* being made a manager of a business.

5. Write an essay on the subject "Every cloud has a silver lining" or "It's the last straw that breaks the camel's back."

LESSON 12

GREAT BRITONS (2): **Oliver Cromwell**

MR. PRIESTLEY: One of the chief threads that make up the pattern of English history, a thread that runs through it from the earliest times almost to our present day, is the struggle between the king and the people (or the Parliament) to decide which should be supreme. At first and for many centuries the king was all-powerful, but gradually his powers were reduced and those of Parliament built up until now it is the Parliament that, in all but name, is the chief power in the land.

And in this long struggle one of the most decisive moments came in the seventeenth century. It was during this period that the political parties as we know them today began to take shape. Charles I was on the throne. His portrait, painted by Van Dyck, has given us a vivid impression of his handsome face with its sad, thoughtful eyes, his kingly manner and his charm. We know that as a man he was admirable, sincerely religious, a faithful husband and a loving father. As a king he was dishonourable, and untrustworthy. He was brought up to believe in the "Divine Right of Kings", and hated the idea of a Parliament, believing that its only purpose was to vote the money that he thought necessary. To get the money he lightly gave any promise that Parliament asked for, and just as lightly broke that word of honour. Time and again he was trusted and time and again he was false to that trust, until it was forced on the people that no promise that he gave was of any value. At last, when Charles entered the House of Commons itself with the intention of arresting the five men who were the leaders of the party that opposed him, people realised that if freedom and truth and justice were to live at all there was no other choice but to resist him by force.

The actual fighting in the Civil War broke out in 1642. At first the tide of battle went completely against the Parliamentary forces, and they were hopelessly defeated in almost every battle. It was natural that they should be. The majority of the country landowners and the wealthy men, most of whom had been trained in arms and had weapons and horses, supported Charles. He had, too, skilful leaders like Prince Rupert of the Rhine; he had all the gay, pleasure-loving, fashionable gentlemen of England, the Cavaliers as they were called, on his side. The Royalists were far more attractive than the Parliamentarians. They had learning, courtesy and good manners. They loved poetry and music and art; their long, curled hair and gay-coloured clothes were the outward expression of an inward gaiety and love of the beautiful.

The Parliamentarians had none of this charm. They were mostly Puritans, men who wanted a simpler and plainer form of religion, and,

CAVALIER FAMILY

among the extremists at least, only too often this showed itself in an actual dislike of the beautiful merely because it was beautiful. It led them to destroy pictures, the lovely stained-glass windows of churches and often the churches themselves.

The Puritans, too, bore the outward signs of their beliefs; their dress was plain and dull in colouring; their hair was cut close—the Cavaliers called them "Roundheads"—their faces were habitually sour. To them all pleasures, even the most innocent, were sinful things. They scorned learning and art; they were bitterly intolerant of the opinions of their enemies and the pleasures of their friends.

But—on the other side of the picture—they had a courage that no defeats could crush; they had a religious faith that inspired every act of their lives. For them God was a living, daily reality. "If they knew nothing of the works of philosophers and poets they were deeply read in the writings of God; if their names were not found in the book of courtiers they were written in the Book of Life. Their palaces were houses not made with hands; their crowns were of

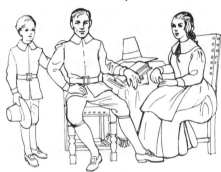

PURITAN FAMILY

glory that should never fade away. On the rich and the learned, on nobles and priests, they looked down with scorn, for they knew themselves to be rich in a more precious treasure, nobles by a greater right, priests by the laying on of a mightier hand. Thus, the Puritan was made up of two different men; the one all humbleness, gratitude, feeling; the other proud, calm, unbending. He humbled himself in the dust before his Maker; but he set his foot on the neck of his king. The intensity of their feelings on one subject made them calm on all others. They had their smiles and their tears, but not for the things of this world. For them death had lost its terrors and pleasure its charm."[1]

[1] Macaulay (1800–59), *Essay on Milton* (adapted to Essential English).

But courage and religious faith alone are not enough to win battles. Leadership and training are necessary too, and it was the hour—the darkest hour for the Parliamentary forces—that brought the man, Oliver Cromwell.

Cromwell was a country gentleman, a farmer of Huntingdonshire, with no desire to be known in the world. He had wanted to leave England and find a new home in America where he would be free to worship as he wished, but the king had forbidden him to leave England. He had been in Parliament, a rough, ungraceful figure, unskilful as a speaker but known for his strength of character and his deep sincerity and religious feeling. Cromwell saw that if the Parliament army was to be victorious it must not only be as fearless and as full of faith in its own cause as the Cavaliers were in theirs, but it must be as well trained as Charles's army—and, if possible, better trained.

He went to the eastern counties and gathered soldiers there, men specially picked for their courage, strength, horsemanship and religious feeling. He said: "A few honest men are better than numbers. If you choose good, honest men to be captains of horse, honest men will follow them." He trained his men in complete obedience, filled them with the desire to fight for freedom, Parliament and religion, combining the spiritual and the practical as in his famous order: "Trust in God, and keep your powder dry."

Then when they were ready he led them into

battle, and on that day his army—the Ironsides as they came to be known—did not give way. For the first time the Cavaliers had been held.

Several battles were won by the Parliamentarians, and finally at Naseby, 1645, the king's forces were completely defeated.

Cromwell was now leader of the whole Parliamentary forces; the king's army was scattered and the king himself was in flight. Seeing that his cause was lost, he gave himself up, and was imprisoned in Carisbrooke Castle in the Isle of Wight. Finally he was brought to trial in London for having made war on his people and for being an enemy of his country. He was found guilty and sentenced to death. At his trial he behaved nobly and firmly, refusing to defend himself before a court which, he said, had no power to try him, and he received the death sentence with a calm courage.

Four days later, after a sad farewell to his younger children[1] in St. James's Palace, he walked across St. James's Park through the snow to Whitehall and there, outside the palace, he was beheaded. Whatever may have been his faults in life, he bore himself like a real king in his last moments:

> He nothing common did or mean
> Upon that memorable scene,
> But bowed his comely[2] head,
> Down as upon a bed.

[1] His wife and eldest son had already gone to France.
[2] *Comely* ['kʌmli] = handsome (*poetic*). From a poem by Andrew Marvell (1621–78).

Cromwell now became ruler of England, not as king but as "Protector of the Commonwealth", and for ten years he ruled England firmly but well. He could be merciless—his treatment of Ireland is one of the blots on his character—yet he loved mercy, and in an age that was bitter with religious intolerance he was nobly tolerant. "The State, in choosing men to serve it," Cromwell wrote before the battle of Marston Moor, "takes no notice of their opinions. If they are willing, faithfully to serve it, that is enough." And from the field of Naseby, just after the victory, he wrote to the Speaker of the House of Commons: "Honest men served you faithfully in this action. Sir, they are trustworthy. I beg you in the name of God not to discourage them. He that risks his life for the liberty of his country, should have liberty of his conscience. In things of the mind we look for no compulsion but that of light and reason."[1]

It was he who really united England, Scotland and Ireland, who enforced justice and order at home and made England stronger and more respected abroad than she had ever been before in the whole of her history, and if he at times acted like a tyrant, he did it because in this, as in the execution of Charles, he saw that this was the only means of bringing order and peace in England.

His rough, harsh nature, like his stern, harsh face, did not inspire affection—though under

[1] Slightly modernised and written in Essential English.

the rough outward appearance there was kind-
ness—but his strength, his unshakable honesty
and his sincere religion made him respected as
one of the greatest Englishmen.

VERB STUDY (9): **bring**

On pp. 104, 107 and 109 you have the sentences:

He was *brought up* (= educated, trained) to believe in the
"Divine Right of Kings".

It was the hour that *brought* the man.

He was *brought to trial* in London.

The essential meaning of *bring* is "to carry to the
place where the speaker is", e.g.

Bring me your book.

Jack will *bring along* some colour photographs (page 23).

but there are numerous variations from this meaning.
Here are some:

What *brings you* (= why have you come) here today?

That remark *brought* his guilt *home* to him (= made him
realise it).

His work has *brought* him fame and riches.

What *brought about* (= caused) the failure of the business?

The sight of that heather *brings back* (= reminds, calls to
mind) the happy days we spent in Scotland.

The jury *brought in* (= gave) a verdict of "not guilty".

His illness was *brought on* (= caused) by poor feeding.

The publishers are going to *bring out* (= publish) a new
edition of that book.

EXERCISES

I. *Word Study: Use the following:*

thread, pattern, history (what is the difference between
history and *story*?), struggle, supreme (use also *supremacy*),

reduce (what is the opposite?), decisive (use also *decide*, *decision, indecisive*), portrait (what is the difference between a *portrait* and a *picture*?), vivid, handsome (what is the difference between *handsome, pretty* and *beautiful*?), admirable (use also *admire, admiration*), trust (*noun* and *verb*) (use also *trustworthy, untrustworthy, entrust*), vote, false (use also *falsely, falseness, falsehood*), arrest, oppose (use also *opposition, opposite*), resist (use also *resistance*), yield, majority (what is the opposite?), weapon, learning (*noun*), extreme (use also *extremist, extremely, extremity*), stained-glass, philosopher (use also *philosophy*), courtier (use also *courtesy*; what is meant by "the King's court"?), palace (compare with *place*), humble (*adjective* and *verb*) (use also *humbly, humbleness*), gratitude (the corresponding adjective is *grateful*) (use also *ungrateful, gratefully, ingratitude*), calm (note the silent "l"), forbid, county (compare *country*), obedience (use also *obey, disobey, disobedience*), scatter, imprisoned (use also *prison, prisoner, imprisonment*), sentence (*verb*), mercy (use also *merciful, merciless*), blot (*noun* and *verb*) (what is *blotting-paper*?), enforce, tyrant (use also *tyranny, tyrannical*), harsh (use also *harshly, harshness*), affection (use also *affectionate, affectionately*).

II. *Explain the following words or phrases from this lesson:*

1. the king was *all-powerful*.
2. it is Parliament that, *in all but name*, is the chief power.
3. one of the most *decisive moments*.
4. he *lightly* gave any promise.
5. *it was forced on the people* that no promise he gave was of any value.
6. their gay-coloured clothes *were an outward expression of an inward gaiety*.
7. their faces were *habitually sour*.
8. they were *deeply read in the writings of God*.
9. their palaces were houses *not made with hands*.
10. *for them death had lost its terrors*.
11. *it was the hour that brought the man*.

12. horsemanship.
13. *keep your powder dry.*
14. the Ironsides *did not give way.*
15. For the first time the Cavaliers *had been held.*
16. the king *gave himself up.*
17. his treatment of Ireland *is one of the blots on his character.*

COMPREHENSION EXERCISE

III. *Give short answers to the following questions:*

1. "In this long struggle one of the most decisive moments came in the seventeenth century." What struggle is referred to ? Why was this a decisive time ?
2. Why did the Parliamentarians decide to resist Charles I by force ?
3. Why did the Parliamentarians suffer defeat at first ?
4. If you had been living in the seventeenth century how would you have been able to tell a Cavalier from a Puritan ?
5. How did Cromwell bring about military success for the Parliamentarians ?
6. How does Cromwell's order, "Trust in God and keep your powder dry", combine "the spiritual and the practical" ?
7. What were the main things that Cromwell did for England ?

IV. *Express in other words:*

1.   He nothing common did or mean
           Upon that memorable scene,
           But bowed his comely head,
           Down as upon a bed.
2. On the rich and the learned, on nobles and priests, they looked down with scorn, for they knew themselves to be rich in a more precious treasure, nobles by a greater right, priests by the laying on of a mightier hand.

3. He that risks his life for the liberty of his country should have liberty of his conscience. In things of the mind we look for no compulsion but that of light and reason.

V. *Learn by heart the lines of Marvell (p. 109), the words of Cromwell (p. 110), and, if you feel like it, the passage from Macaulay (p. 107).*

VI. *Use in sentences of your own the following idioms with* bring:

bring up; bring about; bring on; bring out; bring the house down; bring to a close; bring (something) off.

VII.　　　　　*Composition Exercises*

1. Write character sketches of (1) a Puritan, (2) a Cavalier.

2. Give your impressions of the character of (1) Charles I, (2) Cromwell.

3. Write an essay on one of the following:

1. "The Divine Right of Kings."
2. "The hour brings the man."
3. "A few honest men are better than numbers."
4. "Trust in God and keep your powder dry."
5. "In things of the mind we look for no compulsion but that of light and reason."

LESSON 13

Great Britons (3): **John Milton**

MR. PRIESTLEY: I spoke to you a day or two ago about the Cavaliers and the Puritans in England in the seventeenth century. I said, you may remember, that the Puritans despised learning and art, that they often showed an actual dislike of the beautiful, and knew nothing of the works of philosophers and poets. But that is not true of one of them at least, the greatest of the Puritans and one of the greatest Englishmen, John Milton. He is in many ways characteristic of the age in which he lived, but he is not limited by it. Like Shakespeare, he belongs not to an age but to all time.

He was born in 1608 at a house in Bread Street, London, almost under the shadow of St. Paul's Cathedral. Shakespeare was living in London then and writing his plays—indeed there is a story that Milton, a boy of six or seven, once met Shakespeare, then a man of almost fifty.

Milton's father was a kind of lawyer, a Puritan but a man of learning and a lover of music. John went to school at St. Paul's, a famous English school, and then when he was seventeen to Christ's College, Cambridge. From his early youth Milton seems to have known, with complete certainty, that God had chosen him for some great purpose to which his whole life had to be devoted. At first he thought of entering the Church as a preacher, but later he decided this was not his chosen work, and after taking his degree he returned to the little village of Horton in Buckinghamshire, 17 miles from London, where his father had retired, and he settled down to six more years of study, to reading poetry, philosophy, music and languages.

There was always in Milton's mind the idea of a great poem that he was to write. What its subject was to be he did not know, but in his determination to choose the noblest of subjects and to write in a style worthy of the subject, he read and studied in order to become familiar with the best that had been written and done by other men. He mastered Greek and Latin literature completely, learned French, Italian and Spanish and studied the latest theories of science. This was followed by travels in France and Italy where he perfected his knowledge of French and Italian. He visited theatres there, listened to music and met great and learned men, including Galileo, now old and blind and in prison. He had intended to go to Greece, but the news of the coming struggle in England brought him home. " I considered it a dishonourable thing," he wrote, " to be travelling for amusement abroad in foreign lands while my countrymen were fighting for liberty at home." So in 1639 he came back, and joined the struggle in the way he thought he could help best, not by fighting but by writing to explain and to defend the Puritan cause. For the next twenty years he wrote practically no poetry. Action had taken the place of poetry. "It is fine and noble," he said, "to sing the ways of God; it is finer and nobler to fulfil them." His prose writings, powerful, fierce, learned, have, generally speaking, lost their interest for us now, but one great work stands out, one of the greatest pieces of prose in our language, his *Areopagitica* defending the freedom of the press.

"As good almost kill a man," he wrote, "as kill a good book: he who kills a man destroys a reasonable creature, God's image; but he who destroys a good book, kills reason itself, kills the image of God. . . . Many a man lives a burden to the earth; but a good book is the precious life-blood of a master-spirit embalmed[1] and treasured up on purpose to a life beyond life. Give me the liberty to know, to utter[2] and to argue freely according to my conscience, above all liberties."

In 1649 he became Foreign Secretary to Cromwell. He worked day and night writing, in Latin, countless letters to foreign rulers, reading and translating their replies. As you have seen, the

[1] embalmed [im'baːmd] = preserved so that it doesn't decay, as dead bodies are sometimes preserved.
[2] utter ['ʌtə] = speak.

cause of Puritanism gained the day. Charles I was defeated and executed and Cromwell became ruler of England. But the price that Milton paid was a terrible one. At the age of forty-three, with the great work (that he knew beyond any doubt he was to write) still unwritten, Milton became completely and incurably blind. The doctors had warned him some years before that if he continued with his work he ran the certain risk of going blind. He decided to go on with his work. He wrote, " My resolution was unshaken, though the choice was either the loss of my sight or the desertion of my duty,"[1]

There are few nobler or more moving poems in the English language than Milton's sonnet *On his Blindness*.

> When I consider how my light is spent
>> Ere half my days, in this dark world and wide,
>> And that one talent which is death to hide,
>> Lodged with me useless, though my soul more bent
> To serve therewith my Maker, and present
>> My true account, lest He returning chide;
>> "Doth God exact day-labour, light denied ?"
>> I fondly ask. But Patience, to prevent
> That murmur, soon replies: "God doth not need
>> Either man's work, or His own gifts. Who best
>> Bear His mild yoke, they serve Him best. His state

[1] *Second Defence of the English People.*
ere = before (Poetic), *talent* = ability (see also Bible, St. Matthew XXV), *bent* = resolved, *chide* = blame for a fault, *fondly* here has an older meaning = foolishly, *doth* = does (old 3rd person singular), *yoke* here = burden or service, *post* = travel.

Is kingly; thousands at His bidding speed,
    And post o'er land and ocean without rest:
    They also serve who only stand and wait."

Still further disasters came upon him. Cromwell died, and in 1660 Charles II, son of the
executed Charles I, was brought back from
France to be King of England. Everything that
the Puritans had fought for was overthrown.
The Puritan leaders were hunted down, imprisoned, put to death. Milton, perhaps because
of his blindness, escaped death, but he left
London and retired to a little cottage in Chalfont
St. Giles, about twenty miles from London.
And here, lonely and blind and in disgrace, he
wrote, or rather dictated to his daughters, his
greatest work—the greatest long poem in the
language—*Paradise Lost*. Its vast imaginative
flight takes in the boundless space of Heaven,
Earth and Hell. Its subject is the fall of Lucifer
(Satan) and the fall of man. It tells with tremendous power of Satan's revolt, and of the
war in Heaven that followed. Satan is defeated
and cast down to Hell. Here in darkness and
pain he forms, with the other fallen angels, a
mighty empire and plans revenge. In the form
of a serpent he comes to Paradise to bring evil
into the world. Adam and Eve are tempted and
fall and Paradise is lost.

But the greatness of the poem lies not in the
"story" but in the supreme power and nobility
of the language, in the mighty music of the
verse, and in the noble spirit that inspires the

whole work. You can see something of this in the opening lines:

> And chiefly Thou, O Spirit! that dost[1] prefer
> Before all temples the upright heart and pure,
> Instruct[2] me, for Thou knowest.
> . . . . What in me is dark,
> Illumine;[3] what is low, raise and support,
> That to the height of this great argument[4]
> I may assert[5] Eternal Providence,[6]
> And justify[7] the ways of God to men.

In 1671 two more great works followed *Paradise Lost*. They were the long poem *Paradise Regained* and the drama *Samson Agonistes*. In the figure of Samson we feel that Milton sees himself. Samson is blind; he, like Milton, has seen his cause defeated and his enemies triumphant. He is

> "Eyeless, in Gaza, at the mill, with slaves."

But, like Milton, he is a rebel, proud and courageous, and, in the face of blindness, disgrace and slavery he can still serve God's purpose. In doing this he brings about his own death; but his death is his triumph.

---

[1] *dost* [dʌst] = old 2nd person singular of *do*.
[2] *instruct* = teach.
[3] *illumine* = make light.
[4] *argument*, here = subject.
[5] *assert* = declare solemnly and certainly.
[6] *Providence* = the care of God for man.
[7] *justify . . . God* = show that the ways of God are just and right.

. . . Samson hath[1] quit[2] himself
Like Samson, and heroically hath finished
A life heroic.

. . . . .

Nothing is here for tears, nothing to wail[3]
Or knock the breast,[4] no weakness, no contempt,
Dispraise or blame, nothing but well and fair
And what may quiet us in a death so noble.

In 1674 Milton died. He is buried in London in the churchyard of St. Giles, Cripplegate, not far from the street where he was born.

[1] *hath* = old form of *has*.
[2] *quit* (acquitted) himself = behaved.
[3] *wail* = cry with sorrow.
[4] To *knock the breast* was a sign of sorrow.

MILTON DICTATING *Paradise Lost* TO HIS DAUGHTER

VERB STUDY (10): **run**

On p. 118 you have the sentence: "He *ran the* certain *risk* of going blind." There are many phrasal verbs with *run*. Here are some of them:

The child was *run over* by a car.

My car was *run into* by a bus.

To *run into* debt is to *run into* danger.

Who(m) do you think I *ran into* (= met by chance) yesterday? Our friend Jack.

If you *run about* in the playground you will soon get warm.

I *ran after* the bus, but couldn't catch it.

The clock has *run down* (= stopped) because you didn't wind it up.

He has been working too hard and eating too little and is *run down* (= weak; in poor health).

The careless motorist *ran down* (= knocked down) a boy on a bicycle.

"Food was *running short*" (= becoming very scarce), p. 232.

PREPOSITIONS (5)

In

The main uses of *in* are to express:

(1) Position or place, e.g.

There are twenty students *in* this room. I was right *in* the middle of the crowd. He lives *in* London.

or, as an adverb,

Has the nine o'clock train come *in* yet?

Go *in*, don't wait outside.

(2) Circumstances or condition, e.g.

In prison; *in* the dark; *in* good health; *in* debt; *in* danger; *in* a bad temper. Jan is *in* love with Frieda.

As an adverb, "Is the fire *in* or has it gone out?"

(3) Dress, covering, e.g.

> She was dressed *in* silk. William was *in* uniform. The book was bound *in* leather.

(4) Time, e.g.

> *In* the morning/afternoon/evening.
> I began work here *in* January *in* the year 1940.

Into

Into shows motion, action or change, whereas *in* shows position or rest, e.g.

> He walked *into* the room *in* which we were sitting.
> The tree was sawn *into* logs.
> He is always getting *into* trouble.
> He changed his Swiss francs *into* English pounds.

Into should not be confused with *in to*, e.g.

> He came *into* the room with his wife and they went *in to* dinner together.

Of

Of expresses:

(1) One of the possessive (genitive) forms, e.g.

> The tail *of* the dog; the love *of* God; the Tower *of* London.

and the "double possessive" (see p. 176), e.g.

> A brother *of* mine; a friend *of* John's.

(2) Origin or authorship, e.g.

> He was a child *of* poor parents; the poems *of* Milton.

(3) Measure; quantity, e.g.

> A yard *of* cloth, a pound *of* sugar; a packet *of* cigarettes; some *of* that cake.

Off

Off expresses the idea "away from", e.g.

   She pushed the books *off* the table. He jumped *off* the train.

Similarly with the adverb *off*, e.g.

   This grass is newly sown. Keep *off!*

Off is contrasted with *on*, e.g.

   Don't take your coat *off*, keep it *on*.

Idiomatic expressions:

   He is very *well off* (= rich; fortunate).

   They visit me *off and on* (= occasionally; now and then).

   I can't answer your question *off hand* (= immediately; without thinking more about it).

On

On expresses:

(1) Position, e.g.

   The book is *on* the desk. London is *on* the Thames.

(2) Time, e.g.

   He came here on[1] May 1st; *on* Thursday.
   He changed his wet clothes *on* reaching home.

(3) The meaning "about", e.g.

   He gave a lecture *on* India. This is a book *on* Roman coins.

As an adverb it often expresses continuance, e.g.

   Go *on*; don't stop. Keep *on* working. Don't waken him; let
   him sleep *on*.

and is contrasted with *off*, e.g.

   Is the gas *off* or *on*? Turn the water *on*.

[1] *On* is used for dates and for particular days, e.g.
On Christmas day; *On* Saturday afternoon.
Compare with *in* and *at*, e.g. *at* three o'clock *in* the afternoon.

Idiomatic phrases with *on*:

Hob is not a bad fellow *on the whole*. I don't dislike him at all; *on the contrary* I am very fond of him. Those passengers came *on board* at Gibraltar. He damaged the picture *on purpose*. The house is *on fire*. We are here *on holiday*. The goods will be *on sale* tomorrow. A policeman is not allowed to smoke *on duty*.

EXERCISES

I. *Word Study: Use the following:*

despise, learning (*noun*; note the pronunciation of *learned* ['lə:nid] as an adjective, e.g. "a learned man"), devoted (use also *devotion*), architecture (use also *architect*), perfect (*verb*; note the stress [pə:'fekt]), abroad, fulfil, "the press", burden, treasure (*noun* and *verb*), argue (use also *argument*), price (use also *prize*), desert [di'zə:t] (use also *desertion*), cure (*noun* and *verb*; use also *curable*, *incurable*), disaster, boundless, revolt (*noun* and *verb*), revenge (*noun* and *verb*), serpent, lofty, triumph (*noun* and *verb*; use also *triumphant*, *triumphantly*), eyeless (what does the *-less* mean; give two similar examples).

II. *Give in another way the explanation of the following phrases as used in this lesson:*

1. a dislike of the beautiful. 2. they knew nothing of the work of philosophers. 3. he is characteristic of the age in which he lived. 4. he is not limited by it. 5. he belongs not to an age but to all time. 6. he perfected his knowledge of French. 7. including Galileo. 8. the coming struggle. 9. he wrote practically no poetry. 10. they have lost their interest for us now. 11. the cause of Puritanism gained the day. 12. the work that he knew he was to write. 13. in the face of blindness. 14. he brings about his own death.

III.   COMPREHENSION EXERCISE

1. How did Milton differ from the majority of Puritans?
2. What do you know of Milton's father?
3. What did Milton know "from his early youth and with complete certainty"?
4. What did he do, whom did he meet in his travels abroad?
5. Why did he suddenly return?
6. What work did he do for the Puritan cause?
7. Why is it "as good almost to kill a man as kill a good book"?
8. What liberty did Milton want "above all liberties"?
9. What did his work as Foreign Secretary consist of?
10. Why didn't Milton cease work when the doctors warned him what would happen if he didn't?
11. What happened to the Puritan leaders when Charles II was brought back to the throne?
12. What is Milton's greatest poem?
13. What is the subject of this poem?
14. In what way was Milton like his figure of Samson?
15. Where was Milton born? Where is he buried?

IV. *Express in your own words:*

1. "It is fine and noble to sing the ways of God; it is finer and nobler to fulfil them."
2. "A good book is the precious life-blood of a master-spirit. . . ."
3. "My resolution was unshaken though the choice was either the loss of my sight or the desertion of my duty."

V. *Use in sentences of your own:*

run down; run after; run over; run into; run out of; run through; in running order; run away with; run short of; on the run; in the long run.

VI.   *Composition Exercises*

1. Write an account of Milton in about 450 words.
2. Write an account of a great poet of your country.

LESSON 14

"Wanted—Mr. Stuart"[1]

Charles I had been executed in 1649 and Cromwell became the ruler of England, but Charles Stuart (afterwards Charles II), the eldest son of Charles I, came to England secretly in 1650 and, aided by the Scots, attempted to regain the crown. On September 3rd, 1651, he fought a battle at Worcester; he was completely defeated and fled from the field. This is the background to the play that follows.

SCENE: *The Coffee-Room of The White Hart, Evesham. September 10th, 1651.*

ROBERT, *a waiter, has just shown in* SIR EDGAR HARCOURT. *A confused noise of voices is heard from the next room.*

ROBERT: You'll find it quieter in here, sir.

HARCOURT (*by the fireplace*): Quieter! I can hardly hear myself speak. Shut those doors.

ROBERT: They are shut, sir.

HARCOURT: What a mad-house! I've tried three times to get a drink, four to get a room. . .

ROBERT: I'll see about a room, sir.

HARCOURT: If that terrible noise is going on, you can save your breath. Where's the landlord?

[1] No performance of this play may be given in public unless written permission has been obtained from Messrs. Samuel French Ltd., 26 Southampton Street, London, W.C.2.

ROBERT: He's serving, sir.

HARCOURT: Inform him Sir Edgar Harcourt has
arrived. If that doesn't stir him, you can saddle
my horses and I'll be off.

ROBERT (*moving up to the doors*): Yes, sir.

HARCOURT: And bring me some wine.

(ROBERT *goes out. The* LANDLORD *enters.*)

LANDLORD: Sir Edgar, forgive us. We don't know
where to turn.

HARCOURT: Your inn's a mad-house, man.

LANDLORD: It's the Ironsides. Returning every hour
from Worcester. Foot soldiers, cavalry, gunners.

HARCOURT: And they call this peace!

LANDLORD: I'll get you a room at the back.

HARCOURT: You'll get me some dinner.

LANDLORD: Yes, Sir Edgar.

HARCOURT: Soup, beef, chicken.

LANDLORD: Beef, chicken.

HARCOURT: Your best Château-Latour.

LANDLORD: Château-Latour.

HARCOURT: Stilton cheese and white wine.

LANDLORD: At once, sir. And you'll bear with us
tonight. . . .

HARCOURT: Plague on it, man, I'm a Roundhead.
I'll drink with your noisy crowd. To Cromwell
and victory!

LANDLORD: Cromwell and victory.

HARCOURT: Well, we've waited long enough for it
Ten years to put these scoundrels in their
place.

LANDLORD: We've seen the last of them now, sir.

HARCOURT: We've seen the last of more than them, Henry. (*In a quieter tone.*) We've seen the last of . . . Charles Stuart. (*He laughs softly to himself.*) Dead on the field of Worcester! There'll never be a king in England again.

LANDLORD: Never a king in England.

(ROBERT *enters with the wine.*)

ROBERT: The gentleman's wine.

LANDLORD: Put it on the table, Robert. And order Sir Edgar's dinner. Soup, beef, chicken and Château-Latour.

ROBERT (*putting the wine on the table*): Yes, sir.

LANDLORD: And keep those doors closed.

ROBERT: Yes, sir.

(*He goes out.*)

HARCOURT (*moving to the table for his drink*): Well, it's good to see you even in this mad-house. . . .

LANDLORD: Sir Edgar . . .

HARCOURT: What is it?

(*There is a slight pause.*)

LANDLORD: There's no question, is there . . . about Prince Charles . . . ?

HARCOURT: Question?

LANDLORD: I mean, it is quite certain?

HARCOURT: What the devil do you mean?

LANDLORD: I'd like to have it from your own lips.

HARCOURT (*angrily*): Charles Stuart's body was found on the field of Worcester. He was thrown from his horse and cut down.

(*There is a pause.*)

Does that satisfy you?

LANDLORD: Yes, Sir Edgar.

HARCOURT: Then why do you ask? (*He goes back to the fire.*)

LANDLORD: Because in the sitting-room they were betting three sovereigns to one . . . that he is alive.

(PHILIP MAUNSELL *enters.*)

MAUNSELL: Is this coffee-room private . . . ?

LANDLORD: No, sir. This way, if you please.

MAUNSELL: Your sitting-room's a little noisy.

HARCOURT: Charles Stuart alive!

LANDLORD: Yes, sir.

HARCOURT: Are they out of their senses?

MAUNSELL: Why should they be?

HARCOURT: I beg your pardon?

MAUNSELL: I said "Why should they be?"

HARCOURT: I haven't the pleasure of knowing you.

MAUNSELL: My name is Philip Maunsell. In Tewkesbury they're betting four to one.

(*There is a moment's silence.*)

HARCOURT: Four . . . to one!

MAUNSELL: Yes.

HARCOURT: That Charles Stuart is alive?

MAUNSELL: Yes.

HARCOURT: It's nonsense.

MAUNSELL: No doubt.

HARCOURT: Absurd! The body's been found——

MAUNSELL: They say it was his double.

HARCOURT: His double . . . ?

MAUNSELL: A special bodyguard. The Prince was

seen crossing the Severn the same evening—and two days after in Ludlow.

HARCOURT: What's the evidence?

MAUNSELL: Sentries on the river, townsfolk in Ludlow.

HARCOURT: Why have they kept silent?

MAUNSELL: They haven't. They were ordered to say nothing.

HARCOURT: It's a lie! A lie, I tell you, set about by Royalists to keep their cause alive. Charles Stuart's body rots on the field of Worcester.

MAUNSELL: I'll bet you five to one it does not.

HARCOURT: Five to one!

MAUNSELL: Here in this room.

HARCOURT: I don't bet, sir.

MAUNSELL: A pity.

HARCOURT: If I did, I'd bet you a hundred sovereigns—that it does.

MAUNSELL: A pretty sum! Couldn't the landlord introduce us?

HARCOURT: I'll trouble you, sir, not to joke on this matter. If there's one word of truth in the rumour you're spreading, a shadow lies over England. The dawn of peace is being blotted out. . . .

MAUNSELL: That's a matter of opinion, sir.

HARCOURT: Opinion, sir!

MAUNSELL: Charles was a gay prince. He should be alive, to keep the Roundheads on their toes.

HARCOURT: Treason, I say!

LANDLORD: Now, gentlemen——

HARCOURT: A sword.

LANDLORD: Sir Edgar!

MAUNSELL (*putting up his hand*): One moment, sir. If you want to do me an injury . . . why not rob me of five hundred sovereigns?

HARCOURT: Five hundred . . .

MAUNSELL (*quietly*): I'll take your bet . . . at the terms I offered.

HARCOURT: I've already told you——

MAUNSELL: I am a poor man. I'd feel five hundred more than your sword.

(*There is a slight pause.*)

HARCOURT: You would, sir?

(HARCOURT *faces* MAUNSELL.)

Very well, then. I'll not rob you of five hundred. I'll rob you of five thousand.

LANDLORD: Five thousand . . .

HARCOURT: I'll bet you a thousand sovereigns to five. . . that Charles Stuart is dead.

LANDLORD: Sir Edgar, I beg you——

HARCOURT: Keep out of this, Henry! (*He turns to* MAUNSELL.) You hear me, sir? One thousand sovereigns to five that Charles Stuart is dead.

MAUNSELL: I hear you, sir. (*After a pause.*) There is one small point. How will the bet be decided?

HARCOURT: In this way. If Charles Stuart is not proved alive in a fortnight, he will be taken as dead.

MAUNSELL: If Charles is not proved alive in a fortnight, he will be taken as dead.

HARCOURT: Is that clear?

MAUNSELL: Quite clear.

HARCOURT: Is the bet taken?

(*There is a slight pause.*)

MAUNSELL: Taken.

(*There is a moment's silence. The two men
stand facing each other.*)

HARCOURT: My name is Edgar Harcourt. My address
is Cheveley Manor, Devizes. I shall return there
tomorrow.

MAUNSELL: I am Philip Maunsell. I live at seventeen
High Holborn in the City of London. I am at
your service.

HARCOURT: Landlord, you are witness to this bet.

LANDLORD: But, gentlemen, I beg . . .

VOICE (*from the parlour*): In the name of the Parliament of England . . . silence for a proclamation
from Hampton Court.

HARCOURT: What the devil——

VOICE: Given under the hand of Oliver Cromwell,
Commander-in-Chief of the Puritan Forces.

(*The sound of voices dies to a murmur.*)

HARCOURT: Open those doors.

(*The* LANDLORD *moves up and opens the doors.*)

SERGEANT TRYON: "WANTED—MR. STUART."

HARCOURT (*below his breath*): . . . Dear heaven . . .

SERGEANT: "Although it is commonly accepted that
Charles Stuart, Leader of the Royalist Forces,
was cut down and left for dead on the field of
Worcester, a measure of doubt now exists.
Evidence has been received that Mr. Stuart
crossed the Severn on the night of September 3

and was seen two days later in the Town of Ludlow. Mr. Stuart may be at large or in hiding in the counties of Worcester, Shropshire, Hereford or Oxford.

"For his capture or information leading to it, a reward of one thousand pounds. For hiding his whereabouts or helping his escape, the penalty of death.
                    "Given under our seal.
                              "Hampton Court.

"September 9th, 1651."

HARCOURT (*slowly*): It isn't possible . . . it can't be . . .

SERGEANT: Corporals Britton and Fox, search the inn.

HARCOURT: At large or in hiding. . . .

LANDLORD (*hastily*): Excuse me, gentlemen.

MAUNSELL: Close those doors.

(*The* LANDLORD *goes out, closing the doors. There is a moment's pause.*)

One thousand sovereigns. . . .

HARCOURT: Nothing is proved, I tell you!

MAUNSELL: Nothing yet.

HARCOURT: It's a trick, a Royalist plot. . . .

MAUNSELL: No doubt.

HARCOURT: It'll break down, they'll have to confess.

MAUNSELL: Shall we increase the bet?

HARCOURT: We'll increase nothing. . . .

                    (ROBERT *enters.*)

MAUNSELL: Ah, waiter, a drink.

ROBERT: Glass of wine, sir?

MAUNSELL: Two glasses.

HARCOURT (*to* ROBERT): What's—what's happening in there?

ROBERT: They're searching the inn, sir.

HARCOURT: This inn?

ROBERT: Yes, sir.

HARCOURT: Do they imagine he's here?

ROBERT: They're searching every inn in the country.

HARCOURT: Satan, don't they know what the man looks like? He wears a full-bottomed wig, a moustache no gentleman would dare, has black eyes, and sunken cheeks— you could pick him out of a thousand. And they're looking for him here?

FULL-BOTTOMED WIG

ROBERT: Yes, sir.

HARCOURT: Well, tell 'em they're mad! Mad, d'ye hear me? If they want Charles Stuart, they'll have to dig for him.

ROBERT: Yes, sir.

MAUNSELL: And bring two glasses of wine.

(ROBERT *goes out.*)

HARCOURT: Completely mad . . .

MAUNSELL (*after a pause*): You know, Sir Edgar, it wouldn't be out of the question to shave off that moustache.

HARCOURT: Let him shave it!

MAUNSELL: Or to remove a full-bottomed wig.

HARCOURT: Remove it!

MAUNSELL: It would make a difference.

HARCOURT: He can't change his face.

MAUNSELL (*thoughtfully*): I don't know. Wax and plaster have worked wonders. I heard of a Huguenot who lived two years in his own town

unrecognized. The Marquis de Charron served
as a footman at the Tuileries under sentence of
death.

HARCOURT: This is England, sir! We've eyes in our
heads.

MAUNSELL: We shall need them.

(SERGEANT TRYON *enters*.)

SERGEANT: Your names, gentlemen. . . .

HARCOURT (*sharply*): Who the devil are you, sir?

SERGEANT: Sergeant Tryon of the Oxford Garrison.
In the name of the Parliament.

HARCOURT: Now look here——

SERGEANT: Names, business and destination.

HARCOURT: If you think you've come to any purpose——

SERGEANT: I must trouble you, sir.

MAUNSELL: Philip Maunsell of High Holborn,
London. Gentleman. Travelling to Shrewsbury.

SERGEANT: When did you arrive?

MAUNSELL: Five minutes ago.

SERGEANT: On horse?

MAUNSELL: By coach.

SERGEANT: And leaving?

MAUNSELL: Tomorrow.

SERGEANT (*to* HARCOURT): Yours, sir?

HARCOURT: Edgar Harcourt. Knight. Cheveley
Manor, Devizes.

SERGEANT: Arrived?

HARCOURT: This moment.

SERGEANT: A guest?

HARCOURT: For the night. Now look here——

SERGEANT: Have you knowledge of the whereabouts
of Charles Stuart?

HARCOURT: First hand.

SERGEANT: What is it?

HARCOURT: Feeding the worms of Worcester.

SERGEANT: Speak to the point, sir.

HARCOURT: It is the point, sir.

SERGEANT: Then it may interest you to know . . .
that Charles Stuart was reported last night . . .
in this town.

(*There is a moment's complete silence.*)

HARCOURT: In this town?

SERGEANT: You heard me.

MAUNSELL (*after a pause*): Has he been seen?

SERGEANT: No.

MAUNSELL: Then how——

SERGEANT: A Royalist gave evidence in Hereford.
(*He pauses.*) The town is being searched from
top to bottom. No one may enter or leave with-
out permission. If he is here, we shall get him.
(*He turns to the door.*) That is all, gentlemen.
Good-night.

(*He goes out. The two men stand facing each other.
The* LANDLORD *hurries in.*)

LANDLORD: Forgive me, gentlemen. I was kept back
by the Sergeant. Your drinks are coming . . .

MAUNSELL: You heard, landlord, what he said?

LANDLORD: The Prince reported in Evesham! It
sounds like a fairy tale . . .

HARCOURT (*mechanically*): A fairy tale. . . .

MAUNSELL: Where do you imagine he could be?

LANDLORD: I don't know, sir. There are some great houses in the neighbourhood, the Trevors, the Mainwarings, the Blakeneys. They'll be turned inside out. God help them, if they find him.

MAUNSELL: God help me, landlord . . . if they don't!

LANDLORD: You, sir?

MAUNSELL: I shall lose five thousand pounds.

LANDLORD: Five thousand pounds . . .

MAUNSELL: Have you forgotten . . . the bet?

LANDLORD: By our Lady, sir!

MAUNSELL: If Charles is not found alive in a fortnight, I have lost. Those are the terms, Sir Edgar?

HARCOURT: Those are the terms.

MAUNSELL: So Godspeed to the arrest of Charles!

LANDLORD: Godspeed . . .

MAUNSELL: And I tell you, he won't make it easy. He's the cleverest man in England and will beat us yet.

LANDLORD: He won't beat me, sir.

HARCOURT: Nor me.

MAUNSELL: He's beaten us all for a week. Slipped through four counties and kept an army guessing. . . . Why? (*He faces them.*) I'll tell you. Because they are looking for a ghost. They are looking for the ghost of Charles Stuart. And there is not one trace of Charles Stuart left. Every detail has been changed, clothes, voice, features, manner of walking, character, every mark and detail of the man we know . . . (*his voice dropping*) except one . . . (*He pauses.*) The one thing a man may never change, because he does not know he possesses it.

HARCOURT: What is that?

(ROBERT *enters with drinks.*)

ROBERT: The gentlemen's drinks . . .

LANDLORD: On the table, Robert.

HARCOURT: What is that?

MAUNSELL: A mannerism . . .

(*There is a pause. He smiles quietly at them.* ROBERT *puts the drinks on the table.*)

Some trick of the hand, the slight movement of an eyelid, unknown to each of us and with us all our days. . . . Charles Stuart has a mannerism.

(MAUNSELL *and* HARCOURT *go to the table for their drink.* ROBERT *crosses the room to attend to the fire.*)

LANDLORD: He has!

HARCOURT: What is it?

MAUNSELL (*smiling*): There's a reward . . . for the answer.

LANDLORD: But if you know——

HARCOURT (*sharply*): How do you know?

MAUNSELL: I was two years in the Palace of Whitehall, teacher to Prince Henry. I had time to observe . . . Prince Charles.

HARCOURT: It is your duty to the Parliament to speak.

MAUNSELL (*gently*): My duty to myself . . . for six thousand.

HARCOURT: Then there's no fear you'll forget it.

MAUNSELL (*smiling*): No fear. And yet, Sir Edgar, I wonder . . .

HARCOURT: Wonder, sir!

MAUNSELL: Whether future generations would approve.

HARCOURT: This is treason.

LANDLORD (*between them*): Sir Edgar——

HARCOURT: Explain yourself!

MAUNSELL: A man who can defy England for a week . . . has the makings of a king.

HARCOURT: I tell you, sir, England is tired of kings.

MAUNSELL: She is tired of tyranny. She will never tire of kings. The people will respect a Parliament—they will die for a king. (*Putting down his empty glass.*) Shall we go in to supper?

HARCOURT: I think it is high time. (*He puts down his glass.*)

LANDLORD (*moving up*): I'll show you to your rooms.

HARCOURT (*about to follow, but stops*): And one last word, sir. I thank heaven that the betrayal of a king will save you six thousand sovereigns. It assures me our Parliament is safe.

LANDLORD: This way, sir . . .

(HARCOURT *goes out, followed by the* LANDLORD. *There is a moment's silence.*)

MAUNSELL (*smiling*): Sir Edgar underrates me. He values "a dream" at six thousand. Don't you reckon that cheap, Robert?

ROBERT: I see his point of view, sir.

MAUNSELL: You see his point of view? Then I am a fool and a madman. Do you read Mr. Shakespeare?

ROBERT: Mr. Shakespeare, sir?

MAUNSELL: A playwright who died thirty years ago.

ROBERT: I'm afraid not, sir.

MAUNSELL: He has a line in "The Prince of Denmark" . . . Ophelia, speaking of Prince Hamlet, says:

> "The expectancy and rose of the fair state,
> The glass of fashion and the mould of form. . . ."

Could you betray . . . such a one?

ROBERT: I'm afraid I could, sir.

MAUNSELL: You could?

ROBERT: His father was a traitor. Like father, like son.

MAUNSELL: Cold reasoning, Robert. May it reap its reward. The way to the supper-room?

ROBERT (*moving to the doors*): This way, sir.

(MAUNSELL *goes to the door and turns.*)

MAUNSELL: And by the way, Robert, when you do your evil deed . . . perhaps you'll inform the King that there was one man who would not betray him . . . for six thousand.

ROBERT: I will inform him, sir.

MAUNSELL: Tell me, Robert, do you believe that?

ROBERT: I'm afraid, sir, you would have to prove it.

MAUNSELL: It has been my privilege.

(*He pauses, his hand on the door, facing* ROBERT.)

(*To* ROBERT). Good-night . . . Your Majesty.

The curtain falls.

VERB STUDY (11): call

"And they *call* this peace" (p. 128).

Here are some other idioms with *call:*

His son is *called* (= named) William.

The drowning man *called* (*out*) (= cried) for help.

The ship *calls at* (= stops at) Gibraltar.

When you are in the village will you please *call at* the green-grocer's and get some oranges?

The play at the theatre starts at 7.30. I will *call for* you at 7.0.

I want breakfast at 8.0 so will you please *call* (= waken) me at 7.30?

Mr. Smith is not at home; he was *called away* (= asked to go somewhere) on business.

I know his name but I can't just *call it to mind* (= remember it).

A strike of railway men has been *called* (= ordered) beginning on November 1st.

If you are near my home any time *call in* (= come) and see me.

PREPOSITIONS (6)

Over

The various uses and meanings of *over* can be seen in the following sentences.

There was a mirror *over* the fireplace. Clouds came *over* the sky.

There were dust-sheets *over* the furniture.

That picture cost *over* £10,000.

He couldn't enter for the examination because he was *over* age (= more than).

There is a bridge *over* the river. He jumped *over* the wall (= above and across).

The King is ruler *over* the whole nation. A captain is *over* a lieutenant.

They sat a long time *over* their dinner (= while having dinner). He fell asleep *over* a book (= while reading).

Over is often used as an adverb expressing:

(1) Distance, e.g.

Here, in Britain, we are having hot weather, but *over* in America they are having snowstorms.

(2) Movement, the exact meaning depending on the verb used with *over*, e.g.

to fall *over*; to knock *over*; bend *over*; hand *over*; turn *over*; the milk boiled *over*, etc.

(3) "finished", e.g.

The war is *over*. All your troubles are now *over*.

(4) "remaining", e.g.

I paid the bill and have three pounds *over*.

(5) "too much", "more than is proper", e.g.

The meat is *over*-cooked. I was *over*-charged for these goods. He is *over*-worked.

Past

Past (preposition) has the meaning "beyond", e.g.

It is *past* six o'clock; half-*past* three. The old horse is *past* work. She walked *past* my door (= up to and beyond).

Past (adverb).

The years went *past*. He saw me but walked *past* without speaking.

Round

Round expresses: (1) position, e.g.

There was a rope *round* the tree.

(2) movement (more or less circular), e.g.

He walked *round* the house. Drake sailed *round* the world.

Similarly as an adverb:

He went into the garden and walked *round*. Turn *round*.

ADVERTISEMENT: Our dresses not only make you look slim, they make men look *round*.

Since

Since expresses "from a definite *point* of time in the past until now", e.g.

I have been here *since* 4 o'clock.

Since is generally used with a perfect tense.
Compare this with *for* which expresses "a *length* of time till now", e.g.

I have been here *for* two hours.

Since is also an adverb, e.g.

I saw him last Christmas; I haven't seen him *since*.

Through

Through (preposition and adverb) expresses:
(1) Position or movement usually from one side to the other, e.g.

He knocked a nail *through* the wood. The train rushed *through* the tunnel. Look *through* the window. Air comes in *through* the ventilator. We went *through* France on our way to Switzerland. He has come *through* a lot of difficulties. He read the book *through*. Will you please read *through* my essay.

(2) Time, e.g.

> He talked about it all *through* dinner. The railway line was repaired *through* the night when the trains were not running.

(3) Agency, e.g.

> He bought the property *through* a house agent. He got the job *through* (= by the influence of) his uncle.

To

To expresses:

(1) Direction of movement, e.g.

> I am going *to* London. Come *to* me.

(2) A limit, e.g.

> Classes are from 9 o'clock *to* 5 o'clock. He was faithful *to* the last/end. He read the paper from beginning *to* end.

(3) Comparison, e.g.

> This car is superior/inferior/equal *to* that one. What he said to you is nothing *to* what he said to me.

To is used:

(*a*) as part of the infinitive, e.g.

> I want *to* go home. He said that *to* frighten you.

(*b*) with an indirect object, e.g.

> Give that *to* me. I lost a lot of money *to* him.

To is not much used as an adverb. It is an adverb in:

> Pull the door *to*. The work must be done, so set *to* (= get to work).

Towards (toward)

reposition only.

Towards expresses (1) "in the direction of", e.g.

Go *towards* the window. Their house faces *towards* the south.

(2) approaching (of time), e.g.

I hope to arrive *towards* six o'clock. Shakespeare's best comedies were written *towards* the end of the 16th century.

(3) with regard to, e.g.

I have always felt kindly *towards* him.

EXERCISES

I. *Word Study: Use the following words or phrases in sentences of your own:*

confused (use also *confusion*), landlord (What is the feminine form ?), inform (use also *information*), saddle (*verb*). (*Saddle* is also a noun. It is part of the *harness* of a horse. Where does one put the saddle ? Find out the meaning of *reins*, *stirrups*, *spurs*), forgive (What are the principal parts of this verb ?), sideboard (name six other articles of furniture), sigh (note the pronunciation [sai]), scoundrel, corpse, bet, sovereign (two meanings of this word), private (use also *privacy*. What is the opposite of a private room in a hotel ?), evidence, sentry, fraud, rot, introduce, rumour, dawn (What is the opposite ?), toes (use the idioms "from top to toe"; "to tread on someone's toes"; "to walk on tip-toe"), treason, residence, witness, proclamation, murmur, accept, county (don't confuse with *country*. Note the pronunciation of each ['kaunti] ['kʌntri]), capture, whereabouts, penalty, trick, increase (What is the opposite ?), imagine, moustache (Is this the same as *whiskers*? How do we describe a man who has neither moustache nor whiskers ?), wig, *sunken* cheeks (this is one form of the past participle of *sink*, give the other one), exile, destination, a fairy tale, inside out (use also *upside down*, *from top to bottom*, *back to front*), slip, ghost, mannerism, eyelid (use also *eyebrow*, *eyelash*, *eyeball*), generations, approve, defy (note the pronunciation [di'fai]. Use also *defiance*, *defiantly*), tyranny (use also *tyrant*, *tyrannical*), underrates (What is the opposite ? Use it in a sentence), playwright, mould, reap (What is the opposite ?), evil, privilege.

II. *Explain, or say in another way, each of the following expressions which occurred in the play that you have just read:*

1. Are they out of their senses ? 2. There is no question about Prince Charles being dead. 3. I'd like to have it from your own lips. 4. I beg your pardon. (*This can be used in several situations. State what you think it meant when used on page* 130.) 5. They are betting four to one. 6. No doubt (page 130. *See remark on No.* 4). 7. They say it was his double. 8. Why have they kept silent ? 9. They were hushed up. 10. A pity! (page 131. *See remark on No.* 4). 11. I'll trouble you not to joke on this matter. 12. That is a matter of opinion. 13. To keep the Roundheads on their toes. 14. If he is not proved alive, he will be taken as dead. 15. A proclamation given under the hand of Oliver Cromwell. 16. It is commonly accepted that Charles Stuart is dead. 17. A measure of doubt now exists. 18. Mr. Stuart may be at large. 19. For helping his escape the penalty of death. 20. You could pick him out of a thousand. 21. It wouldn't be out of the question to shave off that moustache. 22. Under sentence of death. 23. We have eyes in our heads. 24. His voice dropped. 25. There is no fear you'll forget. 26. He has the makings of a king. 27. I think it is high time. 28. Don't you reckon that cheap ? 29. Like father, like son. 30. It has been my privilege.

III.   COMPREHENSION EXERCISE

Answer the following, in your own words as far as possible, using only material contained in the play. Use ONE *complete sentence for each answer.*

1. Who is "Mr. Stuart"?
2. Why did the landlord think there was some doubt about Prince Charles being dead?
3. What was Maunsell's "evidence" that the Prince was alive?
4. What were the terms of the bet that Maunsell made with Harcourt?
5. What were the terms (for reward or for penalty) in Cromwell's proclamation?
6. Give Harcourt's description of Prince Charles.
7. How did Maunsell think that Charles could change his appearance?
8. What was the one thing he thought the Prince could not change? Why couldn't he change that?
9. Why did Maunsell know that he could recognise the Prince?
10. What was the "dream" that Maunsell thought was worth more than £6,000?
11. Explain Maunsell's final remark.

IV. *Use the following idioms in sentences of your own:*
    call out; call at; call in; call off; call for; call away; call up; call on; call a spade a spade.

V.   *Composition Exercises*

1. Tell, in your own words, the story of the play.
2. Write a short story or play of your own, having as title: "Loyalty".

LESSON 15

The Story of Hob

*(A letter from the author of this book
to a teacher in Greece)*

LONGMANS, GREEN & CO. LTD.,
48 GROSVENOR STREET,
LONDON, W.I.
18th January 19—

DEAR MISS ——,

I was very pleased to receive your letter and to hear of the work you had been doing with *Essential English*. And so your students have been asking questions about Hob! They have been asking what is his nationality, why he should be learning English, etc., etc. So, too, have quite a lot of other people.

The problem about Hob was not an easy one. You see, in these books I could teach all the "favourable" adjectives easily enough. Lucille could be beautiful, gay and well-dressed; Frieda could be charming; Olaf could be clean and manly, Pedro could be the handsome, well-travelled man of the world; Jan could be clever and hard-working and attractive; and no Poles or Frenchmen or Swedes would rise up in anger against me. But how could I teach the opposites of these ? Who ever knew a Pole, Frenchman, Swiss, Swede, or South American who was lazy, badly-dressed, careless, untidy ? What storms I should have brought on my head if a character of *any* recognisable nationality had all these bad qualities. It was then that I thought of Hob. He, like all my " characters ", had been a student in one of my classes. I knew his story though I didn't want to tell it just then. However, I can do so now without hurting anyone.

．　　　．　　　．　　　．　　　．

The story goes back many years now to the Lancashire town of Manchester. In a little house there, in a small street, Southbank Street, lived the Hobdell family. It was a large family, but the only ones I knew were Eliza[1] and Berta,[2] Ben[2] and Albert and Irene. Theophlius,[3] Tom[4] and Aggie[5] I never met. Albert (familiar to readers of *Essential English* as "Uncle Albert") was a fine-looking fellow, six foot two in height, broad-shouldered and strong as a horse. He was no scholar—he couldn't even write his own name (he was, as he himself said, no credit to his teachers), but he was shrewd and sharp-witted and the merriest, liveliest and most warm-hearted companion you could wish for. Many are the Lancashire hot-pots[6] and many the plates of fish and chips I've

---

[1] See *Recollections and Adventures*, p. 62.
[2] See *Essential English*, Book I, p. 204.
[3] See *Essential English* III, pp. 137–141.
[4] See *Essential English* III, pp. 151–5.
[5] See *Essential English* II, pp. 40–42.
[6] *hot-pot* = a Lancashire dish made with meat, potatoes and onions cooked slowly.

eaten in Southbank Street, and many are the stories with which Albert kept us all roaring with laughter. But it's not Albert so much as Irene that my story is chiefly concerned with. Irene was the youngest of the family. She was about twenty when I first knew her, gay, laughing, full of life and high spirits (she had Albert's nature), and the prettiest girl in Manchester. She was, I'm afraid, a sore trial to Eliza—the oldest of the family—a sour-faced woman of forty odd. Eliza had always been full of " don'ts " and " mustn'ts " —" Ben, don't eat so much "; " Albert, don't laugh like that ". (Albert said that when he was a boy, she used to say, " Albert, go and see what Irene's doing, *and tell her she mustn't.*") Now, it was, " Irene, you mustn't wear that short dress: it's not proper." Poor Eliza saw impropriety everywhere. She even, so Albert told me, put cotton trousers on the legs of the piano because she thought bare legs were improper. She was about as cheerful as a wet Sunday afternoon in Manchester—which is saying a lot—but her sourness seemed to have no effect on Irene, nor for that matter on Albert and Ben; they just laughed and made a joke of it all. Eliza and Berta, who was even sourer but less talkative than Eliza, thought Irene ought to stay at home in the evenings sewing or knitting; Irene preferred going out with soldiers (this was during the war) to knitting socks for them—and there were always plenty of soldiers coming to Southbank Street to take Irene out.

Amongst them (and her chief favourite) was Ruperto. What his other name was I never knew; everyone just called him Ruperto. He had come to

England with our allies, the Ruritanian forces. He was a corporal, I think, or perhaps a sergeant, a gay, dashing sort of fellow with dark, romantic-looking eyes and black curly hair. He didn't speak much English, but that seemed to be no obstacle to his popularity with the girls of Manchester, and it was

SUPPER AT THE HOBDELL'S

soon quite clear that Irene had eyes for no one except Ruperto. The end of the war came and he went back home to Ruritania. Quite honestly, despite the fact that Irene lost a lot of her gaiety, most of us hoped that we had seen the last of him. But a month or two later Irene got a letter from Ruritania (in hardly understandable English) asking her to come to Ruritania and marry him. Albert looked more solemn about it than I have ever seen him look about anything. He had no high opinion of Ruperto; neither had I, but it was none of my business, so I said nothing. Eliza, of course, hated the thought of Irene marrying *anyone*, and was horrified at the thought of her marrying a "foreigner"; but Irene had no doubts. All her old gaiety came back at once; she was overflowing with happiness and laughed and sang about the house all day. She drew all her savings out of the bank, bought herself pretty clothes, bought things for her new home, presents for Ruperto, and set off in high spirits for Ruritania. A month or two later we had a letter from her. She was married to Ruperto and they had a little home about 10 miles from Strelsau—just on the borders of Ruritania and the Urbanian Republic—they were very happy and everything was wonderful.

.   .   .   .   .   .

I left Lancashire soon after that and took a job in Scotland, and later moved to London. Albert stayed in Lancashire and I lost touch with him. As I told you, he couldn't write and it was no use my writing letters that he couldn't read. Years went by. I married, and had more or less forgotten about the Hobdells. Then one day my secretary came to tell me that a visitor, a Mr. Hobdell, had called to see me. Hobdell! —Albert!—Irene! I went to the entrance hall and there was Albert, older, fatter, prosperous-looking, but the same old Albert. I think he was as pleased to see me as I was to see him. I had finished work for the day and we went to a quiet little tea-room near by to have a good talk and to get all his news. Yes, Albert

6

had done very well—he was making a fortune.[1] Eliza ? Yes, she had a little house of her own. She had softened with the passage of time—but the piano legs still had cotton trousers on them.

"And Irene ?" I said.

Albert's face lost all its smiles. It was as if you had turned off a light inside him.

"Irene's dead," he said. "As a matter of fact that's one reason why I've come to see you."

I was shocked to hear it. I remembered her so full of life and laughter and happiness: and all that was gone.

"Yes," he went on, "it was a bad business. You know I never liked that fellow Ruperto that she married. He left her a year or two after her boy was born. Hob, he's called. Irene never told us about Ruperto leaving her. For a time she wrote a letter home fairly often. They were just short letters saying she was getting on all right. Then the letters came less and less often, then it was just a card at Christmas time, and then they stopped altogether. Eliza and Ben wrote to her (you know I'm no scholar), but the letters were returned 'address not known'. We were all very upset about it, for Eliza in spite of her sharp tongue was really fond of Irene, but there seemed to be nothing we could do. Then about six months ago there came a brief note from her saying she was very ill and asking me to come and see her if I could. I took a plane to Strelsau the very next day. She was lying in a bed in a poor little room, bare and comfortless. I could have cried to see how thin and

---

[1] For the story of Albert see pp. 92–100.

pale and old she looked, but when she saw me she
tried to smile as she used to in the old days at home.
I'd have given all I have if I could have taken her
home with me to Lancashire and brought back her
rosy cheeks and smiles; but she knew, and I knew,
that it was too late. 'Albert,' she said, 'I wanted to
see you about Hob; he'll be all alone when I'm
gone.'

" 'You need have no worry about him, my dear,'
I interrupted. 'He'll come back to England with me
and I'll do all I can for him.'

"Tears came into her eyes. 'I knew you would,
Albert,' she said. Two days later she died.

.   .   .   .   .

"Hob's been living with me for six months now,
and I want some help from you. I want to do the best
I can for the lad. He's a bit of a problem; he's lazy,
untidy and not too particular about being clean
(that's from his father), but he's warm-hearted, good-
humoured and loves a joke."

"I know where that's from," I said.

Albert laughed. "I like Hob; he's a fellow after my
own heart and I think he'll do all right in the end."

"And what is it you want me to do?" I said.
"You can count on me to do anything I can."

"Well," said Albert slowly, "you see when Hob
came here he spoke English with a sort of horrible
Ruritanian accent. He's lived with me for six months
and now they say he's speaking it with a terrible
Lancashire accent. I must say I don't notice it
myself, but then, as you know, I'm not a gentleman.

Can you tell me where I can get a good teacher who can teach Hob to speak English as it ought to be spoken. That's why I called to see you today."

"I can certainly help you there," I said, "and nothing would give me more pleasure. I know a Mr. Priestley who gives English lessons to foreign students."

"But Hob's not a foreign student exactly; he's only half foreign."

"And that's the half that Mr. Priestley will deal with," I said. "Moreover, Mr. Priestley is quite a good phonetician and he'll soon deal with Hob's Lancashire accent."

"And he's really good?" said Albert. "It's not a matter of money. I'm willing to pay for the best."

"In my opinion," I said, "Charles Priestley is the best teacher in England."

"Fine," said Albert, "the best is good enough for me, and for Hob."

.   .   .   .   .

And that's how Hob became one of Mr. Priestley's pupils.

All good wishes,
Yours sincerely,
C. E. ECKERSLEY.

P.S. I realise that this story doesn't agree with Hob's own account of his coming to England (Book III, pp. 2–5), but what I have told you is the true story. Hob is shrewd like Albert; he doesn't tell you more than he wants you to know. He loves to tell a story—not necessarily true by any means, even when, as in Book II, p. 40, he *tells* you it's a true one!

VERB STUDY (12): say and tell

The meaning of *say* and *tell* is roughly the same, but the grammatical construction used with each is different, and each verb has special idiomatic uses.

The patterns with *tell* are:

1. *Tell* + a direct object (i.e., tell something), e.g.

He can *tell the time*.
Will you *tell us the story* about the fire of London?

But more frequently it is:

2. *Tell* + indirect object + direct object (i.e., tell somebody something), e.g.

Subject	Verb	Indirect Object	Direct Object
	Tell	me	a story/the truth/your name.
I	told	Hob	what to do.
He	told	us	that he was going away.
I	told	the gardener	to cut the grass.

The patterns with *say* are:

1. Say *something*, e.g.

Every night the child says *her prayers*. He said, "*I am very busy.*" He said *that he was very busy*.

2. Say *something* to *somebody*, e.g.

> He said "*Good-morning*" to me. I said *to the gardener*, "*Cut the grass*." (Compare with: I told the gardener to cut the grass.)
>
> When I see him I shall say *to him*, "*What have you done with my money?*"

NOTE: (1) *Say* is used when we are reporting the actual words spoken. *Tell* is never used with the actual words spoken.

(2) With *say* the person spoken to need not be mentioned; with *told* the person spoken to must be mentioned, e.g.

> The teacher *said*, "Do all the exercises."
> The teacher *told the class* to do all the exercises.

(3) In reported speech *say* is followed by a noun clause, not, as *told* can be, by the infinitive.

Compare: I said *that he must leave the house*.

I told him *to leave* the house.

VERB STUDY (13): **go**

In Lesson 15 you will find several expressions with *go* (*went*, *gone*) in them, e.g.

> The story *goes back* many years now. *Go* and see what Irene's doing. Irene preferred *going out with* soldiers. He *went back* to Ruritania. Years *went by*. "Yes," he *went on* (= continued), "it was a bad business." He'll be all alone when I'm *gone* (= dead).

Here are a few other common usages:

> My watch kept *going* slow; now it won't *go* at all.
> "How did the concert *go*?" (= was it successful?). "I *went* (or *went down*) very well."

The apples have *gone* bad. I think it is *going* to rain. I'm
going in for my examination in July. The fire has *gone out.*
"It is love that makes the world *go round.*" (*Proverb.*)

EXERCISES

I. *Word Study: Use the following:*

lively (use also *liveliness*, to *liven up*), companion (use also
company), chips, roar (most English people pronounce this
like *raw* [rɔː]), proper (note also *improper*, *impropriety*), talkative, knit, romantic (use also *romance*), obstacle, solemn,
horrified (use also *horror*, *horrible*, *horribly*), overflowing,
border, secretary, prosperous (use also *prosperity*), nation
(use also *nationality*; note the difference in accentuation),
recognisable (use also *recognise* and *recognition*; note accentuation), good-humoured.

II. *Explain the following words or phrases:*

1. a dozen *or so.* 2. he's a *bit of a problem.* 3. I'm *no scholar.*
4. I would *do my utmost.* 5. Pedro was a *well-travelled man of
the world.* 6. no one would *rise up in anger.* 7. The story
goes back many years now. 8. he was *sharp-witted.* 9. Albert
kept us *roaring with laughter.* 10. Irene was *a sore trial* to
Eliza, a sour-faced woman of *forty odd.* 11. Irene *had eyes
for no one* except Ruperto. 12. we hoped we had *seen the last
of him.* 13. in *hardly understandable* English. 14. He *had no
high opinion* of Ruperto. 15. Albert stayed in Lancashire and
I lost touch with him. 16. it was *a bad business.* 17. We were
all *very upset* about it. 18. Hob is a fellow *after my own
heart.* 19. You can *count on me.* 20. *It's not a matter of money.*

III. In the story you had the expressions—Albert
was *broad-shouldered* and *warm-hearted.* Give
similar compound adjectives to describe (*a*)
persons who have: blue eyes; red cheeks; brown
hair; a dark skin; a long-nose; big bones; long
legs; flat feet; travelled a lot; (*b*) a person whose

spirits are high; whose heart is warm; whose
tongue is sharp; whose wits are quick; whose will
is strong; whose temper is hot, (c) a man who
has neither beard nor moustache; a suit made by
a good tailor; a book whose binding is made of
leather.

IV. *Use the following in sentences of your own:*

1. go out. 2. go in for. 3. go down. 4. go on. 5. go with.
6. go out with. 7. go by. 8. go about it. 9. on the go. 10. go
down. 11. go over. 12. it goes to show.

V. *Use the following in sentences of your own:*

(a) it goes without saying; that is to say; what do you say
to . . . ?; to say one's say; a saying; they say.

(b) tell the truth; tell their own tale; telling; to tell on someone; all told.

VI. *Make sentences using the word* tell *with the
meanings*

(a) to express or show, (b) to discover, (c) to order,
(d) to have an effect.

VII. *Rewrite the following sentences using* tell *instead
of* say:

1. Eliza said to Albert, "Go and see what Irene's doing."
2. Pedro said to Lucille, "You sing very well."
3. I said to him, "Open the door."
4. She said to me, "I am sorry I can't speak English better."
5. Eliza said, "Albert don't laugh like that."
6. He said to me that he was very busy.
7. You had better say to George what you have said to me.
8. I said to the gardener that he must cut the grass.
9. He said to me, "I have lost your money."
10. Mr. Priestley said to his students, "There will be a
holiday tomorrow."

VIII. *Composition Exercises*

1. Write a composition or short story having for its title one of the following:

(*a*) Tales our mothers told us.

(*b*) The boy who couldn't tell a lie.

(*c*) Some old sayings in your language and what they mean.

2. What qualities would you expect from (*a*) a good doctor, (*b*) a business man, (*c*) a nurse, (*d*) a lawyer? Write a character sketch of each of these.

3. Tell in about 300 to 400 words the story of Hob.

4. Invent a short story in which the chief character is Uncle Ben, *or* Aunt Eliza, *or* Aunt Aggie, *or* Uncle Theophilus.

5. Write a short account of some person (real or imaginary) that you have known.

LESSON 16

Bonnie[1] Prince Charlie

Characters—MR. PRIESTLEY, LUCILLE, FRIEDA,
OLAF, PEDRO, HOB

OLAF: I was in Edinburgh in September for the
Festival.

LUCILLE: Did you enjoy it?

OLAF: Oh yes, it was splendid.

PEDRO: Edinburgh's a beautiful city, isn't it?

OLAF: Lovely both by day and by night. You know
the castle, don't you, Pedro; and you too, of
course, Mr. Priestley.

MR. PRIESTLEY: Yes, I know it well. It stands on a
huge rock, like a great cliff towering over the
city.

OLAF: Well, during the Festival it was flood-lit every
night. Just as it got dark a gun was fired and at
that moment the lights went on. But the flood-
lights were only on the castle building; the rock
was in the darkness. The effect was magical.
The castle looked like a castle in the air, something fairy-like out of the old romances.

[1] *bonny*: a Scottish word for "handsome"; "beautiful". *Charlie* is a
familiar and affectionate form of *Charles*.

PEDRO: And yet the Scots are supposed to be matter-of-fact unromantic people. That wasn't my impression.

OLAF: Nor was it mine. Look at all that romantic feeling they still have for Bonnie Prince Charlie. Why, when I was there there was practically a whole exhibition devoted to him—his portraits, letters that he had written (incidentally with more spelling mistakes to the

A HIGHLANDER

page than ever Hob made), clothes that he wore, his sword, a piece of his hair. To tell you the truth, I must admit I caught some of the fever myself and made a tour of the country to see the places associated with him—Inverness, Glenfinnan and Culloden. It was really quite fascinating.

HOB: Who was Bonnie Prince Charlie?

MR. PRIESTLEY: I think you ought to know the story. If you don't you won't fully understand a good deal of Scottish (or, for that matter, English) history or literature, for in addition to there being many Scottish songs about him, Sir Walter Scott used his story in at least two of his novels —and to my mind two of the best.[1]

[1] *Waverley* and *Redgauntlet*.

FRIEDA: Will you tell us about him, please?

MR. PRIESTLEY: It seems to me Olaf is the most suitable person to tell it. Will you do it, please, Olaf?

OLAF: Well, sir, I'll try. The story begins, I suppose, in 1688 when James II, the last of the Stuart[1] kings, was driven off the throne of England. James went abroad, and never returned to England. But he had many followers in England[2] who sympathised with him and wanted him back on the throne of England. His son James Edward (whom the English called "The Old Pretender") made an unsuccessful attempt to get back the throne in 1715, but the most important attempt was made by his grandson Charles Edward, "Bonnie Prince Charlie" to the Scots, "The Young Pretender" to the English. This was in 1745. Charles was a real prince of romance; young (he was twenty-five when he landed in Scotland), handsome, tall and fair, brave and adventurous. He was coming, he said, to gain the crown of England and place it at his father's feet. England was at war with France at the time and Louis XV was planning an invasion of England. Charles went to Paris, eager to join the French fleet that was to land him at Dover. Once there, he believed that the Jacobite sympathisers would flock to his side and that George II, the English king, would be forced to surrender or flee to Germany. But

[1] The Stuart kings were James I (1603–25), Charles I (1625–49), Charles II (1660–85), James II (1685–88).
[2] These were called *Jacobites* from the Latin "Jacobus" (James).

disaster overtook the French fleet; a great storm struck them in the Channel and they returned beaten and broken to the shores of France. It was a terrible blow to Charles Edward; but not for long. He was a man of spirit, a born adventurer, burning with ambition and courage. If the French couldn't help him, he would invade England by himself—not across the Channel but from Scotland. There he was sure of support; he was not quite so sure of the English Jacobites. England under George II was prosperous, and to the matter-of-fact English, the Stuarts were merely a sentiment, and hard-headed business men don't risk their prosperity for a wild dream. But the Scots, or at least the Highlanders, were different. The Highlands was the wild home of the poor but high-spirited men to whom loyalty to their king was a passion. They were adventurous, romantic men who loved fighting and danger. The Stuarts had come originally from Scotland, and to the Highlanders the Stuarts were not just a sentiment—they were a religion for which they were prepared to fight and die.

Disguised as a clergyman Charles went aboard a small French ship, the *Doutelle*, to sail for Scotland. With him was a French warship, the *Elizabeth*, of sixty-eight guns, and in the *Elizabeth* were loaded the stores, guns, swords, powder and shot with which he hoped to defeat the English. In June 1745 they slipped quietly out of harbour and headed for Scotland. On the fourth day they were seen by a British warship which opened fire on the *Elizabeth*. For five hours a battle went on and both ships were damaged. The English ship turned for England and the *Elizabeth* for Brest. Most of his stores were gone, but Charles, with only six followers, determined to go on. Two British vessels were seen near the coast of Scotland but the *Doutelle* escaped in the mist and made her way among the rocky islands off the west of Scotland. A golden eagle was flying just above them. "The king of birds welcomes your Royal Highness to your Scottish kingdom," said one of his followers; and Charles Stuart set foot on the land of his ancestors.

The news spread quickly throughout the Highlands and Charles crossed from the island where he had landed and with his six faithful followers set up his standard at Glenfinnan. I saw the monument that marks the spot, an impressive if not particularly beautiful, tower. He expected the shore to be lined with Highlanders to welcome him. Hardly a soul was there. It was an anxious moment. Would the Highland chiefs, above all would Cameron of Lochiel, the most powerful of them all, come to his aid? If he didn't, the attempt must end in failure. For two anxious hours the Prince and his followers waited. Then they heard the sound of the pipers, and pouring over the hills came the Camerons, 800 of them headed by Lochiel. The Royal Standard was raised in the name of James, "King of Scotland".

George II issued a proclamation offering £30,000 to anyone who could capture "the eldest son of the Pretender". Charles answered with a similar notice offering £30,000 to anyone who would capture "the Elector of Hanover"![1]

Then began the march on Edinburgh. More Highlanders, wild-looking savages with their swords, knives tied to poles, or any other weapon that they could lay hands on, joined his army as it marched southwards. News of the fierce forces that were coming struck terror in Edinburgh and Stirling. The few soldiers there withdrew in panic. The Highlanders were at the gates of Edinburgh. Almost without a blow being struck the city surrendered and Charles entered in triumph. For a few weeks he held court at Holyrood Palace, the ancient home of the Scottish kings—I saw the room where he received his guests—and then the invasion of England began, through Carlisle, Preston, Manchester, right down to Derby, only four days' march from London. Success was almost within his grasp. There was panic in London; a ship was ready to take George II to Hanover. And then Charles decided not to advance but to retreat to Scotland again. If he had gone on instead of going back the whole course of English history might have been changed. Charles, as a matter of fact, was all for advancing on London, but practically all his followers were

---

[1] The name the Jacobites gave to George II, who they didn't consider was the King.

against it. The English Jacobites had not come to his aid as Charles had hoped. Three hundred men from Manchester was practically all the support he got, and many of the followers who came first had gone back home. Very unwillingly Charles saw that he must give the order to retreat. So they went back and back until they came to Culloden, six or seven miles from Inverness. Here his army was faced by the army of the Duke of Cumberland.

* * * * *

I walked over the field of Culloden, a wild, bare moor, little different from what it was on that fateful day in 1745. You can still see the little weather-worn stones that mark where the men of the clans who died there are buried. I spelled them out, "Clan Cameron", "Clan Mackintosh", "Clan Maclean", "Clan Stuart". Almost the whole flower of the Scottish Highlands fell at Culloden.

Charles had only 5,000 men, weary, hungry and badly armed, against Cumberland's 9,000 regular soldiers, drawn from the Continent where they had been fighting the French, well-trained, well-fed, well-armed, supported by cavalry and artillery.

The Highlanders rushed fiercely against the lines of the English redcoats, threw down their fire-arms and leaped upon the soldiers with swords and knives. They fell under the steady fire of Cumberland's soldiers and the deadly aim of his cannon. But others came on just as fiercely to continue the attack. The slaughter was dreadful as wave after wave of the Highlanders threw themselves on the English lines. But even all that bravery and loyalty could not win the day. The disciplined forces of the English soldiers held the attack, the drums sounded the advance, the redcoats moved forward, the clans were beaten back. Prince Charles saw that the day was lost and galloped from the field on which 1,200 of the clansmen lay dead. No mercy was shown to the survivors. Those who escaped from the battlefield were hunted down and when they were captured were put to death.

FRIEDA: And what happened to Prince Charles?

OLAF: For months he was hunted through the Highlands. A huge reward was offered for anyone who would capture him dead or alive, but though many Highlanders knew where he was—men without a shilling in the world—not one betrayed him. Loyal, faithful followers hid him in the mountains and after many hairbreadth escapes the young, high-spirited Flora Macdonald took him, dressed as her servant-maid, in a boat to the island of Skye, right under the very noses of the English soldiers who were looking for him. After five months of almost hourly perils they managed to get him to the coast where a ship was waiting to take him to France and safety.

LUCILLE: Did he ever come back to Scotland?

OLAF: Yes. Twenty years later he made one more attempt. But it was quite hopeless. The Stuart cause and the clan system had found their grave at Culloden. But Scottish people still sing old Jacobite songs. Here's one of them (*see p.* 171).

> Bonnie Charlie's now awa'[1]
> Safely o'er the friendly main.[2]
> Many a heart will break in twa[3]
> Should he ne'er[4] come back again.
> Will ye no'[5] come back again?
> Will ye no' come back again?
> Better loved ye canna[6] be;
> Will ye no' come back again?

MR. PRIESTLEY: Thank you, Olaf. I think you told the story very well.

* * * * *

And now we have to say good-bye to one of our little group. This is the last time we shall have Pedro with us. I think you all know that he has been accepted at Cambridge University and goes up next week to read English History. We all congratulate Pedro on his success ("Hear, hear") and wish him good luck at Cambridge.

PEDRO: Thank you all for your good wishes. I shall miss you all. I have been very happy in Mr. Priestley's class.

MR. PRIESTLEY: Thank you, Pedro. We shall miss you

---

[1] *awa'* = away. [2] *main* = sea. [3] *twa* = two. [4] *ne'er* = never.
[5] *will ye no'* = will you not. [6] *canna* = cannot.

WILL YE NO' COME BACK AGAIN

Words by
LADY NAIRNE (1766-1845)

Air attributed to
NEIL GOW Jr. (1795-1823)
Arr. PATRICIA MURRAY

Bon - nie Char-lie's now a - wa, Safe - ly o'er the friend-ly main

Ma - ny a heart will break in twa Should he ne'er come back a-gain

CHORUS

Will ye no' come back a - gain? Will ye no' come back a - gain?

Bet-ter loved ye can-na be. Will ye no' come back a-gain.

too. I am sure you will be very happy at Cambridge, and I hope you will write to us sometime.

PEDRO: I certainly will?

VERB STUDY (14): **see**

There are two common uses of *see* both of which are illustrated in Lesson 16.

1. (= look at; observe.) I made a tour to *see* the places associated with him. I *saw* the monument. Two British vessels *were seen* near the coast of Scotland.
2. (= understand.) Very unwillingly Charles *saw* that he must give the order to retreat. Prince Charles *saw* that the day was lost.

But *see* has numerous idiomatic uses. Here are examples of some of them:

A friend came to *see* (= visit) me.

You should go and *see* (= consult) a doctor about your cough.

Who is going to *see you home* (= go with you) after the dance?

He can never *see* (= understand) a joke.

We haven't much money but we do *see life* (= have lots of experiences).

Write to him and *see* (= find out) what he thinks.

Have you *seen* (= read) the paper this morning?

"Will you come to the cinema tonight?" "Well, I'll *see* about it" (= perhaps; I'll consider it).

I'll go at once and *see about* (= attend to, enquire about) the tickets.

Will you come to the station to *see me off*.

There are three common patterns with *see*:

(1)

Subject	see	(Pro)noun	Infinitive (without to) etc.
I We	*saw* *saw*	the boy him	break the window. take the money.

(2)

Subject	see	(Pro)noun	Participle etc.
The policeman I	*saw* *saw*	the man the ship	*driving* the car in a dangerous manner. *dashed* on the rocks.

(3)

Subject	see	Noun Clause
I	*saw*	that there was going to be an accident.

EXERCISES

I. *Word Study: Use the following:*

cliff, tower (note its use here as a verb), flood-lit, magic (use also *magical, magician*), romance (use also *romantic*), blaze (*noun* and *verb*), exhibition, associated (use also *association*), fascinating (also *fascinate, fascination*), throne (compare with *thrown*), pretend (use also *pretence*), land (note its use as a verb), flock (*verb*; use also as a noun), ambition (use also *ambitious*), sentiment, risk (*verb* and *noun*), loyal (also *loyalty*), origin (also *original, originally, originality*), disguise (*noun* and *verb*), aboard, slip (*noun* and *verb*; use also *slippery, to make a slip, a slip of the tongue, to slip one's memory*), mist (how does mist differ from *fog*?), eagle, ancestors, standard (here it means *flag*), soul (note its use here for *person*), issue (*verb*), panic, grasp (*noun* and *verb*), moor (*noun*) (compare with *more*), weary, slaughter (give another word ending in -*aughter* that rhymes with *slaughter*), discipline, drum, gallop, capture (use also *captive, captivity*), betray.

II. *Explain in your own words the meaning of the following phrases:*

1. towering over the city. 2. a blaze of colour. 3. I caught some of the fever. 4. to go abroad. 5. sympathisers would flock to his side. 6. disaster overtook the French fleet. 7. a great storm struck them. 8. Charles went aboard a French ship. 9. the *Doutelle* made her way among the rocky islands. 10. he expected the shore to be lined with Highlanders. 11. they came pouring over the hills. 12. any other weapon they could lay hands on. 13. struck terror. 14. withdrew in panic. 15. success was almost within his grasp. 16. Charles was all for advancing. 17. weather-worn stones. 18. the whole flower of the Scottish Highlands. 19. could not win the day. 20. held the attack. 21. many hairbreadth escapes. 22. under the very noses. 23. almost hourly perils. 24. found their grave.

III.   COMPREHENSION EXERCISE

Answer the following:

1. Why did Olaf say the effect of the flood-lighting of the Castle was "magical"?
2. Why did Pedro and Olaf think the Scots are not "matter-of-fact"?
3. What did Olaf notice about Prince Charles's letters?
4. Who were the Jacobites?

5. Why was Prince Charles surer of support from the Scottish Jacobites than from the English ones?

6. Why was it so important for Charles to get the support of Lochiel?

7. Who was "the Elector of Hanover"?

8. How near did Charles get to London? Why did he turn back?

9. Why were the forces of Prince Charles defeated at Culloden?

10. How did Prince Charles get to the Island of Skye?

11. What happened to the Scottish Jacobites after Culloden?

12. Why is Pedro leaving Mr. Priestley's class?

IV. *Use each of the following in sentences of your own:*

see about; see him off; to see the last of; to see red; to see one's way; seen better days; to see through a person; to see eye to eye.

V. *Composition Exercises*

1. Write a short character sketch of "Bonnie Prince Charlie".

2. Tell the story of "Bonnie Prince Charlie" in about 450 words.

LESSON 17

THE DOUBLE POSSESSIVE

On page 32 you had the sentence:

He's a friend of Uncle *Albert's*.

This use of *'s* and *of* together is an idiomatic construction, e.g.

That's an old hat of my *brother's* (*NOT* "of my brother").
We saw a play of *Shaw's* at the theatre last week (*NOT* "of Shaw").

There is a similar construction with *of* + a possessive pronoun, e.g.

A friend of *ours* (NOT: "of us") will be with us (page 23).
How much do they want for this house of *yours* (page 6).
A cousin of *mine* (NOT "of me") and his wife have *invited* me (p. 210).
It was no fault of *ours* that we took the wrong road.

The construction is of importance as it enables us to make a difference in meaning between:

A portrait of *Rembrandt* (= one portraying him).
A portrait of *Rembrandt's* (= one painted by him or belonging to him).

VERB STUDY (15): **fall**

On page 169 you had the sentence: "Almost the whole flower of the Scottish Highlands *fell* at

Culloden." Here are further examples of the usage with *fall*:

> The little boy was running and *fell down*; I think he *fell over* a stone.
>
> In this office most of the work seems to *fall on* (= has to be done by) me.
>
> The question to be answered *falls into* (= can be divided into) four parts.
>
> Jan *fell in love with* Frieda.
>
> Mary and Ellen have *fallen out* (= are no longer friends with each other).
>
> He had great plans for his business but they *fell through* (= came to nothing).
>
> We hadn't any bread in the house and the shops were closed so we had to *fall back on* (= use instead) biscuits.

PREPOSITIONS (7)

Under

Under is similar in meaning to *below*, e.g.

> Children *under* the age of twelve are not admitted. His income is *under* £1,000 a year.

But there are differences in usage. If the meaning is "lower than and covered by" we use *under* not *below*, e.g.

> He put the letter *under* a book that was lying on the desk.

On the other hand if the distance lower is mentioned we generally use *below*, e.g.

> The submarine travelled 100 feet *below* the surface of the water.

Under meaning "less than" is used to express time, e.g.

> We went from our house to Cambridge in *under* an hour.

Under means also "governed by", "protected by", e.g.

> In 1890 that country was *under* British rule and its soldiers served *under* the British flag.

It is also used to express certain states of being, e.g.

> He is *under* treatment for rheumatism. The prisoner is *under* guard. That farm has 200 acres *under* (= sown with) wheat. He is *under* sentence of death. The soldier showed great bravery *under* fire.

Under is used to express cover or disguise, e.g.

> Samuel Clemens wrote *under* the name of Mark Twain.

Under is used as a prefix with the meaning "below", "not enough", "too small", e.g.

> *Under*ground; *under*done meat; an *under*sized boy.

Under is an adverb in such sentences as:

> The people were kept *under* by the tyrant. A huge wave struck the ship and it went *under* (= sank).

Until (till)

Until (more usually *till*) can be a preposition, e.g.

> We won't be home *till* morning. He stayed *till* (*until*) long after midnight.

or a conjunction, e.g.

> I will wait *till* (*until*) you come.

Up

In most cases *up* expresses the opposite of *down*, e.g.

He walked *up* the hill. They put *up* a flag.

It is very often used as an adverb with a variety of meanings, e.g.

The sun is *up*. Look *up*. The house is *up* at last. Plants come *up* in the spring. Wake *up*. Hurry *up*. Speak *up*. What time did you get *up* ? I was *up* all night. The car is not far behind us, it will soon catch us *up*. Prices are going *up*. My time is *up*. You will have to pay *up*. The room is dirty; help me to clean *up*.

With (preposition only)

With suggests (1) Accompaniment, e.g.

He came *with* all his family. Don't wear brown shoes *with* a blue suit.

(2) Agreement (or disagreement),

I agree/disagree *with* him on most matters. I don't want to quarrel *with* you.

(3) An instrument, e.g.

Cut the bread *with* this knife. He hit the dog *with* a stick.

(4) Cause, e.g.

The old man was bent *with* age and dying *with* hunger.

(5) Manner, e.g.

He fought *with* bravery. He stood *with* his hands in his pockets.

(6) Possession (= " who (which) has "),

A girl *with* golden hair. A house *with* a large garden.

(7) Contents.

His pockets were filled *with* money.

Within

Within has the meaning "inside", e.g.

"Is anybody *within*?"

but is formal rather than colloquial English.

Within as a preposition is used to refer to time, e.g.

I'll be there *within* (= in less than) an hour.

and in such expressions as:

to live *within* one's income; to be *within* hearing; *within* sight of home; *within* the law.

Without

Without in modern English does not mean "outside" (e.g. Who is *without*?). *Without* means "not having", e.g.

Hob travelled *without* a ticket because he left home *without* money.

It is used with a gerund to give a negative meaning, e.g.

He left *without* saying (= and did not say) good-bye.
Hob travelled *without* buying (= and did not buy) a ticket.

EXERCISES

I. *Make six sentences of your own using* fall *as a different phrasal verb in each.*

II. *Use each of the following* (a) *as a preposition,* (b) *as an adverb:*

on, in, up, about, after, before, behind, over, round, since, off, through.

III. *Put in the prepositions or adverbs that have been omitted:*

1. The man who spoke was standing — me. 2. There are others — me who believe that. 3. Put the two books side — side. 4. Everyone was listening — Richard. 5. He lived here — the years 1940 and 1941. 6. Their plans have completely broken —. 7. The soldiers came in two — two. 8. That book was written — Dickens. 9. That is a book — Russia and the Russian people. 10. I ran — the thief but couldn't catch him. 11. He who is not for us is — us. 12. He has written ten books and there is not a single good one — them. 13. The mother divided the apple — the two boys. 14. Who is looking — you ? 15. Jan is very good — English. 16. He did that — my wishes. 17. I bought that — the butcher's. 18. He put his hands — his back. 19. That ought to cost sixpence or — the very most ninepence. 20. I hoped it would be fine but it poured — all afternoon. 21. My shoes are made — leather; the box is made — iron. 22. I can't get this ring — my finger. 23. He put the book — the table and sat — a chair. 24. He has 10,000 men working — him. 25. What country do you come — ? 26. He walked — the room and sat — his desk. 27. I shan't be away long; I'll be back — a year. 28. The ship rocked — side to side. 29. I don't like to be — debt; that is to be — danger. 30. It is cold — this room now that the fire has gone —. 31. You must make the best — it. 32. The petrol is all running —; turn the tap —. 33. There are houses — both sides — the street. 34. I bought a bicycle — £4. 35. He tried to look at it — my point of view. 36. I shouldn't be — such

a hurry if I were — your place. 37. A friend — mine went with me to the Tower — London. 38. Help me — — my coat. 39. I went there — business; I have to work — my living. 40. — reply — your letter — the 15th of November, we wish to state that we are — need — a traveller — the London district. If you will come here — Saturday the 12th — April we can give you our ideas — the subject and it will then depend — you whether you accept and try to make a success — it or whether — the contrary the whole matter must be considered as definitely —. 41. Someone left a box — the garden and I fell — it — the dark. 42. I stood — the corner — the road and hundreds — cars went —. 43. Walk — the town — me and then we will come home and sit — the fire. 44. I have been — London — the 25th — July. 45. We went — France — our way — Spain. 46. This coat is wet. Hold it — the fire — a few minutes. 47. That is the first step — getting the matter cleared —. 48. I can't use my office — business — present; it is — repair. 49. I had never had a lesson — English until I came — London. 50. That stream never dries — even — the middle — summer. 51. Come and stay — us — a few days — Christmas and bring your wife — you. 52. I did not approve — his action and what he did was done — my consent. 53. You don't need to pay — the money you borrowed all — once. The repayment can be spread — a number — years. 54. Drake sailed — the world — the reign — Queen Elizabeth I. 55. I have been — England — six months but have had lessons only — April. 56. The motor boat cut — the water — a terrific speed. 57. I live quite close — the church; in fact next door — it. 58. It was somewhere — five o'clock — the afternoon when he called — me. 59. — the circumstances, I will not give you any extra work. 60. You could see — a glance there was someone — home; the house was all lit —. 61. I like beef — done rather than — done. 62. They walked — the new road, then — the hill — my house. 63. Orders — the new car came — — a rush. 64. He walked — his hat — the back — his head. 65. — regard — that business, I don't want to do anything more — it, but I'll keep — touch — you.

LESSON 18

Roger's First Day at School

FRIEDA: A short time ago I had a very pleasant week-end at my friend Phyllis Cooper's[1] house. Young Roger, that's Phyllis and Frank Cooper's little boy, had just had his fifth birthday. It was a rather special birthday for him since, as soon as an English child reaches the age of five he must start attending school. I was very interested to hear Frank and Phyllis discussing his education and I thought you might like to hear about it.

MR. PRIESTLEY: I'm sure we shall. I think you will all like to get a little sidelight on English education. Please go on, Frieda.

FRIEDA: Well, it was only after a good deal of thoughtful discussion between Phyllis and Frank Cooper that they had finally decided that Roger should go to his local Primary School. Phyllis, to begin with, would have preferred Roger to go to one of the small "private" schools in the district.

"The fees aren't very high," she had said to her husband, "and he'll mix with much nicer children than he'll meet at the ordinary State Primary School."

[1] See *The Gardiners and the Coopers*, by C. E. Eckersley and L. C. B. Seaman (Longmans).

"I know the fees aren't high," had been Frank's answer, "but don't forget we *have* to pay for State schools through our rates and taxes. I don't hold with the idea of paying for the upkeep of a school and then not making use of it. Besides, when you talk about the 'nicer' children at the private school don't you merely mean that their parents have got more money than most people?"

"Perhaps I do, but some of the children at the Primary School don't come from very good homes, do they? I don't want Roger to pick up any bad habits of speech or a lot of bad manners."

Frank laughed. "Let's risk it. You mothers do so want your boys to be nice, clean, well-spoken little creatures, don't you? Personally, I think that if you and I give him an example of good speech and good manners, what he happens to see and hear at school won't really harm him very much."

"I'm afraid that argument doesn't hold water," answered Phyllis with a smile. "The things you said this morning when you couldn't find a fresh pair of socks in your drawer weren't exactly examples of polite speech, were they?"

"That's a very unfair remark, my dear," said Frank with a laugh; "but I didn't feel quite as fresh as a daisy first thing this morning."

"Besides," said Phyllis, "there's another thing about these State schools: the classes are so large. Mrs. Robinson says they have over forty in a class. Classes are much smaller at the private schools. Isn't that very much better for the children?"

"I'm afraid," replied Frank, "that children of all ages do find themselves in larger classes in State schools than if they went to private schools; but I do know this, that nowadays Infant Teachers in State Primary Schools are very good. I do think they know their job and I believe they work wonders sometimes—even if they do have classes of over thirty. Look here, why don't you go to the Primary School and have a look round? They'll be quite glad to let you see the school."

So Phyllis and I called to see the Head Teacher of the Infant's Department and came away quite charmed. We both liked the Head Teacher's enthusiasm and quiet efficiency and above all we liked the teacher who was in charge of the five-year-olds' class. The thirty children in the room were seated in small chairs around a number of low tables. They were all of them very busy and very interested in what they were doing. Some were cutting out small pictures with scissors (special blunt scissors, for hands and fingers that were not yet expert); some were solemnly colouring-in outline pictures with chalks; others were working with modelling clay. But when the teacher told them to stop what they were doing they did so with what seemed to me quite unusual rapidity—after all, I thought, there are thirty of them and there aren't any of them a day over five. The friendly but not over-excited conversation that took place as the scissors and other things were collected and put away gave us both the impression that here was a happy school which Roger would enjoy and in which any habits he learned would certainly be good ones.

The Head Teacher told us that in the Infants' Department the object was to introduce the children to the art of living together and to develop not only the skill of reading and writing and counting but also to train the hands, the body and the imagination. Drawing with coloured chalks and painting, dancing in time to the music of the piano, the handling of scissors and modelling materials, the acting of little plays— in all these ways it seemed that Roger's day at school would be filled both usefully and happily. After that Phyllis talked no more of paying fees to a private school.

"Will you want Roger to stay to school dinner?" the Head Teacher asked Phyllis.

"What do you advise?"

"I think it's best if they start staying to school dinner right from the beginning," the Head Teacher said, "even though it does make the day seem rather long to them at first. As you know, the cost is very little and we take particular care that the infants, above all, get a really satisfying meal."

"Yes, I see," said Phyllis, a little doubtfully, "but Roger is rather fussy about his food. I'm afraid I've always tried to give him just the things I know he particularly likes."

The Head Teacher smiled. She had heard remarks such as this a hundred times before.

"Don't worry, Mrs. Cooper. We don't *force* the food down their throats, you know. I think it does them good sometimes to eat things they're not used to. Of course, he's bound to grumble — children always do grumble about school dinners. But after all, if Roger

"... THINGS THEY'RE NOT USED TO"

came home every day and said he liked school dinners better than your dinners I think you'd be quite upset, wouldn't you?"

Phyllis laughed.

"They have milk in the morning, too, don't they?" she asked.

"Yes. A third of a pint—that's free, of course. By the way (it's a small point, I know, but then children's lives are made up of small points), you might give him a little practice beforehand in the art of drinking through a straw. That's how we drink our milk in school. It's said to be the cleanest and healthiest way of doing it."

The great day arrived. Roger, having become an expert at the art of drinking cold milk through a straw and now looking as clean as a new pin—far cleaner and neater than he will ever look again for the rest of his schooldays—is about to begin the great adventure. It will never be known which of the two was the more nervous, Roger or his mother.

"I do hope he'll like it, Frank," she had said several times to her husband. And Frank had said cheerfully, "He'll just have to like it, my dear. After all, he's got to go to school on most days of the year for another ten or twelve years!"

"Yes, but some people have such trouble. Peter next door was very difficult about going to school when he first started."

"Only for a little while. They say he's as keen as mustard on school now and can hold his own with any of the boys. Stop worrying, my dear, and remember he'll·be in the hands of people who are probably much better at handling children than you or I will ever be."

Phyllis recalled to mind the teacher she had seen on her visit to the school and felt happier for a while, But even though she told herself she was being silly, she was still as anxious as ever. So, holding his mother's hand very tightly, Roger walked with Phyllis and me along the road to Greenfields County Primary School.

On the way to the school we were joined by a friend on a similar job. Mrs. Jenkins was taking her little girl Susan to school for her first day

The two mothers spent the rest of the ten-minute journey assuring Roger and Susan in bright, cheerful voices that nothing in the world was nicer for them than that they should be going to school together.

"You can play with Susan at playtime," Phyllis told Roger.

And Susan's mother said to Susan, "You can sit next to Roger at dinner-time, can't you? That'll be nice for you, won't it?"

Both children dutifully agreed that it would indeed be very nice, but what views they really held about it nobody would ever know.

In a fairly large room at the school the Head Teacher was receiving the newcomers. As each child's name was called the mother was told to slip quietly away. Susan was as quiet as a mouse but one small boy was protesting against the whole educational system by roaring at the top of his voice.

"Take him away," said the Head Teacher quietly to one of her assistants. The small boy was led off to a distant class-room, his roars getting gradually fainter, and the remaining mothers eyed their own children, each secretly hoping that *her* child would *not* "make a scene".

Roger's name was called. He, too, passed into the class-room and into the charge of the pleasant young woman whom we had seen on our first visit, and Phyllis went home to a house that seemed, after five years of Roger's daily presence in it, strangely quiet.

*   *   *   *   *

Phyllis and I were at the school gate well in time to meet Roger when his day ended at half-past three. She was bursting with impatience to see him, and even began to worry when he was not one of the first five children to come through the school door. He came at last and, thank goodness, all smiles. His teacher, who came to see him across the road, said he had been as good as gold. He had had, he said, a lovely time and a lovely dinner and teacher had told them all a lovely story. And they were to bring some flowers to school to decorate the class-room and could he please pick some from the garden as soon as he got home. . . . And so ended Roger's first day at school.

* * * * *

HOB: Do you know the story of the little boy who went to school for the first time? When he got there, there were three entrances: on one it said GIRLS, on the second BOYS and on the third MIXED INFANTS (because small boys and girls worked together in that department). When he got home he said, "Mother, I'm not a little boy now; I'm a mixed infant."

IDIOMATIC ENGLISH (3): COMPARISONS

In Lesson 18 you probably noticed these idiomatic comparisons:

Roger was *as clean as a new pin*. Peter is *as keen as mustard*. Susan was *as quiet as a mouse*. Roger had been *as good as gold*.

There are many of these comparisons. Here are some of the ones most frequently used:

as black as coal, as black as ink; as bold as brass; as brave as a lion; as brown as a berry (usually said of a person who is very sunburnt); as busy as a bee; as clear as a bell (for a sound, e.g., a person's voice); as clear as crystal, as clear as day (for things seen or understood); as cold as ice; as cool as a cucumber (for a person who doesn't lose his head); dead as a door-nail; deaf as a post; dry as a bone, dry as dust (usually said of a book, a talk, a lesson); drunk as a lord; as easy as A.B.C.; as firm as a rock; as green as grass; as happy as the day is long; as hard as iron; as heavy as lead; as hot as fire; as hungry as a hunter; as light as a feather; as like as two peas; as mad as a hatter; as old as the hills; as quick as lightning; as regular as clockwork; as sharp as a needle; as strong as a horse (for work), as strong as a lion (for fighting); as weak as water; as wet as a drowned rat; as white as snow, as white as a sheet (for a person who is ill or badly frightened).

VERB STUDY (16): **hold**

In Lesson 18 you had the sentences:

Holding his mother's hand tightly Roger walked . . . to school.
But what *views they really held* (= what they really thought) about it nobody would never know.
I *don't hold with the idea* of (= I don't believe in, am not in favour of) paying for the upkeep of a school and then not making use of it.
Peter can *hold his own* with (= compete with, is as good as) any of the boys.
I'm afraid that argument doesn't *hold water* (= is not a good one; will not bear close examination).

The chief meanings of *hold* are:

1. "to keep in the hand"; "to grip".

The child *held* a pair of scissors in her hand.
The man *held* a pipe between his teeth.

2. "to contain".

These shelves *hold* all my books.
We can't tell what joys or sorrows the future will *hold* for us.
I *held my breath* as the car turned the corner at 60 miles an hour.

3. "to support".

The walls of the house *hold up* the roof.

4. "to keep in position or condition".

Hold your head up and keep your back straight.
You must *hold yourself ready* to go to South America at a day's notice.

EXERCISES

I. *Word Study: Use the following:*

week-end, birthday (what do you say to a person on his or her birthday ?), attend (note its use in Lesson 18), sidelight, local, primary, fee, taxes (compare *taxis*; how do *taxes* differ from *rates* ?), daisy, scissors (note this word is a plural), blunt (what is the opposite ?), chalk (note the pronunciation [tʃɔːk]), clay, habits, skill, satisfy (also *satisfaction*, *satisfactory*), fussy, (use also *fuss*, noun and verb), throat, grumble, practice (use also *practise*), pin (what's the difference between a *pin* and a *needle* ?), neat, mustard, roar, eye (as a verb), infant.

II. *Note the sentences:*

Some of the children at Primary Schools don't come from very good homes (p. 184).
Some were cutting out small pictures ... *some* were colouring pictures (p. 185).

Copy out these sentences putting some (someone, something, somewhere) *or* any (anyone, anything, anywhere)[1] *in the places marked by a dash:*

1. I should like to hear — about English education.
2. So should I. I don't know — about it.
3. Is there — here who does know — about it?
4. Have your friends — children?
5. Are — of the children over five? Yes, — of them are six.
6. I can't find my book —. Look again; it must be — in this room.
7. Have you — cigarettes. No, I haven't; I must go and buy —.
8. I want — cigarettes, please. Have you — Turkish ones?
9. — is wrong with my car, it won't go. Perhaps it needs — more petrol; look and see if you have —.
10. Can't you give us — more difficult exercises. — can answer these easy ones.

III. *Explain, or give another word or phrase with, roughly, the same meaning as the following phrases from Lesson* 18:

1. he'll *mix with* nicer children. 2. I don't want him to *pick up* bad habits. 3. *first thing* this morning. 4. they *work wonders* sometimes. 5. the *five-year-olds'* class. 6. they were colouring-in *outline pictures.* 7. they did so with *quite unusual rapidity.* 8. he's *bound* to grumble. 9. I think you'd be *quite upset.* 10. Phyllis *recalled to mind* the teacher. 11. both children *dutifully agreed.* 12. receiving the *newcomers.* 13. one small boy was *protesting against* the whole educational system. 14. he roared *at the top of his voice.* 15. her child would not *make a scene.* 16. Phyllis was at the school gate *well on time.* 17. she was *bursting with impatience* to see him.

[1] If you are not sure about *some* and *any*, see *Essential English*, Book I, p. 129, and Book II, p. 172.

IV.   COMPREHENSION EXERCISE

1. Why is five an important age to an English boy or girl?
2. At which schools in England do you generally pay fees? At which schools do you generally *not* pay fees?
3. Why did Phyllis want Roger to go to a "private school"?
4. What arguments did Frank use for sending Roger to a state school?
5. When Phyllis and Frieda went to visit a class-room what were the children doing?
6. What did the Head Teacher say were the objects of the Infants' Department?
7. In what way was Roger's time at school going to be "filled both usefully and happily"?
8. What reasons did the Head Teacher give why Roger should have his dinner at school?
9. How did she answer Phyllis's doubts?
10. How much milk did Roger get at school, what did he pay for it, and how did he drink it?

V. *Complete the following idiomatic comparisons:*

(a) as black as —.   as hard as —.   as green as —.
     as brown as —.   as white as —.   as cold as —.
     as clear as —.   as cool as —.   as firm as —.
     as easy as —.   as dead as —.   as strong as —.

(b) — as a sheet.   — as a needle.
     — as water.   — as the hills.
     — as a lion.   — as a drowned rat.
     — as lightning.   — as a hatter.
     — as two peas.   — as clockwork.
     — as the day is long.   — as a post.

VI. *Use each of the following in sentences of your own:*

1. hold the view. 2. hold with. 3. hold one's own. 4. hold water. 5. hold one's breath. 6. hold up. 7. hold oneself ready. 8. shareholder. 9. hold a person back. 10. hold out hope. 11. hold in respect.

VII.   *Composition Exercises*

1. Describe (in about 150 words) Phyllis's and Frieda's first visit to the Greenfields Infants' School.

2. Describe (in about 250 words) what happened on Roger's first day at school.

3. Write a short essay on one of the following:

   1. Your first day at school.
   2. The true aim of education.
   3. The educational system in your country.

VIII. *Study this picture and write the story.*

(Reproduced by permission of the proprietors of " Punch ").

THE BANK ROBBERY

LESSON 19

Word Order

1. The normal word order in an English sentence is:

Subject	Verb	Object	Adverbial¹
Mr. Brown	answers	his letters	promptly.
She	sees	him	every day.
The students	meet	Mr. Priestley	in his study.
I	like	wine	very much.

2. If there is an indirect object as well as a direct one, the order is:

Subject	Verb	Indirect Object	Direct Object	Adverbial
The boy	gives	the dog	a bone	every day.
I	bought	him	some sweets	at the shop.
Mary	cooked	John	a good dinner.	
They	paid	me	the money	this morning.

¹ The term *adverbial* covers adverbs, adverb phrases, adverb clauses.

196

3. In a few sentences the adverbial may come before the object or after it, e.g.

> Turn off (*adverbial*) the gas (*object*), OR: Turn the gas off.
> Put on your coat, OR: Put your coat on.
> I have locked up the house, OR: I have locked the house up.
> Ring up John, OR: Ring John up.
> The firemen put out the fire, OR: The firemen put the fire out.

But note that the adverbial cannot come before the object if the object is a pronoun. So you can say:

> "Ring up John," but NOT: "Ring up him."

The pronoun construction would be *Ring him up*.

4. The usual place for the "Adverbs of Frequency", i.e., such adverbs as *always*, *often*, *never*, *sometimes* etc., is before the verb, e.g.

Subject	Adverb of Frequency	Verb	Object	Other Adverbials
He	always often never sometimes, etc.	sees	people	in his office. in the evening. before lunch.

but if the verb is in two parts, these adverbs come after the first part, e.g.

He **has** { *always* *often* *never* *sometimes* } **seen** people { in his office in the evening before lunch }

INVERSION

There are a number of occasions, however, when the usual order SUBJECT + VERB is changed to VERB + SUBJECT. These occasions are:

(1) when the subject is introduced by *there is/are, was, were*, etc. Compare:

> A burglar (*Subject*) is (*Verb*) in the house;
> *and*: There is (*Verb*) a burglar (*Subject*) in the house.

Similarly:

> *There was* a good play on television last night.
> *There are* fifteen students in the class.
> *There will be* six people for dinner tonight.
> *Are there* any cakes on the plate?
> *There were* ten cakes when Hob came in, now *there is* only one.

There is (*was*) is used with a singular subject; *there are* (*were*) with a plural one.

(2) When the sentence begins with certain words or expressions:

(*a*) words or phrases suggesting a negative, e.g.

> **Never** *have I* heard such a silly story.
> **At no time** *did he* ever say that he was not satisfied with my work.
> **Nowhere** in the world *will you* find a higher standard of living.
> **Seldom** *has such a thing* been done before.

(*b*) with *no sooner, hardly, scarcely, rarely*, e.g.

> **No sooner** *had they been given* one increase in pay than[1] they asked for another.
> **Hardly (Scarcely)** *had we begun* the climb when[1] the snow began to come down.

---

[1] Note that after *no sooner* (which is a comparative), *than* is used; after *scarcely, hardly* you should use *when*.

(c) with *only* followed by an adverbial usually of time or place, e.g.

> **Only now** *are we beginning* to realise how great a man he was.
> **Only then** *did they* fully *understand* what he meant.
> **Only by the end of the year,** *shall we know* whether the business has made a profit.
> **Only in north-west Scotland** *have I seen* such scenery as that.

If *Only when* begins a subordinate clause, inversion occurs in the main clause, e.g.

> **Only when** I had the man's story, *did I* realise that you were in danger.

(d) with *so* followed by an adjective or adverb, e.g.

> **So important** *was the news* that the messenger was taken instantly to the King.
> **So deafening** *was the noise* that I could hardly hear myself speak.
> **So seriously** *was he* injured that he was taken to hospital at once.

(3) With the "short answer" beginning *Neither (Nor)*, e.g.

> Pedro can't speak Russian, **neither (nor)** *can Olaf*.
> Frieda didn't go to the dance, **neither (nor)** *did Jan*.

(4) When a direct quotation is divided or when the principal clause of a direct quotation follows the subordinate clause,[1] e.g.

> "That reminds me," *said Hob*, "of a good story."
> "What shall we do?" *said Jan*.

---

[1] But not usually where the subject of *said* is a pronoun.

(5) In exclamatory sentences introduced by *there* or *here*, e.g.

> There *goes our train*! Here *comes the bride*!

(6) When an adverbial which does not usually begin a sentence is used to begin one, usually for emphasis, e.g.

> **Now** *comes my great news* (p. 13).
> **Over the hills** *came the Camerons* (p. 166).
> **Often** *have I heard* it said that he is not to be trusted.
> **Near the church** *was an old cottage*.
> **By his side** *sat his faithful dog*.
> **Such** *was the story* he told me.

(7) With certain old subjunctive forms, e.g.

> *May you* be very happy. *Come* what may.

Or the rather formal construction with *had* (= if . . . had), e.g.

> *Had I* known that you were coming, I would have stayed at home to welcome you.
> *Had the news* reached me earlier I could have done something about it.

Note how a change of word order can completely alter the meaning. For example: a *garden flower* is not the same as a *flower-garden*; a *racehorse* as a *horse-race*; a *glass eye* as an *eyeglass*, or a *foot long* as a *long foot*. And there is a good deal of difference between:

> "*He doesn't like wine very much*," AND: "*He doesn't like very much wine*."

EXERCISES

I. *Explain* (a) *the meanings of the following words and expressions as they are given, and then* (b) *their meanings when the two words in each are put the other way round. In each case illustrate by sentences.*

  1. playing card. 2. grammar school. 3. flower garden. 4. eyeglass. 5. village green. 6. house dog. 7. bicycle pedal. 8. pocket-book. 9. oil-lamp. 10. bus-station. 11. tobacco-pipe. 12. lawn tennis.

II. *Rewrite each sentence to make it begin with the word or phrase in brackets and make any necessary changes.*

  1. That has been said before. (Never.)
  2. We had reached home when it began to rain. (Hardly.)
  3. You will get better cakes than these. (Nowhere.)
  4. I said that you were dishonest. (Neither yesterday nor at any other time.)
  5. We knew how badly hurt he was. (Only after the doctor had seen him.)

III. *Something has gone wrong with the word order here! Put it right.*

  1. The ball hit him on his head, which was made of solid rubber.
  2. ADVERTISEMENT: Bed-sitting room to let, suit single gentleman, twelve feet square.
  3. The boys said that the school meals were bad and would not obey their masters.
  4. LOST: Dark green lady's handbag.
  5. During the struggle the burgler dropped his gun near the door which Bill kicked under the table.

LESSON 20

Great Britons (4): **Florence Nightingale**

FRIEDA: Mr. Priestley, you have told us about a number of great English *men*. but you've said nothing about great English *women*.

MR. PRIESTLEY: Well, I mentioned Queen Elizabeth and Queen Victoria.

FRIEDA: I wasn't thinking so much about kings and queens. They are sometimes great only owing to their position.

LUCILLE: Or because writers or courtiers wanted to flatter them and make them out to be great.

FRIEDA: Yes, I wondered if there were any who had become great by what they did.

MR. PRIESTLEY: Oh yes, quite a lot. Of course, until fairly recently women hadn't the education or the opportunity for winning fame that men had, but just speaking from memory I could mention Jane Austen, the Brontë sisters, Elizabeth Barrett Browning, George Eliot, Christina Rossetti.

OLAF: All these were writers. It's natural, I suppose, that women should become great by writing.

MR. PRIESTLEY: Yes, I suppose so, but there have been others. Elizabeth Fry, for example, who did a great deal of prison reform; Grace Darling who, with only her father to help, took out the lifeboat and rowed across a mile of wild, stormy sea to rescue shipwrecked sailors. Above all, perhaps, there is Florence Nightingale.

OLAF: I read a play about her—I enjoyed it very much.[1]

FRIEDA: Could you tell us something about her, please ?

MR. PRIESTLEY: Certainly if you wish. The story goes back to the middle of the nineteenth century. England was at war with Russia, and an English army was fighting in the Crimea. Disturbing reports, chiefly from the pen of William Russell, *The Times* reporter, began to come to England of the terrible conditions in the hospitals where our wounded men were being treated. The chief hospital, the one at Scutari in Turkey, was an old barracks. It was built over a vast drain up which the wind blew evil-smelling air. The floors were broken and the building was swarming with rats and mice. But even this horrible place was overcrowded. There were hardly any beds, and men were lying on the floor, in the passages, anywhere. There were no clean shirts for the men, and they lay in their blood-soaked rags. They were dying in thousands, not of their wounds so much as of sickness. The only nurses were old soldiers long past fighting age, who knew nothing of nursing and were quite unable to do the work.

[1] *The Lady with the Lamp*, by Reginald Berkeley (Essential English Library).

That was the terrible position when Sidney Herbert, the Minister for War, wrote to Florence Nightingale asking if she would go out to the Crimea with a band of nurses. His letter crossed hers in the post offering her services. Within a week she was ready, and with thirty-eight nurses she sailed for Scutari.

FRIEDA: But why did Sidney Herbert choose Florence Nightingale? Was she already working as a nurse or had she already organised any work like this?

MR. PRIESTLEY: No woman had already organised work like this, and the home of Florence Nightingale was almost the last place that you would have expected a nurse to come from. In her day, nursing was done only by women of the lowest moral class, dirty, drunken creatures such as Dickens had drawn in his picture of Mrs. Gamp.[1] In fact, when women were charged in the police-courts they were often given the choice of going to prison or to hospital service.

The Nightingales moved in the highest social class. Cabinet Ministers were frequent visitors to their house. They were very wealthy; they had two large country houses and a town house in London. They travelled a good deal, and Florence (she was so called because she was born in the city of Florence in 1820) was highly educated in music, art, literature, Latin and Greek. She spoke Italian, French and German with ease, was attractive, and was expected to

[1] In *Martin Chuzzlewit*.

marry one of the numerous admirers who came to the Nightingales' home. But ever since she was a child she had nursed the villagers and the sick dogs and cats and horses round her home and had had a passion to be a nurse. Her parents were horrified and did all they could to prevent it, but Florence was

FLORENCE NIGHTINGALE

not to be turned aside. Whenever she was abroad she visited hospitals, she read, secretly, books on nursing, reports of medical societies, histories of hospitals. She spent some weeks as a sister in a hospital in Paris and three months in a nursing school at Kaiserwerth in Germany, and kept up a constant struggle with her parents. Finally her singleness of aim and her resolution won the day. Her mother—with tears in her eyes—agreed to Florence becoming superintendent of an "Establishment for Gentlewomen during illness" in Harley Street, the fashionable street of London's most famous doctors. She had been there a year when the Crimean War broke out. It was from there that she wrote to Sidney Herbert, whom she knew personally, offering her services.

When she arrived at Scutari she found conditions even worse than the reports had stated. The War Office had told her "nothing was lacking at Scutari". She found that everything was lacking, furniture, clothes, towels, soap, knives, plates. There were no bandages and no linen to make bandages, few medicines and scarcely any proper food. Luckily (or perhaps it wasn't luck but good organisation) she had brought with her large quantities of food, soups, wines, jellies and medical supplies. Everywhere she met with inefficiency and confusion, and everywhere difficulties were put in her way by the officials in charge. As the officials working "according to Army Regulations" could not, or would not, supply the necessary stores, she did so out of her own money. She bought boots, socks, blankets, shirts by the thousand. "I am a kind of general dealer," she wrote, "in shirts, knives, forks, tin baths, cabbages, operating tables, towels, soap." She was the only one who cared nothing for regulations and red-tape.[1] To the stone wall of officialdom she opposed a will of iron. "It can't be done," said a doctor, objecting to an order that she gave. "It must be done," she said quietly. And it was.

HOB: She sounds more like an eagle than a nightingale!

MR. PRIESTLEY: She spared no one, least of all herself.

[1] *red-tape*. Papers in Government offices, lawyers' offices, etc., are often tied with pink or red tape (i.e., thin band of cotton cloth). So the phrase is used to mean rules and regulations in Government affairs that make it difficult to get business done quickly.

She often worked for twenty-four hours on end, dressing wounds, helping surgeons in their operations, easing the pain of the sick, comforting the dying. Every night, carrying a little oil-lamp to light her way, she walked by the beds, four miles of them. To the soldiers she was the "Lady with the Lamp", and they worshipped her. One of them wrote: "What a comfort it was just to see her pass. She would speak to one, smile to many more. She could not speak to all, you know. We lay there by hundreds, but we could kiss her shadow as it fell on the wall." But that is only one side of the picture. The "Lady with the Lamp" was also the hard, practical woman. She and her nurses got down on their knees and scrubbed floors and walls. She organised the cooking of the men's food and the washing of their clothes. Instead of badly-cooked, badly-served food she gave the men well-cooked, well-served meals. She wrote letters to the Government in England, stinging letters to waken them out of their self-satisfied dreams. "When I wrote politely," she said, "I got a polite answer—and nothing was done. When I wrote furiously I got a rude answer—but something was done." Out of hopeless confusion she brought order. The rate of deaths fell from sixty per thousand to three per thousand.

In 1855 she was made Inspector of all hospitals in the Crimea. It meant long, uncomfortable journeys in snow and rain and cold. She took fever but continued her work from her bed.

She refused to go home until the last soldier went. It was not until after peace was declared in 1856 that she returned home—an invalid for life.

But she lived fifty-four years longer. Though she couldn't leave her house, often not even her bed, she worked as fiercely as she had done at Scutari and brought about more changes in English life than perhaps any other private person of her time. At home she met with the same opposition from " officials " as she had met in the Crimea but she had great support, too. Queen Victoria was a great admirer of her. " Such a clear head," she said. " I wish we had her at the War Office."

And the British public was always solidly at her back. Now it was not only a hospital at Scutari that needed her, it was a whole world that was sick and needed help. She changed the whole system of hospital organisation of the army. She began the reform of the health service in India. She wrote books on nursing. She started the Nightingale Training School for nurses at St. Thomas's Hospital, now one of the finest in the world. She changed the whole idea of hospital planning and is the founder of modern nursing. Foreign governments consulted her on the health services for their countries, and their representatives crowded to the ceremony in 1907 when she was given the Order of Merit, the highest civil honour the Government can give and the first ever given to a woman.

Three years later, a very old, tired woman of ninety, she died quietly in her sleep.

EXERCISES

I. *Word Study: Use the following:*

flatter (use also *flatterer*, *flattery*), row (as a verb, and with a quite different meaning as a noun), shipwreck, hospital, barracks, drain (*noun* and *verb*; use also *drainage*), swarm (*noun* and *verb*), soak, charge (to be *charged* with a crime), admirer (use also *admiration*), superintendent, lack, bandage (*noun* and *verb*), jelly, soup (not *soap*), regulations (use also *regulate*), nightingale, dress (note its use here, "to *dress* a wound"), scrub, sting (*noun* and *verb*; give the parts of this verb), rate (compare this use of the word with that on p. 184), invalid ['invəliːd], founder (what is the difference between to *found* and to *find*?; give the parts of each verb), mysterious (what is the corresponding noun?).

II. *Express in other words the meaning of these words or phrases as used in Lesson 20:*

1. speaking from memory. 2. disturbing reports. 3. long past fighting age. 4. his letter crossed hers. 5. Florence was not to be turned aside. 6. the Crimean War broke out. 7. offering her services. 8. red-tape. 9. the stone wall of officialdom. 10. she spared no one. 11. hours on end. 12. self-satisfied dreams. 13. sixty per thousand. 14. peace was declared. 15. an invalid for life.

III.   COMPREHENSION EXERCISE

Answer the following:

1. Why is it natural there should have been fewer famous women than famous men ?
2. What did Grace Darling do ?
3. In what ways was the *building* at Scutari unsuitable to be a hospital ?
4. What was wrong with the *conditions* there before Florence Nightingale arrived ?
5. Who invited Florence Nightingale to go to the Crimea ?
6. Mention the conditions of nursing in England before Florence Nightingale's time.
7. What kind of people were the Nightingales ?
8. Give a short account of Florence Nightingale's education.
9. In what ways had she prepared herself for her task ?
10. "Nothing was lacking at Scutari." How far was this true ?
11. How did she overcome the shortage of supplies ?
12. "I am a kind of general dealer." How far was this true ?
13. What did Hob mean by saying, "She sounds more like an eagle than a nightingale" ?
14. Mention some of the duties she did (*a*) as a nurse, (*b*) as "a hard, practical woman".
15. Why was she called "The Lady with the Lamp" ?

IV. *What prepositions or adverbs are used after the following verbs? Illustrate your answer by an example.*

1. deal	6. entrust	11. laugh	16. play
2. debate	7. glance	12. listen	17. present
3. depend	8. hear	13. live	18. preside
4. differ	9. increase	14. long	19. quarrel
5. divide	10. inquire	15. object	20. refer

V.   *Composition Exercises*

1. Tell in about 450 words the story of Florence Nightingale.

2. Write an essay on " A day in the life of a nurse ".

3. Give an account of a great woman in your or any other country.

*   *   *   *   *

LUCILLE GOES

LUCILLE: Mr. Priestley, I'm afraid this is the last lesson I shall have with you. A cousin of mine and his wife who live in America have invited me to go there and stay with them for three or four months so I am flying there next week. I am very sorry to leave. I have enjoyed our class very much and have learned a great deal.

MR. PRIESTLEY: And we are sorry to lose you, Lucille. Out little circle is breaking up. Jan is going to London University, Pedro to Cambridge, Frieda is going to be married, and now you, Lucille. Well, it is only to be expected. We shall often think of you, Lucille, and of the pleasant times we have had here, and I am sure we all give you our heartiest good wishes for the future. If ever you come to England again, please come and see me. I shall always be glad to see you again.

OLAF, FRIEDA, PEDRO, JAN, HOB: Hear Hear! Good-bye, Lucille, and the best of luck.

LESSON 21

Idiomatic English (4): ANIMAL IDIOMS

MR. PRIESTLEY: A sentence in Lesson 20 about Florence Nightingale as a child nursing animals, "cats and dogs and horses", and the remark about "rats and mice"—not to mention nightingales and eagles—led me to thinking how many idioms there are in English that are drawn from animal life. For example, when we do two things at one and the same time we "kill two *birds* with one stone", or, if we are greedy and foolish, we "kill the *goose* that lays the golden eggs". A bad-tempered person is "like a *bear* with a sore head", an awkward, heavy-footed person is "like a *bull* in a china shop". But let us leave the foolish person, or the bad person, "the *black sheep*", the man who has "gone to the *dogs*" . . .

HOB: I once went to the "dogs"[1] with Uncle Albert.

MR. PRIESTLEY: Yes, some people do "go to the dogs" by going to "the dogs". As I was saying, let's leave the foolish person and consider the wise man. He never "counts his *chickens* before they are hatched" or "buys a *pig* in a poke"[2]—

[1] "the dogs" = dog-racing.
[2] poke = bag (a word no longer used with this meaning except in this phrase).

he always examines carefully what he is buying before he pays his money. He will always, of course, do things in the right order and not try to "put the cart before the *horse*". He will leave alone things that might cause trouble; as he would say, "let sleeping *dogs* lie"; nor will he waste good things on people who can't appreciate them; he doesn't believe in "casting[1] pearls before *swine*".[2] There are some people who always take safety measures when it is too late and "lock the stable door after the *horse* is stolen". That, he considers, is as foolish as putting the cart before the horse. When bold decisive measures are necessary he takes them and "takes the *bull* by the horns", and when an ill-tempered, sharp-tongued friend says something unpleasant, he doesn't worry too much, he knows "his bark is worse than his bite". If he knows a secret, he keeps it; he is not one to "let the *cat* out of the bag". He is full of sound common sense, "*horse* sense" he calls it, and he doesn't believe in making changes while a job is in progress; that would be "changing *horses* in midstream"—a risky business. He knows, too, that there are some things you can't force people to do. As he would say, "you can lead a *horse* to the water, but you can't make it drink". And he would, of course, be too generous-hearted to "look a gift *horse* in the mouth". He's a cheerful, hard-working fellow, "works

[1] cast = throw.
[2] *swine* is an old word for *pigs*.

like a *horse*". He hopes he will always be like that and "die in harness". He isn't proud, "riding the high *horse*", and is always willing to help others in difficulty, "putting his shoulder to the wheel" or "helping lame *dogs* over stiles".

He pities the poor fellow who has "never had a *dog's* chance" and "leads a *dog's* life", perhaps because misfortune has always "*dogged* his footsteps".

OLAF: Oh yes, the policeman always "dogs"[1] the criminal in the crime stories.

MR. PRIESTLEY: Yes, and the criminal tries to "throw him off the scent", perhaps by "drawing a *red herring* across the track", and the poor policeman goes on *dogging* him until he is "*dog* tired".

Our hero and his wife get on very well together; they don't lead a "*cat* and *dog* life". She, of course, never makes "catty"[2] remarks, nor will she fuss "like a *cat* on hot bricks" if he goes out when it is "raining *cats* and *dogs*". She doesn't worry too much; she knows that "care killed a *cat*". She has her independence of mind, too, and knows that the humblest have their rights even in the presence of the greatest. As she says, "a *cat* may look at a king".

Our wise man isn't easily deceived, for when you try to trick him with a *cock-and-bull* story he, like his dog, "smells a *rat*". He's careful

---

[1] to dog = follow closely behind, as a dog does.
[2] catty = spiteful.

what company he keeps. "*Birds* of a feather flock together," he says, and he mixes with people of his own kind, not with "queer *fish*". With them he'd feel "like a *fish* out of water".

He's making a success in life, too. If you give him a difficult job to do you'll find you've "backed[1] a winner". Three or four other men tried for a job he's doing but they were just "also rans"; he "left them at the post". I know that for a fact, I got it "straight from the *horse's* mouth"; from a man who had entrusted him with a big job.

But I'd better stop or you'll think I am "riding my *horse* to death".

VERB STUDY (17): **pull**

Here are examples of usage with *pull*:

I went to the dentist to have a tooth *pulled out*.

They are going to *pull* that building *down* (or: *pull down* that building).

The man has been very ill but I think he will *pull round* (= get better).

The child ran in front of the car and I had to *pull up* (= stop) quickly to avoid an accident.

The boy *pulled a face* when he took the unpleasant-tasting medicine.

Take the car a little further along the street; you will find a place to *pull in* there.

[1] to back = to put a bet on. The idioms in this paragraph are, of course, taken from horse-racing.

IDIOMATIC ENGLISH (5): COLOUR IDIOMS

We have numerous "colour" idioms in the language. Here are some grouped under the various colours:

red

When I hear of cruelty to animals it makes me *see red* (= become violently angry).

I caught the thief *red-handed* (= in the very act).

You are not answering my question. You are trying to *draw a red herring across the track* (= lead the attention away from the real point).

As soon as he led the conversation round to borrowing money I *saw the red light* (= was aware of approaching danger).

On boat-race night the College students *paint the town red* (= have a gay, high-spirited, noisy time).

The mention of that man's name to him is like a *red rag to a bull* (= something that causes violent anger).

Red-tape (see p. 206).

pink

His behaviour was *the pink of perfection* (= perfect).

"How are you?" "Oh, I'm *in the pink*" (= very well). (*Slang*)

He looks at life through *rose-coloured spectacles* (= optimistically, seeing everything in a pleasant light).

blue

He was *blue* in the face with cold.

I'm feeling rather *blue* (in the *blues*) today (= rather miserable, "down in the mouth").

He got his *blue* for football. (At Oxford or Cambridge a man who has been chosen to represent his University at football, rowing, cricket, etc., is given his "colours", light blue for Cambridge, dark blue for Oxford).

He spends all his time reading *blue books* (= Government publications).

A thing like that only happens *once in a blue moon* (= very rarely).

You can talk *till all is blue* (= as long as you like) but I shan't believe you.

The news was a great shock to me; it *came* absolutely *out of the blue* (= was quite unexpected).

green

I hope you live to a *green old age* (= age full of youthful strength).

He's very *green* (= easily deceived). (*slang*)

She was *green* with jealousy (= very jealous).

white

Jan's factory[1] is an absolute *white elephant* (= something valuable but useless, of which the owner would be glad to be free[2]).

Though I believe in telling the truth I think a *white lie* (= a lie told for a good purpose) is sometimes justified.

He boasted a lot about his courage but when danger came he *showed the white feather* (= was a coward).

Many attempts have been made to *whitewash* the man's reputation (= to make it appear good and honourable) but the fact remains that he is a rogue.

black

I won't believe it unless I see it in *black and white* (= in writing).

After the fight one of the boxers had a *black eye*.

You can never believe what he says; he will swear *black is white* if it suits his purpose.

If Hob doesn't work harder he will get in Mr. Priestley's *black books* (= out of favour).

England's wealth was built up on diamonds—*black diamonds* (= coal).

He got many *black looks* (= looks of displeasure) for his speech criticising the Government.

[1] For Jan's factory see *Essential English*, Book III, Lesson 37.
[2] It is said that the King of Siam used to give a white elephant to courtiers that he wanted to ruin.

8

The men tried to persuade the *blacklegs* not to work while they were on strike (= men who are not in a trade union and who work while their fellow workers are on strike).

They tried to force the men to give money by *blackmail* (= threats, often a threat to reveal some guilty secret).

They are rather ashamed of George; he is the *black sheep* of the family (= person with a bad character).

EXERCISES

I. *Explain the following:*

1. to go to the dogs. 2. the black sheep of the family. 3. to put the cart before the horse. 4. to lock the stable door after the horse is stolen. 5. to take the bull by the horns. 6. to let the cat out of the bag. 7. to die in harness. 8. his bark is worse than his bite. 9. to ride the high horse. 10. a cat and dog life. 11. a cat on hot bricks. 12. a bull in a china shop. 13. to smell a rat. 14. a fish out of water. 15. an "also ran". 16. straight from the horse's mouth. 17. raining cats and dogs. 18. a red herring. 19. misfortune dogged his footsteps. 20. a cock-and-bull story.

II. *Why shouldn't you:*

1. Count your chickens before they are hatched. 2. Kill the goose that lays the golden eggs. 3. Buy a pig in a poke. 4. Cast pearls before swine. 5. Change horses in midstream. 6. Look a gift horse in the mouth?

III. *Why should you:*

1. Let sleeping dogs lie. 2. Put your shoulder to the wheel?

IV. *Complete the following and explain:*

1. "You can lead (take) a horse to the water . . ."
2. "Help a lame dog . . ."
3. "Birds of a feather . . ."

V. *Make six sentences of your own using* pull *as a different phrasal verb in each.*

VI. *Explain and use the following:*

to see red; red-handed; a red herring; a red rag to a bull; rose-coloured spectacles; in the blues; once in a blue moon; out of the blue; a green old age; a white elephant; a white lie; to show the white feather; to whitewash; to be in someone's black books; to give black looks; a black-leg; to blackmail.

VII. *Study the pictures below and write the story they tell.*

(Reproduced by permission of the proprietors of "Punch").

TAKING THE DOG FOR A WALK

LESSON 22

Cambridge

MR. PRIESTLEY: I have just received a letter from Pedro at Cambridge. You will remember he promised to write and I'm sure you will enjoy his letter. Here it is.

KING'S COLLEGE,
CAMBRIDGE.

DEAR MR. PRIESTLEY, FRIEDA, OLAF AND HOB,

My coming to Cambridge has been an unusual experience. From whatever country one comes as a student one cannot escape the influence of the Cambridge traditions—and they go back so far! Here, perhaps, more than anywhere else, I have felt at one and the same time the Past, the Present and even the Future. It's easy to see in the old grey stone buildings how the past has moulded the present and how the present is giving shape to the future. So let me tell you a little of what this University town looks like and how it came to be here at all.

The story of the University begins, so far as I know, in 1209 when several hundred students and scholars arrived in the little town of Cambridge after having walked 60 miles from Oxford.

These students were all churchmen and had been studying in Oxford at that city's well-known schools. It was a hard life at Oxford for there was constant trouble, even fighting, between the townsfolk and the students. Then one day a student accidentally killed a man of the town. The Mayor arrested three other students who were innocent, and by order of King John (who was quarrelling with the Church and knew that the death of three student clergymen would displease it) they were put to death by hanging. In protest, many students moved elsewhere, some coming to Cambridge; and so the new University began.

Of course there were no Colleges in those early days and student life was very different from what it is now. Students were of all ages and came from anywhere and everywhere. Those from the same part of the country tended to group themselves together and these groups, called "Nations", often fought one another.

The students were armed; some even banded together to rob the people of the countryside. Gradually the idea of the College developed, and in 1284 Peterhouse, the oldest College in Cambridge, was founded.

Life in College was strict; students were forbidden to play games, to sing (except sacred music), to hunt or fish or even to dance. Books were very scarce and all the lessons were in the Latin language which students were supposed to speak even among themselves.

In 1440 King Henry VI founded King's College,

and other colleges followed. Erasmus, the great Dutch scholar, was at one of these, Queens' College, from 1511 to 1513, and though he writes that the College beer was "weak and badly made" he also mentions a pleasant custom that unfortunately seems to have ceased.

"The English girls are extremely pretty," Erasmus says, "soft, pleasant, gentle, and charming. When you go anywhere on a visit the girls all kiss you. They kiss you when you arrive. They kiss you when you go away and again when you return."

Many other great men studied at Cambridge, amongst them Bacon, Milton, Cromwell, Newton, Wordsworth, Byron and Tennyson.

Practical jokes seem always to have been common, and there is an amusing tale of one played on the poet Gray[1] by the students of Peterhouse College where he lived. Gray was a rather nervous man with a fear of fire, and every night he used to hang a rope-ladder from his window for use in case a fire broke out. One night there was a great noise and shouts of "Fire! Fire!" Dressed only in his nightgown Gray opened his window, climbed onto his ladder and slid down as fast as he could—into a barrel of cold water put there by a joking student!

Now let me give you some idea of what you would see if you were to walk around Cambridge. Let us imagine that I am seeing the sights for the first time. It is a quiet market town and the shopping centre for quite a large area, but I notice more bookshops than

---

[1] *Thomas Gray* (1716-71). His poem *Elegy in a Country Churchyard* is one of the best known in the English language.

one normally sees in country towns, and more tailors' shops showing in their windows the black gowns that students must wear, long gowns that hang down to the feet for graduates and shorter ones for undergraduates.

In the centre of the town is the market-place where several times each week country traders come to sell their produce. Everywhere there are teashops, some in modern and many in old buildings, reached by climbing narrow stairs. The streets are narrow and crowded, and here and there among the modern shops and offices a quiet opening tempts one away from the rush of the shopping centre. There is a great deal of bicycle traffic, mainly undergraduates who race along thoughtless of safety, with long scarves (in various colours to denote their College) wound round their necks.

Continuing, I find my way to the river which flows behind the College buildings and curls about the town in the shape of a horseshoe. This narrow river (a good jumper could almost leap it) is the Granta, and a little farther on it changes its name to the Cam. It flows slowly and calmly. The "Backs", as this part of the town behind the Colleges is called, have been described as the loveliest man-made view in England. It is indeed beautiful. To the left, across the stream, there are no buildings, merely meadows, College gardens and lines of tall trees. Everything is very green and peaceful. On the river-bank are willow trees[1] with their branches bending into the

---

[1] willow tree = a tree that grows near water and whose branches bend down to the water; it is known as the "weeping willow".

water, and at intervals along the river, stone bridges cross the stream and lead into the Colleges which line the right bank. The deep-coloured brick or stone of the College walls, sometimes red and sometimes grey, is 500 years old. The walls rise out of their own reflection in the water and their colour contrasts charmingly with glimpses of the many green lawns.

Walking along the river-bank, where the only sound is the noise of the gentle wind in the tree-tops, I come to my College, King's College. Across a bridge and beyond a vast carpet of green lawn stands King's College Chapel, the largest and most beautiful building in Cambridge and the most perfect example left of English fifteenth-century architecture. (*See Frontispiece*).

The Colleges join one another along the curve of the river. Going through a College gate one finds one is standing in an almost square space of about 70 yards (the size varies from College to College) known as a "court". Looking down into the court on all sides are the buildings where the students live. The Colleges are built on a plan common to all. There is a chapel, a library, and a large dining-hall. One court leads into another and each is made beautiful with lawns or a fountain or charming old stone path. The student gets a good impression of all the English architectural styles of the past 600 years—the bad as well as the good.

There are nineteen Colleges, excluding two for women students, which were built near the end of the last century (women students do not play a very active part in University life at Cambridge, by the way. But they work harder than men and one seldom sees them outside of the classrooms).

It is difficult to walk around the quiet courts of the Colleges without feeling a sense of peace and scholar-ship. And the sense of peace that green lawns always suggest to me is found in the town too, for often one is surprised to meet open stretches of grass in the midst of the streets and houses giving a charmingly cool countryside effect and reminding one of the more graceful days of the eighteenth century. I'll finish as I began on that note, the feeling one has here of the past in the present, of continuing tradition and firm faith.

Kind regards and best wishes,

Your sincere friend,

PEDRO.

VERB STUDY (18): **put**

The usual meaning of *put* is "place", as for example on p. 222.

He fell into a barrel of cold water *put* there by joking students.

But their are a great many idiomatic uses, as for example on p. 221.

"The three students were *put to death*."
"You *put down* a portion of the money" (p. 5).

Here are some common usages:

I want to *put in* (= do) an hour or two's work before dinner.
Olaf is going to *put in* (= apply) for a job with a business firm.

They have *put up* (= raised) the price of coal again.

We *put up* (= stayed) at a very good hotel in Paris.

I have *put off* (= postponed) my holidays until September.

Put the light *out* (*off*) before you go to bed.

His modesty is all *put on* (= pretence).

The hotel is not good but we are only staying for two days so we can *put up with* (= endure) it.

"Never *put off* till tomorrow what you can do today." (*Proverb*.)

The Non-Finites (1): **The Infinitive**

MR. PRIESTLEY: When you look up a verb in the dictionary, the form of it that is given is the infinitive, and when we speak of a verb we generally use this form (with *to*), e.g. "the verb *to be*", "the verb *to go*", etc. The infinitive cannot form a predicate by itself but it plays an important part in many sentences. Here are some examples of it in action:

> *To grow* roses one must have good soil. I want *to know* the answer. You must learn *to work* hard and *to save* money. Frieda and Jan are *to be* married soon. She has come here *to learn* English. You should eat *to live*, not live *to eat*. He likes having nothing *to do*. They gave him something *to eat*. I was very glad *to see* you. Richard is sure *to be* at the party; he will be the first *to come* and last *to go*. He helped me *to do* my work. I asked her *to write* to me.

The infinitive is also used after *know* (and one or two other verbs) together with an interrogative word like *how*, *where*, *what*, e.g.

I don't KNOW **how** *to do* this exercise.

If you want me you KNOW **where** *to find* me.

I don't KNOW **what** *to say*.

When the verb *know* is followed by a simple infinitive it must always have one of these interrogative words after it.

Such a sentence as,

"He KNOWS *to drive* a car" is WRONG.

Change it to:

He KNOWS **how** *to drive* a car.

THE NON-FINITES (2): **The "Bare" Infinitive**

In some cases the infinitive is used without *to*; this form is the "bare" infinitive. The bare infinitive is used with all the "special" verbs except *ought* and *used*, e.g.

Henry **can** *speak* French.
Do you *understand* this?
I **will** *help* you with your work.

but:

Hob **ought** *to work* harder.

HOB: I **used** *to work* harder when I **didn't** *know* so much as I do now.

MR. PRIESTLEY: The bare infinitive is used also after a number of other verbs, e.g.

She **saw** him *take* the money.
I **heard** her *sing*.
The boys wanted to **watch** the train *go* out.
Let me *have* your homework now.
That **made** me *laugh*.

We have just seen the infinitive used without *to*, but sometimes the *to* is used without the infinitive, e.g.

> I shall go if I want *to* (go).
> Hob never works harder than he needs *to* (work).
> "Will you come and see me?" "I should love *to*" (come).

HOB: I know a story with a lot of infinitives in it. May I tell it, please?

MR. PRIESTLEY: Very well, Hob.

HOB'S STORY

My aunt Aggie[1] used to think that she was able to sing; I'm sorry to say her singing was terrible. Well, one day she asked a piano-tuner to come and tune her piano. He went, and when he tried to tune the piano it seemed to be all right. However, he thought he had better do something though he would rather have gone away, so he went over it carefully and made a very good job of it. A few days later Aunt Aggie rang up again to say she didn't think the man had done it properly. The man's employer was very angry, and I need hardly say the piano-tuner himself was very surprised. However, he went again to the house. Aggie said, "Let me play it"; so he heard her play it. It was perfectly in tune but she made him tune it again. He swore to himself (it was the first time he had ever been heard to swear) but he did the job again.

[1] You met Aunt Aggie in Book II, pp. 40–42.

The next day she rang up again and said, "It is easy to see that your man doesn't know his job. The piano seemed to be all right when he was here, but as soon as I begin to play it and sing at the same time, it gets all out of tune."

EXERCISES

I. *Word Study: Use the following:*

influence (*noun* and *verb*; use also *influential* and *influenza*—formerly believed to be caused by the "influence" of the stars), tradition, mould (*verb* and *noun*), innocent (what is the opposite? Use also *innocence* and its opposite), tend ("they tended to group themselves together"), amusing (use also *amuse, amusement*), ladder, slide (give the parts of this verb), barrel, display (*verb* and *noun*), produce (*noun*; note the stress; it is different in the verb *produce*), scarf (write the plural), flow (give the principal parts of this verb and of the verbs *fly, flee*), meadow, intervals, reflection, contrast (*noun* and *verb*; note the difference in stress; what is the difference between *contrast* and *compare*?), lawn, scholarship (p. 225; compare this meaning with that on p. 48).

II. *What preposition or adverb is generally used after the following verbs? Illustrate your answer by an example. In some cases more than one preposition may be used[1] according to the meaning required, for example,* agree:

I *agree to* your proposal.
I *agree with* you that we ought to do this.

---

[1] With verbs like *get, make, put*, etc., there may be a dozen or more.

Are we all *agreed about* this matter ?

1. account	6. approve	11. borrow	16. compare
2. accuse	7. ask	12. break	17. complain
3. aim	8. attend	13. call	18. consist
4. answer	9. believe	14. care	19. correspond
5. apply	10. blame	15. come	20. cut

III. In this lesson you had the words: *un*usual, *un*fortunately, *dis*pleased, where the PREFIXES *un*- and *dis*- give the meaning "not" or "opposite of". You had also: thought*less* where the SUFFIX -*less* gave the meaning "without".

    (*a*) *Give six words (and use each in a sentence) using the prefix* UN-, *six using the prefix* DIS- *and six using the suffix* -LESS *with these meanings.*

    (*b*) There are other prefixes used to express the negative of adjectives or adverbs. *Using prefixes, make the following negative:* happy, pleasant, attentive, possible, patient, regular, legal, obedient, loyal, responsible, *and use each of the words you make in a sentence.*

IV.   COMPREHENSION EXERCISE

    1. What does Pedro say is his first impression of Cambridge ?
    2. Which is the older University, Oxford or Cambridge ?
    3. How did Cambridge University begin ?
    4. In the Middle Ages "life in College was strict" (p. 221). Illustrate this statement.
    5. Who was Erasmus ? What "pleasant custom" at Cambridge does he mention ?
    6. What was the practical joke played on the poet Gray ?
    7. If you visited Cambridge how would you know which of the young men there were students ?

8. What does Pedro say is "the loveliest man-made view in England"? Describe it briefly as you have imagined it from his description.

9. What is the "common plan" on which the Colleges are built?

10. What does Pedro say of the women students at Cambridge?

V. *Use each of the following in sentences of your own:*

1. put into words. 2. put away. 3. put down to. 4. put down for. 5. put one's foot down. 6. put in a fix. 7. put back. 8. put aside. 9. put a stop to. 10. put to death. 11. put forward. 12. put money on. 13. all put on. 14. put off. 15. put in. 16. put up at. 17. put one in mind of. 18. put into force. 19. put in a word. 20. put in an appearance. 21. put two and two together. 22. put a person up. 23. put out. 24. put up with. 25. put upon. 26. put someone's back up.

VI. *Find all the infinitives in Hob's story on pp. 228-9.*

VII.   *Composition Exercises*

1. Pedro has described a walk round Cambridge. Describe a walk round any pleasant town or city that you know.

2. Write an account, mentioning any interesting customs, of a University in your country or of any other University.

3. What do you think ought to be the aim and ideals of a University?

LESSON 23

Great Britons (5): **Captain Scott**

MR. PRIESTLEY: You know, I am sure, about one Scott, Sir Walter, who will be immortal as long as the English language is read. Here is another Scott, immortal, too, as long as men still admire heroism and endurance.

In 1910 Captain Robert Falcon Scott and his crew set sail in the *Terra Nova* in an attempt to discover the South Pole. They made their base at Cape Evans and planned the journey to the Pole in three stages.

First there was the crossing of the Barrier, a great plain of ice of nearly 500 miles. Over this Scott planned to send as much food and other stuff as he could by motor sledges. When these could go no farther, dogs and ponies would take the loads as much farther forward as they could. The motors took them the first 50 miles, then the ponies and dogs and men continued the journey south. Some of the ponies had to be shot as food for them was running short, but at last the plain was crossed. An even more difficult stage lay before them now, for towering in front of them rose a great range of mountains, in parts over 9,000 feet high and covered with ice. But through the range flowed a glacier, the Beardmore Glacier, and to climb this would be the next stage of the journey.

At the foot of the glacier they killed the remaining ponies (some of them had already died), cut up the meat and buried it so that it would provide food for the return journey. The dogs and some of the men now went back, but three sledges, each pulled by four men, set off on the next stage. It was a terrible journey; the snow was so soft that often they sank to their knees in it, and the heavy sledges—each carried 800 lbs.—were very difficult to move through it. Some of the men suffered from snow blindness, and most of them were already feeling the strain of the journey. Still they struggled on, nine hours a day, with resolute courage. It was the hope of reaching the Pole that made the journey endurable.

Scott watched the men carefully. He had decided that the final dash of 150 miles would be made by four men and himself, and he had to make up his mind which of the men he would choose. Finally he made his choice. In addition to Scott himself there was Dr. E. A. Wilson ("Uncle Bill"), surgeon and artist, a deeply learned man of a most lovable nature, brave, gentle and saintly. Then there was Lieutenant Bowers, small in body but a giant in soul; Captain L. E. G. Oates of the Royal Inniskilling Dragoons, and finally there was Edgar Evans, a British seaman, a huge fellow, as strong as a horse and unfailingly cheerful. These were the immortal five.

On 3rd January 1912, when the South Pole was 150 miles away, the seven men left behind said good-bye and cheered the five who were to go on, and watched them set off harnessed to their sledges, five brave souls who would never again see living faces except one another's. Scott expected they would be at the Pole in a fortnight. For thirteen months nothing was heard of them, but from Scott's diaries we know all there is to be known.

On 18th January they reached the Pole. Three of the men were frost-bitten; all were hungry and weak. And at the Pole, in the midst of the waste of snow, stood a tent, with the Norwegian flag flying above it. Amundsen, the Norwegian explorer, had been there a month before and had gone. In the tent was a letter addressed to Scott saying: "Welcome to 90 degrees. With kind regards. I wish you a safe return. Roald Amundsen."

Bitterly disappointed, Scott and his companions set out on the return journey. It had taken them seventy-six days to get there; it would take at least as long to get back, and there were no ponies at the Barrier, only their frozen flesh, and they might not even find that. It was still the Antarctic summer but the weather was bitter, the wind was blowing at blizzard force, the ice was rough and food was short. They got at last to the top of the glacier. "I wonder if we can do it," wrote Scott. The conditions were terrible; their sleeping-bags never really thawed out, ice formed on the inside of their tent, and then, a month after they left the Pole, Evans collapsed. When he could no longer walk he tried to crawl on hands and knees down the glacier. Their only hope of success was to go on and leave Evans. But they did not go on. They stayed by him and, "we did not leave him till two hours after his death," writes Scott.

Without Evans' mighty strength it was almost impossible for the others to pull the sledge. The weather grew worse, with hurricanes, blizzards, intense cold, and they had not enough fuel to warm their food. Oates was suffering terribly from frost-bite and could not pull the sledge; indeed he could hardly walk. "What shall I do?" he said to Dr. Wilson. "Keep on, keep on," said Wilson. But Oates knew he was slowing down the progress of his friends and making their death certain too. He slept through the night, hoping that he would not wake, but in the morning he was still alive. He said to his friends, "I am going outside and I may be some time." They knew he was walking out to his death in order that they might live, and tried to dissuade him, "but," says Scott, "we knew it was the act of a brave man and an English gentleman. We all hope to meet the end with a similar spirit, and assuredly the end is not far."

They came at last to a spot only 11 miles from their "One-Ton Camp", but the blizzard was so fierce that they had to camp where they were with fuel for one hot meal and food for two days only. Only 11 miles to safety but they could not reach it. The blizzard blew more fiercely than ever. Despite the cold and hunger, Scott and his companions lived for four days longer, and they died there in their tent, three friends who did not fail one another.

Scott was the last to die. He filled in his diary almost to the last day and wrote a noble last message:

"We are weak, writing is difficult, but for my own sake I do not regret this journey, which has shown that Englishmen can endure hardship, help one another and meet death with as great a fortitude as ever in the past.

"Things have come out against us; we have no cause for complaint but bow to the will of God, determined still to do our best to the last.

"But if we have been willing to give our lives to this enterprise, which is for the honour of our country, I appeal to our country to see that those who depend on us are properly cared for. Had we lived I should have had a tale to tell of the endurance and courage of my companions which would have stirred the heart of every Englishman. These rough notes and our dead bodies must tell the tale."

Eight months later a search party found that silent tent. They were there as they had died.

Scott's arm was outstretched to touch his friend Wilson. The diary and letters were by his side; there was no food whatever, but on the sledges outside were still the rocks, etc., 35 lbs. in weight, for scientific study that they had brought back from the Pole. In that last painful march they had not forgotten that they were scientists as well as explorers. The body of Oates was never found, but somewhere about the place where he went away they put up a heap of stones with the words: "Hereabouts died a very gallant gentleman, Captain L. E. G. Oates, who, on their return journey from the Pole in March 1912, willingly walked to his death in a blizzard to try to save his companions."

VERB STUDY (19): **set**

On p. 232 and p. 234 you have the sentences

Captain Scott *set sail* in the *Terra Nova*.
They watched them *set off*.
Scott and his companions *set out* on the return journey.

But *set* is used in a great variety of meanings. Here are examples of some of the commonest ones:

The sun *sets* in the west.
Tell Susan to *set* the table (i.e., put the cups, saucers, plates, etc., in position on the table).
The child was playing with matches and *set fire to* some papers and the whole house was *set on* fire.
Frieda's engagement ring is a diamond *set* in gold.
Jan broke his leg playing football and the doctor *set* the broken bone.

He opened the cage and *set* the bird *free*.

Mr. Priestley will *set* the examination paper.

Winter has *set in* (= begun) early this year.

Come on, *set* to work (= begin in earnest).

What you said has *set me thinking* (= caused me to think).

THE NON-FINITES (3): **Participles**

There are two participles, the present participle and the past participle. The present participle ends in *-ing*, e.g. *walking*, *speaking*, *reading*. The past participle of regular verbs ends in *-ed*; the past participle of irregular verbs has a variety of endings.

The present participle is used in the continuous tenses of verbs, e.g. He is *writing* a letter. I shall be *going* away tomorrow.

The past participle is used to make the perfect tense, e.g. He *has written* me a letter. Pedro *had studied* English before he came to England.

It is also used to form the Passive Voice, e.g.

The tree was *blown* down by the wind.

All the tickets for the concert have been *sold*.

Participles (both present and past) are partly verbs and partly adjectives and are often used exactly like adjectives, e.g.

An *exciting* story; *disappointing* news; he is a *good-looking* man.

broken bottles; a *well-cut* suit; the workers were *tired*.

Misrelated Participles

In using a participial phrase, i.e., a phrase with a participle in it, take care that the participle is correctly related; it ought to be related to the subject of the verb in the sentence, e.g.

Walking through the park, *I* saw some lovely flowers. (The person *walking* was *I*. Participle correctly related.)

Walking through the park, *the flowers* looked beautiful. (It was not the flowers that were walking. Participle wrongly related.)

Running into the house, *the boy* banged the door (*Running* refers to *boy*. Participle correctly related.

Running into the house, *the door* banged after the boy. (*Running* does not refer to *the door*. Participle wrongly related.)

EXERCISES

I. *Word Study: Use the following:*

immortal (use also *mortal*, *mortality*), hero (what is the feminine form?), endurance, stage, sledge, pony, range, glacier, dash (*noun* and *verb*), blizzard, thaw (what is the opposite?), collapse, crawl (*noun* and *verb*), hurricane, dissuade (how does *dissuade* differ from *persuade*?), enterprise, appeal (*noun* and *verb*), explorer (use also *explore*, *exploration*).

II. *Make each of the following sets of simple sentences into a complex sentence by the use of relative pronouns or conjunctions*:

1. Scott and his companions were three friends. They did not fail one another.
2. I do not regret this journey. It has shown our courage.
3. We have given our lives for this enterprise. It is for the honour of our country.
4. I could tell a tale of courage. It would stir the heart of every Englishman.
5. The rocks were on the sledges. The rocks had been brought back from the Pole.
6. The body of Captain Oates is buried here. He willingly walked to his death.
7. They expected the provisions there. They did not find them.
8. They reached the Pole. They found Amundsen had already been there.
9. Scott wrote in his diary, "Things have come out against us."
10. We leave our children. They will be cared for. We hope.

III. Consider the sentence, "They were so weak that they could not battle against the blizzard." This sentence could be written with another construction using *too* and an infinitive, e.g.

They were *too* weak *to battle* against the blizzard.

Rewrite the following sentences using the too *and infinitive construction. A preposition, e.g.* for, *will sometimes be necessary*:

1. The ponies were so tired that they could not pull the sledges.
2. The snow was so deep that the sledges could not go over it.

3. The blizzard was so fierce that they could not continue the journey.

4. The food was so short that they could not have a proper meal.

5. The rest of the party were so loyal that they would not leave Evans and save themselves.

IV. *Make sentences of your own using the following:*

1. set off. 2. set foot on. 3. set out. 4. set sail. 5. set something right. 6. set something in order. 7. set on fire. 8. set fire to. 9. sunset. 10. set one's teeth. 11. rain set in. 12. set-back. 13. set aside. 14. set about. 15. set an example. 16. set one's heart on. 17. set an examination paper. 18. set a person thinking. 19. set a person at his ease. 20. set to music. 21. set free. 22. set one up. 23. set up in. 24. set to work. 25. set up. 26. set up as. 27. well set up.

V. COMPREHENSION EXERCISE

1. Distinguish between Sir Walter Scott and Captain Scott.

2. How far did (*a*) the motors, (*b*) the dogs and ponies, take Scott's party?

3. How many men continued the journey from the foot of the glacier?

4. Who were the "immortal five" who completed the "final dash"?

5. How do we know what happened on that last stage?

6. When he got to the South Pole why was Scott "bitterly disappointed"?

7. Why did Oates walk out of the tent into the blizzard?

8. How near to safety were they when they died?

9. What did Scott think that this journey had shown?

10. "In that last painful march they had not forgotten that they were scientists as well as explorers." What proof is there of this statement?

VI. *Composition Exercises*

1. Tell the story of Captain Scott in about 450 words.

2. Write about any other great explorer.

3. Write an essay on one of the following:

   1. What benefits are to be gained from Polar exploration?
   2. Heroes of peace.

VII. Study the pictures below, write the story and suggest a title.

(Reproduced by permission of the proprietors of "Punch").

LESSON 24

THE AMERICAN SCENE (1)

A Letter from Lucille

APARTMENT 109,
1717, FIFTH AVENUE,
NEW YORK.

5th April, 19—

DEAR MR. PRIESTLEY,

The address is rather a surprise, isn't it? Yes, I'm actually in America; I've been here for three months, but I've been so busy going about "seeing America" that I have hardly had any time for writing letters. All the same, I haven't been lazy, I've been keeping a "journal". I know you will find this hard to believe after the way I so often wasted my time when you were my teacher, so, to prove what I say I am sending the journal to you, under separate cover. I don't say that my journal is like Swift's[1] or Boswell's[2]; it's perhaps more like those journals or diaries that young ladies used to write in Queen Victoria's time, but I saw and heard so many things that interested me that I wanted to write them down while the impressions were still fresh in my mind. I hope that

[1] Journal to Stella by Jonathan Swift (1667–1745).
[2] Journal of a Tour to the Hebrides with Dr. Johnson by James Boswell (1740–1795).

what I have written may interest you and my old friends Frieda, Pedro, Jan, Olaf and Hob. I often think about you and hope we shall all have a meeting again before very long.

Kind regards and best wishes to you all,

Yours sincerely,

LUCILLE.

Extracts from Lucille's Journal

3rd February.

. . . The first sight of the skyline of New York from the water is really staggering, and it is just as

NEW YORK SKYLINE

impressive when you are in the streets and beside these enormous "skyscrapers" that rise up like great cliffs. To someone accustomed, like me, to buildings in London or Paris four or five storeys high, it takes your breath away to see them here shooting up 70, 80, 100 storeys.[1] They are a sort of vertical landscape

---

[1] But we are getting them in London now (1963) of 40–50 storeys.

instead of the horizontal one that we are accustomed to. They are hard and bare but they give one a feeling of power and have a kind of cold, hard beauty, and at night, when all the windows are lit up, the hardness of the daytime is softened, and the scene becomes a twentieth-century fairyland.

I went up the highest one, the Empire State Building, 102 storeys, more than a thousand feet high, the highest man-made thing in the world. (When you get to the top you can buy a badge for your coat saying " I've been up"!)

Many Americans are terribly impressed with mere size; to them "bigger" and "better" seem to mean the same thing. Within a very short time of being here I was told that the Cathedral in New York is the largest "Gothic" Cathedral in the world; that the finger of the Statue of Liberty in New York Harbour is eight feet long and that forty people can stand inside its head; that the Rockefeller Centre cost 100 million dollars to build, has 13,000 telephones, and its hanging gardens are four times the size of the famous hanging gardens of Babylon that were one of the Seven Wonders of the ancient world; that Macy's (the famous department store) employs 11,000 shop assistants and sells a million dollars' worth of goods every day; and if all the people in the skyscrapers came out at once, the streets couldn't hold them. As for their newspapers there is no doubt at all that, for the number of pages, they certainly take the prize, the daily edition of a newspaper has anything from 60 to 100 pages, and the Sunday editions remind you in size of the Encyclopaedia

Britannica. But, of course, the United States is a big place. As one American said to me, "You can leave New York, fly twice as far as from London to Moscow, and find yourself still in America."

*   *   *   *   *

10th February.

It is easy to find your way about in New York, it is laid out so regularly. Instead of streets wandering and twisting as they do in London, they are all regular and planned. The streets running north and south are called "Avenues" and are numbered, e.g. 1st Avenue, 2nd Avenue, 3rd Avenue, etc., the streets going east and west are called "Streets" and are also numbered, e.g. 51st Street, 63rd Street, etc. It's all very much more logical and sensible than London's street names; but I couldn't help thinking how much more fascinating than these dull, cold numbers are London's illogical but colourful "Paternoster Row" and "Amen Corner", "Drury Lane" and "Petticoat Lane" (which are not lanes at all), "Bishopsgate" (which isn't a gate and hasn't a bishop in it), "Haymarket" or "Corn Market" (where you won't see any hay or corn), "Poultry" (with not a live chicken anywhere in sight) or "Threadneedle Street" where you will find, not little girls learning to sew, but the fortress-like Bank of England.

*   *   *   *   *

15th February.

When I first arrived in America I thought how

English America was; the people speak (more or less) the same language as the English, their dress, houses, food, democratic government are—with, of course, some differences—very similar. After a time I began to realise that there were some differences between England and America; I suppose that isn't surprising when we think of the many nations that have gone to the making of America. I have been told that there are more Irish in America than in Dublin, more Germans than in Hamburg, more Poles than in Warsaw, more Russians than in Kiev, more Scandinavians than in Oslo and Stockholm, twice as many British as in Manchester, and more negroes than the combined population of Ghana, Congo, Guinea, Liberia and South West Africa. And before very long it was the *differences* between England and America that struck me most. For example the American word for many things is not the same as the English one. So *curtains* are "drapes", a *holiday* is a "vacation", a *cinema* is "the movies", a *cookery book* is a "cook-book", a *label* is a "tag" and a *lift* an "elevator". Here, your *luggage* is your "baggage" and instead of *pound notes* you have "dollar bills" (which you put, not into a *note case* but into a "bill fold"). The *pavement* is the "sidewalk", *petrol* is "gasoline" (gas). *Biscuits*, if sweet, are "cookies", if plain, are "crackers"; and instead of posting a letter you "mail" it. You don't live in a *flat* but an "apartment" (you would be unlucky if you had a "flat"; it means a *puncture* in the *tyre*—which they write "tire"—of your motor-car). *Sweets* are "candy", a *tin* is a "can", the *Underground* (railway) is the "subway", and the

Englishman's *trousers* and *waistcoat* are the American's "pants" and "vest".

The Englishman, making an appointment with you, will say, for example, "I will call for you at a *quarter to eight*" or "at *half-past four*"; the American would say "at a quarter before (*or* of) eight" or "a half after four". After an Englishman has 'phoned you, he will *ring off*; after an American has "called" you, he will "hang up".

The well-mannered Englishman at table holds and keeps his knife in his right hand, his fork in his left, cuts his meat and presses his vegetables on to his fork. The well-mannered American first cuts up all his meat, then places his knife down on the right of his plate, takes his fork in his right hand and with his fork lifts the food to his mouth. He will have coffee (generally with cream) half-way through his dinner *before* the pudding (which he calls "dessert"). The Englishman drinks his coffee ("black" usually) *after* the dinner. And, of course, Americans are coffee-drinkers rather than tea-drinkers. The English (among whom tea-making is almost a religious ceremony) would be shocked at the American's idea of how tea should be made. I remember what we said about English coffee.[1] That's nothing to what English people would say about American tea. The popular method is to take a cup or a pot of hot (not necessarily boiling) water and drop into it a cotton bag with tea leaves in it. For a change they will sometimes put a pan of water on the electric stove and, just as the water gets warm, throw in a few

[1] In *Essential English*, Book I, pp. 200–1.

teaspoonfuls of tea and then pour the mixture into a tea-pot (cold, of course), pour it from there into a cup (or glass) and then drink it without turning a hair.

(*Continued on p.* 253)

THE NON-FINITES (4): **The Gerund**

The gerund looks exactly like the present participle, i.e., it is formed from a verb and ends in *-ing*. The difference is that the present participle is a verbal adjective and the gerund is a verbal noun. Here are examples:

> *Smoking* is not allowed in this carriage. Lucille likes *dancing*. *Seeing* is *believing*. Olaf is fond of *walking*. George earns his living by *selling washing*-machines.

After a preposition (like *of* or *by* in the last two sentences) the only part of the verb that can be used is the gerund.[1] The gerund often qualifies a noun just as the participle does, but note the difference in meaning between:

Participle	*Gerund*
a *dancing* girl (= a girl who is dancing or who dances)	a *dancing*-teacher (= a teacher of dancing)
a *sleeping* child (= a child who is sleeping)	a *sleeping*-carriage (= a railway carriage fitted with beds)
a *walking* doll (= a doll that walks)	a *walking* match (= a race for fast walkers)

---

[1] The *to* of the infinitive, e.g. "I want to speak *to* you", is not a preposition.

9

HOB: That reminds me of the boys who put up a notice outside their garden gate

---

NOTICE

If you are interested in water-sports, swimming, diving, floating, etc., come and see the floating match here this afternoon.

Admission 3*d*.

Some people paid their threepences and went inside, and all they saw was a match-stick floating in a saucerful of water.

MR. PRIESTLEY: They expected to see a gerund and all they saw was a participle!

Notice the difference in pronunciation. When a participle qualifies a noun, both words are stressed. When a gerund qualifies a noun, only the gerund is stressed, e.g.

Participle	*Gerund*
a sléeping chíld	a sléeping-carriage[1]
a rúnning stréam	rúnning-shoes

EXERCISES

I. *Word Study: Use the following in sentences of your own:*

actually (use also *actual*), diary (how does this differ from *dairy*?), staggering, storey (not *story*), vertical, horizontal, badge, department store, assistants (use also *assistance*),

---

[1] Note, too, that there is a hyphen between the gerund and the noun.

twist, fascinating, logical (what is the opposite ?), poultry, thread (describe how you would thread a needle), democratic (use also *autocratic*, *bureaucratic*), label, pavement, puncture, vegetable (mention six vegetables), ceremony, stove.

II. *Explain, or express differently, the following expressions from Lucille's journal, and use each in sentences of your own:*

1. under separate cover. 2. all the same. 3. It takes your breath away. 4. it is laid out regularly. 5. I couldn't help thinking. 6. fortress-like. 7. that have gone to the making. 8. a well-mannered man. 9. is nothing to ... 10. without turning a hair.

III. *Translate the following American-English sentences into British-English:*

I called Lucille to see if she was back from her vacation and would like to come out with me to dinner and the movies. She said she would love it, so I said I would come for her at a quarter before eight. I hung up, went home and changed my coat, vest and pants, put some dollar bills in my bill fold and, at half after seven, drove to Lucille's apartment. I went up in the elevator and into her apartment. I admired the new drapes; we ate one or two crackers and cookies and some candy and then went down to my automobile. I had left it (full of gas) by the sidewalk, but when I looked at it I saw I had got a flat, so we had to take a taxi.

What would (a) an Englishman, (b) an American, understand by: "I am mad about my flat" ?

IV. *Rewrite these questions in the indirect form. Begin each answer* "I asked Lucille . . ."

Example: "Have you ever been to America before ?"
I asked Lucille if (whether) she had ever been to America before.

1. Are you keeping a journal? 2. Do you think your journal will interest Mr. Priestley? 3. Did you go to the top of the Empire State Building? 4. How high is that building? 5. Have you been to Macy's department store? 6. Did you go along Fifth Avenue? 7. What do the American call biscuits? 8. Where do you think you will go next? 9. Is there a lift in your flat? 10. Can you find your way easily about New York? 11. Does New York remind you of London? 12. Do you drink tea in America?

V. *Make sentences using these expressions, followed by gerunds:*

1. I am fond of. 2. laugh at. 3. look forward to. 4. think about. 5. believe in. 6. afraid of. 7. instead of. 8. succeed in. 9. tired of. 10. interested in. 11. used to. 12. have difficulty in. 13. in the habit of. 14. in danger of. 15. reason for. 16. ashamed of.

Composition Exercises

VI. Describe briefly—as Lucille does—(*a*) how a well-mannered Englishman, (*b*) a well-mannered American uses his knife and fork, (*c*) how (according to Lucille) Americans make tea, (*d*) how you think it ought to be made.

VII. Give a page or two from your (imaginary) journal.

VIII. Write a short composition on:

(*a*) First Impressions.
(*b*) The pleasures of travel.

LESSON 25

THE AMERICAN SCENE (2)

Lucille's Journal (*continued*)

17th February.

One often hears of the Englishman's "reserve"; how he likes to "keep himself to himself"; and how on a long railway journey, with four Englishmen in the carriage, often there won't be a word spoken during the whole journey. I'm sure that wouldn't be the case in America. The Englishman thinks it is ill-mannered to ask personal questions. The American doesn't feel that at all. In the short ride between the boat on which you arrived in New York and the hotel to which you are being driven, the taxi driver will have told you all about himself, his wife and family and probably the towns in England that he was in during the war. He will inquire where you have come from, what your job is, how you like America and how long you are staying in New York. The Englishman prizes privacy, the American prefers sociability. I think this same feeling shows itself in the houses in the two countries. The Englishman's suburban house has its little garden with a hedge or a fence all round it to shut him off from his neighbours. "The Englishman's home is his castle."

The American houses have no hedges or fences separating them from the pavement or from each other. There are none of those little shut-off gardens; generally just a strip of grass with trees in it. The American in his home doesn't object to being seen by everyone—he actually likes it. And inside the house, instead of the separate hall, living-room, dining-room so typical of the English house, the American has the "open plan" house, just one large room where all the family activities (usually noisy) go on with, perhaps, a "dining recess" or a "kitchen-breakfast-room".

"But, Hank," I said to a young man I know here, "don't you sometimes want privacy, to be by yourself?" "If I want privacy," said Hank, "I go to bed."

With this sociability goes overwhelming hospitality. I don't think any door in the world is more open to the stranger than is the American's. You get taken to parties at the houses of your friends and of your friends' friends; you are invited to theatres, dinners, sports meetings, motor trips; from the first minute you are on "first name" terms with the people you meet ("Hiya Lucille, pleased to meet you"); they all show the keenest interest in your affairs and ask you to let them know if they can help you.

"Yes," said a somewhat cynical young American to me, "and by the following week they have forgotten all about you. They like new things—and they get rid of their friends as they do their cars. No one strikes up acquaintance sooner than we do, and nobody finds it harder to make a real friendship."

Well, that may be what happens to *male* visitors, but I must say the young men here, even after three or four weeks, certainly don't seem to have forgotten all about me! But I agree that they like new things, a new car every year, the latest thing in television, this year's, or, if possible, next year's, washing-machine. In England—and in France—I knew people who had lived in the same house and been in the same job for twenty, thirty, forty years, and who would hate to pull up their roots and change to something new. That's not the American way of life. They love change, they call it "the spirit of adventure", a spirit that they think is more characteristic of America than of Europe. There may be something in this. There was a very interesting remark in a book[1] (written by an Englishman, Kenneth Harris) that I read recently giving what he thought was a reason for this American characteristic. He wrote:

"We in England, and the French, the Germans, the Italians, even the Russians, have all got one thing in common—we are descended from the men who stayed behind. In the States they are descended from the folk who moved away."

And so they still like to "move away", to change homes and jobs. They seem to be constantly pulling down old and often quite beautiful houses or throwing away things merely because they are old. They have none of the Englishman's sentimental love for

[1] *Travelling Tongues*

things because they are old. I thought of that beautiful big old clock that stands in Mr. Priestley's hall. Mrs. Priestley told me that her grandfather had it made, more than a hundred years ago, for his wedding. I used to love to hear it striking twelve, though it usually did so when the hands were pointing to twenty to two! An American would throw out the old clock and have a shining new electric one. It might not be beautiful; it would have no history or "tradition"; it would certainly not be loved, and its life would be short, lasting only until a newer model came out. But as long as it lived it would strike the hour at the right time.

I happened to mention Mr. Priestley's old tweed jacket (you remember it!) to a young American. The jacket was beautifully cut and you could see at a glance that it had been made by a good tailor, but it was at least ten years old, the colour had faded and there were leather patches at the elbows; but how fond he was of it! The young American gazed at me

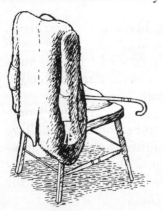

in surprise and said, "I don't want a suit to last me for more than a year. What's the point of wearing an old suit if you can afford to buy a new one? In fact," he added, "I consider your Mr. Priestley a bad citizen. America is a prosperous country; it has the highest standard of living in the world.

There is a car (sometimes two) in practically every home, the ordinary working man has his own television set; there is in his house a washing machine, a refrigerator and 'deep freeze', and probably a dish-washing machine, radios that wake you up in the morning and, at the same time, make you a cup of tea or coffee. There are 'hi-fi' gramophones or tape-recorders. Thousands of people have tennis courts or swimming pools in their gardens. They go for good holidays, cruises or visits to Europe.

"You complained because, when you ordered a steak in a restaurant here, it was so big that you had to leave three-quarters of it and it had to be thrown away." (That's quite true, it covered the whole plate. I don't think even Hob could have eaten it.) "That," he continued triumphantly, "is why we have the highest standard of living in the world. It is because you—and millions of other people—leave three-quarters of your steak uneaten that our butchers and farmers are prosperous. If Americans didn't get a new car every year (though their old one is quite good) thousands of our workpeople would be out of work. I sell clothes, and I'd hate to have three or four million Mr. Priestleys in America saying, 'This suit of mine is three years old, but I can make it last another year.' If, instead of doing that, he and a few thousands more bought a new suit—that they really don't need—I should be more prosperous. I could buy a new and better radio and a new washing machine or go for a longer holiday—and so bring prosperity to the men who make and sell radios or washing machines, to hotel keepers, to the railways or air-lines or shipping companies. America is prosperous *because* it has a 'waste economy'; and the greater the waste, the greater the prosperity."

I have a feeling that there is something wrong in this argument—but I can't see what it is!

There is the point, of course, that the wealth that most people seem to be enjoying, is not theirs in reality. These cars, refrigerators, television sets, the wife's fur coat and the husband's gold watch, the house and the furniture in it are usually bought on hire-purchase and are being paid for by monthly instalments over a number of years. A lot of these people are really living beyond their income "to keep up with the Joneses". If a slump in trade came, like the one in 1931, the greater part of these goods that the people are using could not be paid for. Even in the present period of prosperity many people have a struggle to pay these monthly instalments. There was an interesting sidelight on this struggle in a "commercial" that I heard on the radio (and here you can't help hearing commercials; every few minutes the programme is interrupted to give you one advertising something or other). This one said: "You got[1] money troubles? You being[1] pushed around because you can't pay the instalments on your car, your television, your washing machine or your home? That's bad. But don't worry, friend; I'll tell you what to do. Get right into your car and come and see me at the Omega Bank right here in your town. Just ask for the President. And this is what I'll do—I'll advance you enough money to pay

[1] Colloquial American for "Have you got . . . ?" "Are you being . . . ?"

off all those accounts, and after that you'll only have *one* monthly payment to worry about. Did I say "worry"? With the Omega Bank you won't have any worries, so just ask for me, the President."

Easy, isn't it?

You can't escape from the radio here. Radios are switched on early in the morning and go on all day as a permanent background noise. So you hear them wherever you go—in houses, cars, restaurants, taxis, railway stations. You don't pay for a licence, as you do in England, to have a radio. The money for the programmes is provided by the manufacturers of cars, soap, cigarettes, beauty preparations who "buy time" in which to advertise their products. And advertising is a fine art here; an American said to me: "The best brains in our country go into salesmanship. Any fool can *make* a thing. What takes real brains is to *sell* it when the customer has got one already and doesn't want another." The result is that when you listen to their "commercials" you are more or less told that if you use A——'s soap powder in your kitchen you will remain young and beautiful, if you smoke B——'s cigarettes, women will find you irrestible; if you use "Dento" toothpaste a rise[1] in salary is a

HAVE A SMOG!

[1] They call it a *raise*.

certainty, and by always buying Blobb's Tomato Sauce, you will sing like Maria Callas. I don't suppose anyone believes a word of it—nevertheless, people do buy this particular brand of soap powder, cigarettes, tooth-paste and sauce in large quantities.

(*Continued on p.* 263).

THE NON-FINITES (5): **Gerund and Infinitive**

One of the difficulties in learning English is that after some verbs you must use the gerund, after others you must use the infinitive, and after some you can use either.

Verbs followed by the Gerund

Some of the verbs followed by the gerund are: *avoid, dislike, enjoy, finish, mind* (= object to), e.g.

He couldn't **avoid** *meeting* them.

He **enjoys** *asking* questions but **dislikes** *answering* them.

When you have **finished** *talking*, we will continue the lesson.

Do you **mind** *passing* the salt ?

Verbs followed by the Infinitive

Verbs followed by the Infinitive are: (*a*) All the "Special" verbs, (*b*) the verbs *expect, hope, mean* (= intend), *promise, want* and certain others, e.g.

(*Special verbs*) You **ought** *to try* harder. You **must** *do* this work. I **shall** *see* him tomorrow.

(*Other verbs*) My friends **expect** *to arrive* here on Saturday and I **hope** *to meet* them at the airport. They **mean** *to stay* with us for a month. I **want** *to learn* English and I **promise** *to* work hard.

EXERCISES

I. *Word Study: Use the following in sentences of your own:*

reserve (as a noun (*three meanings*) and as as verb. What is a *reserved seat*?), ill-mannered (What is the opposite?), enquire (and *enquiry*. You will also see *inquire* and *inquiry*), privacy (use also *private*), sociability (use also *social, sociable, society, socialism*), suburban (use *suburbs*), hedge (compare *edge*), strip (compare *stripe*), activities (use also *active*), recess, overwhelming, hospitality (use also *hospitable*. Don't confuse it with *hospital!*), cynical, acquaintance (common noun and abstract. Use an example of each. What is the difference between an *acquaintance* and a *friend*?), descended (What is the opposite of *descend*?), sentimental, brand-new, tradition, obviously, patches, gaze, prosperous, refrigerator, tape-recorder, cruise, triumphantly, economy (use also *economic, economics, economical*), hire-purchase, instalments, slump (What is the opposite?), switch (noun and verb), licence (use also *license*), products (also *producer, production*), irresistible (use also *resist, resistance*).

II. *Explain or express in other words:*

1. To keep oneself to oneself. 2. personal questions. 3. to shut him off from his neighbours. 4. an open-plan house. 5. to be on first-name terms. 6. to strike up an acquaintance. 7. this is the latest thing in ... 8. people don't like to pull up their roots. 9. they have one thing in common. 10. What's the point of ... 11. a deep-freeze. 12. a waste economy. 13. keeping up with the Joneses. 14. a radio "Commercial". 15. I'll advance you money. 16. a background noise. 17. advertising here is a fine art.

III. You had the sentence about Mr. Priestley's old coat, "How fond he was of it!" This is an exclamatory sentence. *Rewrite the following sentences as exclamatory ones*.

1. America is a very big country. (What . . .!) 2. I have been very happy here. (How . . .!) 3. They seem to waste a lot of food. 4. Everyone is very hospitable here. 5. She sings beauti-fully. 6. This car goes at a great speed. 7. He has been very kind to her. 8. He has done a lot for you. 9. Her face is very pale. 10. We are glad to see you. 11. America is a country for cars.

IV. In the reading you had the words: a *dining-room*, a *washing-machine*, i.e. the gerund of the verb *to dine* and *to wash* is used like an adjective to qualify a noun. *Use the gerunds of the following verbs in the same way:*

meet, ride, wait, write, shave, live, play, swim, walk, read.

V.   *Composition Exercises*

Write a short composition on one of the following:

1. The Englishman's home is his castle.
2. "Change proves that we have the spirit of adventure." Discuss.
3. Advertisements OR: Advertising.
4. "Keeping up with the Joneses."
5. "The greater the waste, the greater the prosperity." Discuss.

LESSON 26

THE AMERICAN SCENE (3)

Lucille's Journal (*concluded*)

20th February.

What a country this is for cars! America is a nation on wheels, and I have a feeling that the American man thinks longer and more earnestly about choosing his car than choosing his wife. The words in which the makers describe cars are pure poetry. Looking through the *New Yorker* magazine I met the follow-descriptions of cars: "the car with youthful beauty that surrounds you with silent strength", "balanced beauty", "luxury reflected in every shining inch", "see its clean length knifing through clear, cool air", "jewel-bright beauty", "sculptured in steel", "There's nothing like a new car—and there's never been a new car like this. We proudly invite you to inspect it." One of the cars has a "great deep-breathing engine", the engine of another is "lean-muscled". But the advertisement I liked best showed a picture of the car, and underneath you read:

"If you know the woman who should have this car, you must admire her very much—she's gentle, strong and intensely feminine. Her sense of beauty, of the rightness of things accepts this car easily—

And because she knows and loves fine things she will have an affection for this car. If you know this remarkable women, you'd be well advised to marry her quickly. If you're lucky, you already have."

Almost every American has at least one car, and, as he doesn't believe in walking anywhere if he can go in a car, there are "drive-in" banks where you can cash a cheque without even turning off your engine, drive-in post-offices, or drive-in cafeterias where a meal is brought to you on a tray that fits neatly on to the door of your car; there is even a drive-in church.

*   *   *   *   *

One evening I was taken by a friend to a drive-in cinema about 10 miles out of the city. We set off

DRIVE-IN CINEMA

as it was growing dark and soon you saw cars coming from all directions towards a skyscraper screen that you could see more than a mile away. Then we slowly went past the box office where we reached out to pay for admission and turned along a wide drive towards the curved lines of cars, about 3,000 of them. We switched off our car lights, and attendants waved us on with electric torches to our place (about 100 yards from the enormous screen on which we could see the soundless picture moving) where there was an instrument, a loudspeaker, something like a telephone, hooked to a post. My friend unhooked the loud-speaker, fixed it inside the car, switched it on, and now the dumb figures on the screen were no longer dumb; without leaving the comfort of our car we were at a cinema performance. At the interval a comic figure on the screen announced:

"Ice cream, hot dogs,[1] soft drinks too,
    Sandwiches, coffee, all ready for you."

Car doors opened and people made their way to the refreshment room where they could get the refreshments they wanted on trays which they brought back to the cars.

At last the performance ended; a message appeared on the screen: "Please remove the loud-speaker before starting up your car", and as midnight was striking we were on the road again towards home.

*   *   *   *   *

[1] hot dogs = American term for a split roll enclosing a hot sausage spread with mustard.

I doubt whether England will adopt drive-in cinemas, but I believe they have begun to adopt another American feature, "motels", that is hotels for motorists. You find them all along the great American highways, rows of them, small one-storey buildings, something like Swiss chalets[1] or smart-looking huts, each with a brightly lighted sign at the entrance. You give your name and pay the charge at the little office, drive up to your door and park your car outside. There is no service—you don't see any attendants. The rooms are plain but clean and plea-sant and comfortable. There is a bath—or a shower— a radio (perhaps a television), towels, soap, some-times a pair of slippers or a few books by the bed. You walk down the road to a restaurant where you can get a meal, and in the morning you just step into your car and drive off.

*   *   *   *   *

The big highways are magnificent for the fast driver, and I must say I love them. But even roads like this don't always prevent accidents and I couldn't help noticing some typical American safety-signs:

> "Can your wife afford your funeral?"

> "This is God's country. Don't
> drive through it like hell."

[1] Pronounced ['ʃæliz]

> "Only *one* letter removes DANGER from
> ANGER."

And one frightening reminder, a wrecked car on a
high platform, and under it was written:

> "Three died in this.
> Your turn next?"

*   *   *   *   *

10th March.

There are, of course, wonderful shops here, but
so there are in London, Paris, Rome and a dozen
more great cities. In shop windows here I saw a
magnificent fur coat on which was a card saying,
"Earth has not anything to show more fair", a pair
of ear-rings priced at $3,000 each, a tiny bottle of
scent priced at $65. And, in contrast to all this
magnificence, bread "sprayed with bakery smell",
fish "sprayed with smell o' the sea", little pieces of
"Texas oil stone, 13,000 feet deep, 400,000,000
years old", and, perhaps the silliest of all, empty tins
from Florida labelled "filled with pure air from
Florida's coast; send one to your friends".

But the shops that are most characteristically
American are the "drug stores" and the "supermarkets". A "drug store" is not, as an Englishman
might think, a "chemist's shop", i.e., a place that

sells only—or mainly—drugs. In some of them you can buy drugs, but their main business is to sell stationery, candy, milk shakes, braces, fountain pens, ice-cream, toasters, electric clocks, doormats, paper-backed books or imitation jewellery. Every drug store has a food counter where you can sit on a high stool and have hot chocolate, Coca-Cola, orange juice, hot dogs, coffee, cakes, sandwiches or omelettes.

There are "automats" from which on putting in a coin you can get a plate of cooked ham, cooked beef or cheese,[1] or "the best hand-carved sandwich in town"—all to the constant sound of music from the "juke-boxes"[2] or "canned music" that is telephoned in.

I had already seen supermarkets in England but the ones here are vastly bigger; some covering 40,000 square feet are not uncommon, and they have huge car-parks where the cars of a thousand customers can be parked. I am told that nearly 50% of the groceries sold in America are sold in the supermarkets. As you walk to the doors they automatically open, and as you enter they automatically close after you. Inside, there are bright lights and amusing advertisements to please the children, and on the shelves there seems to be everything, all of it most attractively packed and displayed. You just help yourself as you walk (pushing a wire basket on wheels that is provided to hold the goods you want to buy). What impresses you is the enormous quantities of everything; thus

[1] American: *hamburger, beefburger, cheeseburger*.
[2] *juke-box* ['dʒuːkbɔks] = machine which plays music when a coin is put in.

one huge block of shelves will contain nothing but breakfast foods, another, equally huge, will be filled only with canned fruit or soup or beans. From thousands of cans exactly alike, a cat's smiling face proclaims the delights of "Kitcat—the food all cats love". Vast refrigerators display joints of beef, legs of lamb, packages of pink and white bacon, Maryland chickens or pork pies; you can buy twenty different kinds of bread, fifty different kinds of soap. At the exits polite assistants ("Fred" or "Hank" or "Shirley"—their names are on their white coats) will take the goods you have chosen from your wheel-basket, add up the cost, pack them into a box and take your money in payment for the goods. Then "Joe" or "Ike" will carry the box to your car.

*　　　*　　　*　　　*　　　*

18th March.

A young man I know here called Bud is at Harvard and he took me round his University. It is a wonderful place; the rooms were magnificent, beautifully lighted, sound-proofed and air-conditioned. The furniture, the carpets, the curtains might have been in a first-class hotel. There are splendid libraries and the laboratories are some of the most up-to-date and best equipped in the world. And yet—I know you'll hardly believe it of me, but it's true—I thought longingly of the beauty of those colleges at Oxford and Cambridge with their old, weather-worn stone, their oak-panelled rooms with their long bare dining-table, and above all with their lovely gardens and lawns:—they don't seem to be able to grow lawns in American Colleges!

*   *   *   *   *

20th March.

Yesterday afternoon Bud took me to a football match between Harvard and Yale. I didn't understand the game at all; it wasn't like the rugby that I had seen in France or that soccer match in England when I watched Jan play. To tell you the truth it was more like a battle than a game. But I loved the rest of the proceedings. The ground was packed with spectators—chiefly students, who yelled and shouted in chorus. There were "cheer-leaders" for Harvard and cheer-leaders for Yale. There were two bands, dozens of "drum-majors" and "drum-majorettes" — pretty girls, dressed in very short skirts, knee-high red leather boots and military-looking white jackets decorated with gold and red—who marched to a military band and danced and led the cheering. I have never seen anything like it before, but it seems to be the usual thing at football matches here.

DRUM-MAJORETTES

*   *   *   *   *

MR. PRIESTLEY: Well, that's the end of Lucille's Journal up to date, but this short letter came with it.

3rd. April.

DEAR MR. PRIESTLEY,

Next week I'm going to Washington, the capital of the U.S.A. I believe it is a lovely city, and friends here tell me I shall be seeing it just at the right time when all the cherry trees that run alongside the lake will be in full bloom making a sea of pink blossom, a wonderful, background for the magnificent monuments that the Americans have put up to their greatest sons, George Washington, Thomas Jefferson and—greatest of them all—Abraham Lincoln.

A friend says that he will get me an invitation to the White House, the home of the President. I hear, too, that there are some very gay night-clubs in Washington, so my visit won't be all "history". By the way, do you know why the White House is white? The story I was told is that in 1812 when England was at war with America (a fact which few Englishmen seem to know), the British captured the city, and some of the buildings, including the Capitol and the house of the President, were set on fire. In 1814, in order to hide the marks of the fire, the brown stone walls of the President's home were painted white—and it has been the "White House" ever since.

All good wishes,

Yours sincerely,

LUCILLE.

HOB: When my Uncle Albert was in America, an American said to him, "Did you know that the English burned Washington in 1812?" Uncle Albert said, "Well, I knew we'd burned Joan of Arc, but I didn't know we'd burned *him*."

THE NON-FINITES (6): **Gerund or Infinitive**

Verbs followed by the Infinitive or the Gerund

Some of these are: *begin, hate, learn, like, prefer, stop, forget, remember, hear, see*, e.g.

> The teacher said, "You can **begin** *writing* now"; and the children **began** *to write*.
> Hob **hates** *working* at grammar.

HOB: "I **hate** *to work* at anything!"

> At school children **learn** *reading* and *writing*.
> He is **learning** *to fly* an aeroplane.
> I **heard** him *coming* in late last night.
> I **heard** him *come* in late last night. (Infinitive without *to*.)
> I **saw** him *work/working* in the garden yesterday.

In the examples just given, it doesn't make much difference in meaning whether the gerund or the infinitive is used, but with the verbs *stop, forget, remember* there is a difference. Thus:

STOP

> "He worked for three hours and then **stopped** for half an hour *to eat* his lunch" means that he ceased work in order to eat. BUT:
> "He **stopped** *eating* while he spoke to me" means that he paused in his eating while he spoke.

FORGET

The verb *forget* with the infinitive means "fail to remember", e.g.

I am afraid that he will **forget** *to write*.

With the gerund it means "lose the memory of", e.g.

I shall never **forget** *seeing* the Swiss Alps for the first time.

REMEMBER

The infinitive used with, *remember* refers to a future action, e.g.

Please **remember** *to post* this letter before four o'clock.

The gerund used with *remember* refers to past action, e.g.

I **remember** *seeing* you at the Christmas party last year.

EXERCISES

I. *Word Study: Use each of the following in sentences:*

earnestly, luxury (use also *luxurious*. How does this differ from *luxuriant* ?), muscle (pronunciation [ˈmʌsl]. Compare with *mussel* in Book II, p. 78), lean (two meanings. Here as an adjective. Give its opposite. It can also be a verb), affection (use also *affectionate*, *affectionately*), cafeteria, screen (noun and, with different meaning, verb. Where would you find a *wind-screen* ?), box-office, torch, soundless (give six other adjectives expressing "without" by the ending *-less*), instrument, loud-speaker, dumb, interval, message, adopt, hut, smart (two meanings), danger—anger (only one letter different, but note difference in pronunciation), wrecked, tiny, spray, drug, stationery (compare *stationary*), braces (to the American "suspenders"), automatic, supermarket, huge, vast, sound-proof (use also *water-proof*, *bullet-proof*, *fool-proof*), equipped (use also *equipment*), weather-worn, yell, monument.

II. *Explain or express in other words these phrases from the lesson you have just read:*

1. You'd be well advised. 2. there's nothing like ... 3. he doesn't believe in ... 4. cash a cheque. 5. ... people made their way. 6. soft drinks. 7. to park a car. 8. a bath or a shower. 9. I couldn't help. 10. ... proclaims the delights of *Kitcat*. 11. the rooms are sound-proofed and air-conditioned. 12. I thought longingly. 13. knee-high boots. 14. trees run alongside the lake. 15. by the way.

III. *Write questions to which these could be answers. The material for the questions is in the lesson on pp. 263 to 272.*

1. I met them in the *New Yorker*. 2. It was about ten miles out of the city. 3. By taking the loud-speaker into the car and switching it on. 4. Ice cream, sandwiches, coffee and so on. 5. They are plain, but clean and pleasant and comfortable. 6. It said: "Earth has not anything to show more fair." 7. Some cover 40,000 square feet. 8. Nearly 50%. 9. in a wire basket. 10. they carry the box to your car. 11. at Harvard we went round the University. 12. She is going to Washington.

IV. *You had the sentences:*

I couldn't help *noticing* safety signs (*gerund*).
He doesn't believe in *walking* ... (*gerund*).
We invite you *to inspect* (*infinitive*).
Their business is *to sell* stationery, candy (*infinitive*).

In the following sentences use the correct form (gerund or infinitive):

1. I don't want (buy) a new car without (get) good advice.
2. Lucille remembers (visit) a drive-in cinema and hopes (stay) at a motel.
3. By (take) the loud-speaker into the car we were able (hear) the actors (speak).

4. You liked (meet) Henry; would you like (meet) his brother ?
5. There was a refreshment room for (sell) sandwiches and ice cream for anyone who wanted (buy) them.
6. As we were driving along we saw a good restaurant, so we stopped (have) dinner, and my friend stopped (say) he was hungry.
7. I enjoyed (see) the film in the open air.
8. It's no use (try) to find a place (park) your car in this street.
9. I tried to make him (understand) it was no good (get) angry.
10. I used (drive) on the left in England, but I soon got used to (drive) on the right in America.
11. Lucille didn't feel like (go) to the cinema last night and refused (go) with me, so I didn't try (make) her change her mind.
12. I should like (go) to America because I like (see) new places.

V. *Choose the right form (gerund or infinitive) in these sentences:*

1. I wish you would not keep (ask) silly questions.
2. I don't think we will refuse (help) you.
3. The motorist tried to avoid (run) over the dog.
4. I don't remember (meet) him.
5. I hope Hob will remember (bring) his book.
6. You can't afford (waste) your time.
7. Don't forget (pay) for the papers.
8. We always enjoy (come) to your house.
9. I never mind (see) a good film twice.
10. He stopped (write) while he had a cup of tea.
11. After writing for two hours he stopped (have) a cup of tea.
12. I can't help (feel) sorry for animals in a circus.
13. He went on (talk) until everyone was bored.
14. I prefer (travel) by air to (travel) by sea.
15. I would rather (travel) by air than (travel) by sea.

VI.   *Composition Exercises*

1. Discuss the advantages and the disadvantages of the drive-in cinema compared with the indoor cinema.

2. Imagine you are walking along a street of shops (in whatever town or city you like) and describe in as lively a way as you can, what you see in them.

3. What is each of the following thinking? (*a*) Hank, (*b*) Bud, (*c*) Lucille.

HANK   LUCILLE   BUD

(*Reproduced by permission of the proprietors of "Punch"*)

LESSON 27

THE AMERICAN SCENE (4)
The Greatest American

Characters—MR. PRIESTLEY, FRIEDA, OLAF, HOB

MR. PRIESTLEY: In her letter to us, Lucille spoke of Lincoln as "the greatest American of them all". I think she was right; so, as I have told you about a number of "Great Britons", I thought you might like this account of the Greatest American.

Abraham Lincoln

Abraham Lincoln is the most famous instance of the claim that Americans often make that in their country a man may rise from the lowest to the highest position in their land, "from log-cabin to White House"—for that is exactly what Lincoln did.

He was born in 1809, in a small farm in Kentucky, but while Abraham was quite young, the family moved into the wild forest land of Indiana. Here, his home was what was called a "half-faced camp", that is, a rough shelter of logs and boughs, enclosed on three sides and with the fourth side protected only by a roaring wood-fire. Though "Abe" was young he was big and strong. At eight years of age an axe was put into his hands and he worked with the rest of his family at their main task—clearing the land of trees. Of education he had hardly any. There was no public education in Indiana then; a few teachers got a living from the small fees that they charged, and Abraham went to one or two of these from time to time and learned to read and write and do simple arithmetic. "All told," he once said, "I attended school less than one year."

He grew up tall—six foot four—with huge hands and long arms, but with enormous strength in his leg, arm and chest muscles. He was considered lazy except in his desire to learn. He took a book to read while he was ploughing, and when he had no paper or slate he would lie before the fire at night practising writing and arithmetic on a piece of wood and cleaning it again by shaving the writing off with a hunting-knife.

Among the books that he read were *A Life of George Washington*, *Robinson Crusoe*,[1] and *The Pilgrim's Progress*,[2] but the only book that he owned in his youth was the Bible, and its influence is seen in all his speeches and writings.

The first big experience that opened up the

[1] By Daniel Defoe (1661–1731).
[2] By John Bunyan (1628–1688).

world for him occurred when he was nineteen. He was given a job on a river boat to go with a cargo down the Mississippi to New Orleans, a busy commercial port and the first town that he had ever seen. It was here, in the famous (or infamous) slave market, that he saw men, women and children being sold to the highest bidder, and, greatly moved, he said, "If ever I get a chance to hit that thing, I'll hit it hard."

In 1830 Abraham left his father's farm and went to Springfield, Illinois. Here he became a clerk in a store and worked hard to improve his education. He studied English Language and Literature (he developed a lasting fondness for Shakespeare, learning large portions by heart) and, in 1836, he qualified as a lawyer. A friend of Lincoln's has left an account of him at this period:

"He was very tall, awkward, and badly dressed. He generally wore an old, shabby hat (in the lining of which he often carried letters or law papers); his trousers were too short and his coat and vest too loose. He was never systematic about his papers; they piled up on his desk and work table and overflowed on to the floor. On a large envelope was written—in Lincoln's handwriting—'When you can't find it anywhere, look in this.'" (Lincoln had a very lively sense of humour).

Nevertheless, in spite of this untidiness, he was a great lawyer—not as an expert on legal matters, but as an advocate in court; he was able to present a case simply, powerfully and convincingly—mainly because he himself was completely and fiercely honest.

He had, too, entered politics and in 1832 became a candidate for the Legislature[1] of his State, Illinois; but the election was interrupted by an attack by Red Indians led by "Black Hawk". Volunteers were called for to defend the city. Lincoln volunteered and was made captain of his company. At the next election, in 1834, he was elected to the Legislature of Illinois. He soon became a force in political life and in 1847 he went as a Congressman to the national Assembly[2] in Washington. There, close to the beautiful White House where the President lived, he saw—to use his own words— "a sort of negro stable where herds of negroes were collected, temporarily kept and finally taken to Southern markets exactly like herds of horses", and his hatred of slavery hardened.

Slavery was now becoming a burning question in American politics. A great many people in the Northern states of America wanted to abolish it; a great many in the Southern states bitterly opposed abolition. The prosperity of the South was built largely on cotton growing, and the negroes were able to work in the hot steaming cotton-fields where white men could not. Abolition of slavery would, said the Southerners, mean economic ruin for them and they threat-

---

[1] i.e. the "Parliament".
[2] The National Assembly is the national Parliament.

ened that unless the North ceased its fight against slavery, the Southern states would leave the Union and form an independent "Confederacy". It was in 1860, when the storm clouds had blown up dark between North and South and feeling between them was very bitter that Lincoln was elected President of the United States. South Carolina left the Union, followed shortly after by six other states.[1] They called for "immediate, absolute, eternal separation from the North" and elected their own President, Jefferson Davis.

Lincoln was an unbending foe of slavery; he was even more strongly against the break-up of the Union. If the Union could not be preserved, the struggle for the abolition of slavery was lost. If there was no other way, he would preserve the Union by force. There was no other way. In 1862 the American Civil War between North and South began: four bitter years were to pass before it ended.

At first the war went badly for the North. They had the bigger population, the greater wealth, the more arms factories; but their soldiers were untrained, unready and unwarlike. The Southerners had great skill in riding and shooting; they were brave, gallant and well-led. Their general, Robert E. Lee, was perhaps the greatest soldier alive at the time. He was ably

---

[1] They were Mississippi, Florida, Alabama, Georgia, Louisiana, Texas. They were joined later by Virginia, N. Carolina, Tennessee, and Arkansas.

10

seconded by "Stonewall" Jackson[1] and they won a succession of brilliant victories.

In those early years the North had no soldier to compare with Lee or Jackson. But they had Lincoln. For four years he shouldered an almost unbearable burden of defeats and disasters and of disloyalty in his Cabinet by those he thought were his friends. He was saddened by the terrible slaughter on both sides, and in his personal life, by the death of his elder son and the mental illness of his wife. But he was unshaken by defeats, by sadness or disappointments. Generals failed; he appointed others. Armies fought badly; he sent them reinforcements. The people's courage was failing; his speeches revived it. He never lost courage or faith in the righteousness of his cause.

Gradually the tide turned. He appointed General Grant to take command—not without considerable opposition from the rest of the Cabinet. Grant was of humble origin, shabby in dress, rough in speech and manners, and there were many stories of his hard drinking. Lincoln knew that these stories were exaggerated and, when a member of the Government demanded that, because of his drinking, Grant should be dismissed, Lincoln replied—with a touch of

[1] His name was actually Thomas Jonathan Jackson. At the battle of Bull Run in Virginia in 1861, Jackson was Colonel of the Virginia Volunteers, and the Southern forces were almost on the point of retreat, but another officer, General Bee, shouted, "Look, there is Jackson standing like a stone wall. Stand fast with him." Inspired by Jackson's example, the Southern forces remained firm, attacked, and won a complete victory. The nickname "Stonewall" rang through Virginia, and for ever after was attached to Jackson's name.

humour that was characteristic of him—"Grant wins battles. If I knew what kind of liquor[1] he drinks I would send a barrel or so to some other of my generals."

Grant proved worthy of Lincoln's trust. Jackson had been killed in 1863, and now the armies of Grant and Sherman, Grant's second in command, were advancing everywhere. In November 1864, Sherman with an army of 60,000 men marched off from Atlanta, southwards into Georgia. For a month nothing was heard of them. Then on Christmas Day, Lincoln received a telegram from Sherman:

"I beg to offer you as a Christmas present the city of Savannah."

They had marched 300 miles, from Atlanta to the sea, all the way through enemy country. The enemy forces had been cut in half.

In January Sherman marched northwards again to where Grant was attacking Lee. Final victory could not be far away now; and now that the triumph of his policy was assured, Lincoln issued a proclamation setting free every man, woman and child in the U.S.A. Slavery was ended.

On April 9th, Lincoln received a message from Grant:

"General Lee surrendered this morning on terms proposed by myself."

and, though fighting did not cease until May 26th, the Civil War was over. Lincoln's

---

[1] liquor ['likə], here = strong drink

unconquerable spirit, his steadfast faith in his country's true destiny, his resolute leadership had won the day.

He now turned from leadership in war to reconciliation in peace, and he showed as great a nobility of spirit in reconciling former enemies for peace as he had shown in heartening his country for war. "We must not be enemies," he said. "With malice toward none, with charity for all, with firmness in the right as God gives us to see the right, let us strive to finish the work we are in; to bind up the nation's wounds, to care for him who has borne the battle and for his widow and his orphan, to do all which may achieve and cherish a just and lasting peace among ourselves and with all nations."

On April 14th, after a very busy day, the President and his wife went to see the performance of a play at Ford's Theatre in Washington.

In an inn near the theatre was a 25-year-old unsuccessful actor named John Wilkes Booth. He was a supporter of the defeated South—though he had not fought for her. As the play was going to start again after the interval, Booth entered the theatre and walked slowly towards the President's box and opened the door. The sound of a shot broke in on the play, and Booth leaped from the box on to the stage and hurried out through an exit door. Smoke was seen coming from the President's box and the theatre was filled with shouting, madly excited people. Soldiers hurried in to clear the building, and

Lincoln, shot through the head, was carried unconscious to a house across the road from the theatre, and laid on the bed. He never recovered consciousness and died next morning.

"Now he belongs to the ages."[1]

ABRAHAM LINCOLN

The Complement

FRIEDA: Excuse me, Mr. Priestley, but would you please tell me what the "Complement" of a sentence is.

MR. PRIESTLEY: Certainly, Frieda. There are some verbs that can express an idea quite fully without an object or anything else; for example:

The sun *shines*. The birds *are singing*. The crowd *cheered*.

But that is not the case with some verbs[2]; for example:

Yesterday *was*; The trees *seem*; The boy *became*; Hob *is*.

We must add something to these verbs before the sense is complete, e.g.

Yesterday was *my birthday*. The trees seem *dead*. The boy became *angry*. Hob is *asleep again*.

---

[1] It was in these words that Stanton (the War Minister in Lincoln's government), who was watching at Lincoln's bed, announced the President's death.

[2] These are called "Verbs of Incomplete Predication".

The words *my birthday*, *dead*, *angry*, *asleep again* are Complements. They are not objects; all the verbs I have used there are intransitive verbs, and intransitive verbs don't take an object. You can see the difference between a complement and an object in the following examples:

The child smelt *the flowers* (Object).
The flowers smell *sweet* (Complement).

I grow *strawberries* in my garden (Object).
The boy's face grew *pale* at the news (Complement).

PEDRO: Can't a verb sometimes have an object and also a complement?

MR. PRIESTLEY: Yes, Pedro, it can. There are a number of verbs, e.g. *make*, *call*, *find*, that can take both object and complement. Here is the pattern:

Subject and Verb	Object	Complement
They *made*	him	king
They are going to *call*	the baby	Susan
He *finds*	this work	rather difficult
The boy *set*	the bird	free
This toothache *is* nearly *driving*	me	mad

Do you all know now what is meant by a Complement?

HOB (*suddenly waking up*): One of the nicest compliments I ever heard was paid by my uncle Theophilus—you remember him, he's a professor at Camford University.[1] He has a garden

[1] Hob told the story of him in Book III, Lesson 19.

round his house in Camford and is very proud of the roses that he grows. One day he took a very pretty girl, who was paying a visit, into the garden to see his roses.

"Oh! Professor Hobdell," she said, "you have brought your roses to perfection."

"And now," said Uncle Theo, with a smile and an admiring look at her, "now I have brought perfection to my roses."

MR. PRIESTLEY: Pedro, can you put Hob right? (and that's another example of a verb taking an object and a complement).

PEDRO: Yes, I think so. There are two words both pronounced alike, (1) *Complement* (spelt with an "e") meaning "something that completes", and (2) *Compliment* (spelt with an "i") meaning "an expression of admiration or praise". You, sir, have been explaining (1) and Hob has given us an example of (2), and, if I may say so, a very good one. I think I must get a garden and grow roses so that I can make use of it!

MR. PRIESTLEY: Thank you, Pedro. I couldn't have given a better explanation myself.

EXERCISES

I. *Word Study: Use the following in sentences:*

claim (noun and verb), forest (what's the difference between a *wood* and a *forest*?), bough (note the pronunciation [bau]), fee, hire, cargo, infamous (how does this differ from *famous*?), store (use as a noun and as a verb), awkward, shabby, systematic (use also *system*), legal (what is the opposite?), advocate, present (verb. Compare pronunciation with *present* (noun or adjective), candidate, election (use also *elect*, *elector*), volunteer, abolish (use also *abolition*), eternal, "untrained, unready, unwarlike". (Here are three words showing a negative by the use of *un-*. Give six others), gallant, succession (What's the difference between *succession* and *success* ?), burden, disloyalty (give three other words made negative by *dis-*), slaughter (note the pronunciation ['slɔːtə]), reinforcements, revive, exaggerated, liquor, policy (not *police*), steadfast, destiny (Is this the same as *destination* ?), resolute, reconciliation, malice, charity, strive (use also *strife*), orphan, widow (what is the masculine form ?), achieve, cherish.

II. *Explain or express in different words the following phrases or sentences from this lesson. The words for special attention are in italics.*

1. a half-faced camp. 2. all told. 3. he was *considered* lazy. 4. the experience that opened up the world for him. 5. the highest bidder. 6. he developed a lasting fondness for Shakespeare. 7. *despite* his untidiness. 8. his hatred of slavery *hardened*. 9. slavery was becoming a *burning question*. 10. the prosperity of the South was built largely on cotton-growing. 11. The storm clouds had blown up dark between North and South. 12. Lincoln was an *unbending* foe of slavery. 13. he was ably *seconded* by Jackson. 14. Lincoln shouldered an almost unbearable burden. 15. gradually the tide turned. 16. *not without* opposition. 17. *hard* drinking. 18. on terms proposed by myself. 19. to care for him who has borne the battle. 20. a *just* and lasting peace. 21. the sound of a shot *broke in on* the play.

COMPREHENSION EXERCISE

III. *Answer the following from the pages that you have just read:*

1. What is "the claim that Americans often make" ?
2. How did teachers make a living ?

3. How did Lincoln practise writing?
4. What impressed him most on his first visit to New Orleans?
5. Describe (as a friend of Lincoln's did) Lincoln's appearance and habits as a young lawyer.
6. Why was Lincoln a good advocate in court?
7. What experience as a soldier had Lincoln before the Civil War?
8. Why were the people of the South opposed to the abolition of slavery?
9. What was the cause of the Civil War in America?
10. What, at first, were the advantages of the South, and what the advantages and disadvantages of the North?
11. What were the "almost unbearable burdens" that Lincoln had to bear? What did he do when faced with his many difficulties?
12. What sort of a man was General Grant?
13. Describe what Sherman did?
14. What did Lincoln say were his aims now the war was over?
15. Describe the scene of Lincoln's death.

IV. *Paraphrase (i.e., give in your own words) the passage from Lincoln's speech,*[1] "With malice towards none . . . all nations."

You may like to memorise this passage.

V. *Pick out the complements in the following sentences:*

1. Pedro is a student. 2. The milk tastes sour. 3. These roses smell sweet. 4. The room looks clean and tidy. 5. That is quite true. 6. The exercise seemed easy but it turned out quite difficult. 7. He went as white as a sheet. 8. That remark sounds stupid to me. 9. The man grew weaker every

[1] The Speech is known as The Second Inaugural Address.

day. 10. These shoes have worn thin. 11. They made
Cromwell Protector of England. 12. She called him a thief.
13. Lincoln set the slaves free.

VI. *Make sentences in which the complement is:*

1. a noun	2. a pronoun	3. an adjective
4. an adverb	5. a gerund	6. an infinitive
7. a phrase	8. a clause	9. a participle

VII.   *Composition Exercises*

1. Give an account in about 400–500 words of
Lincoln's life.

2. Write a short character study of Lincoln.

3. Give an account in about 400–500 words of
your country's "greatest son".

SIDELIGHTS ON LESSON 27: A Speech and a Poem.

One of the most terrible battles of the American
Civil War was fought in July 1863 at Gettysburg. In
November of that year a portion of the battlefield was
dedicated as a final resting-place for those men of
both armies who died there. The chief speech on
that occasion was given by Edward Everett, a cele-
brated orator. Lincoln was asked to "make a few
remarks". Everett's speech lasted two hours, Lincoln's for two minutes; it was over almost before the
crowd realised that it had begun. But the Gettysburg
speech[1] is now one of the world's immortal pieces of
literature. Here it is:

[1] Generally called *The Gettysburg Address.*

The Gettysburg Address

" Fourscore and seven years ago our fathers brought forth on this continent a new nation conceived in liberty and dedicated to the proposition that all men are created equal. Now we are engaged in a great civil war, testing whether that nation, or any nation so conceived and dedicated, can long endure.

" We are met on a great battlefield of that war; we have come to dedicate a portion of that field as a final resting-place for those who here gave their lives that that nation might live. It is altogether fitting and proper that we should do this. But, in a larger sense, we cannot dedicate, we cannot consecrate, we cannot hallow this ground. The brave men, living and dead, who struggled here have consecrated it far above our poor power to add or detract.

" The world will little note nor long remember what we say here, but it can never forget what they did here. It is for us, the living, rather to be dedicated here to the unfinished work which they who fought here have thus far so nobly advanced.

" It is rather for us to be here dedicated to the great task remaining before us—that from these honoured dead we take increased devotion to that cause for which they gave the last full measure of devotion; that we here highly resolve that these dead shall not have died in vain, that this nation, under God, shall have a new birth of freedom, and that government of the people, by the people, for the people, shall not perish from the earth."

Barbara Frietchie

And here is a poem, by John Greenleaf Whittier (1807–1892), an American poet who, for the greater part of his life, was engaged in the struggle to put down slavery. He describes an incident during the American Civil War when a "rebel" (i.e. Southern) force, with Lee and Stonewall Jackson, entered the Maryland town of Frederick, probably during Jackson's march to Harper's Ferry in 1862 after defeating the Northern army of General McClellan. The house of Barbara Frietchie no longer exists, but a replica[1] of it, and the flag itself, are in the museum in Frederick.

1. Up from the meadows rich with corn,
   Clear in the cool September morn,

   The clustered spires of Frederick stand,
   Green-walled by the hills of Maryland.

5. Round about them orchards sweep,
   Apple and peach tree fruited deep,

   Fair as the garden of the Lord
   To the eyes of the famished rebel horde

   On that pleasant morn of the early fall
10. When Lee marched over the mountain wall,

   Over the mountains winding down,
   Horse and foot, into Frederick town.

   Forty flags with their silver stars,
   Forty flags with their crimson bars,

---

[1] replica ['replikə] = exact copy.

15.   Flapped in the morning wind: the sun
      Of noon looked down, and saw not one.

      Up rose Barbara Frietchie then,
      Bowed with her fourscore years and ten;

      Bravest of all in Frederick town,
20.   She took up the flag the men hauled down;

      In her attic window the staff she set,
      To show that one heart was loyal yet.

      Up the street came the rebel tread,
      Stonewall Jackson riding ahead.

25.   Under his slouched hat left and right
      He glanced: the old flag met his sight.

      "Halt!"—the dust-brown ranks stood fast.
      "Fire!"—out blazed the rifle-blast.

      It shivered the window, frame and sash;
30.   It rent the banner with seam and gash.

      Quick, as it fell from the broken staff,
      Dame Barbara snatched the silken scarf;

      She leaned far out on the window-sill,
      And shook it forth with a royal will.

35.   "Shoot, if you must, this old grey head,
      "But spare your country's flag", she said.

      A shade of sadness, a blush of shame,
      Over the face of the leader came;

      The nobler nature within him stirred
40.   To life at that woman's deed and word.

      "Who touches a hair of yon grey head,
      Dies like a dog! March on!" he said.

All day long through Frederick street
Sounded the tread of marching feet:

45. All day long that free flag tossed
Over the heads of the rebel host.

And through the hill-gaps, sunset light
Shone over it with a warm good-night.

EXERCISES

I. The Gettysburg Address is not ordinary, matter-of-fact speech; it is emotional, poetic speech. The feeling, the choice of words, the position of the words lift it above everyday speech and give it power and beauty. This is noble prose; no change of words or of word order that we can make can express the feeling or thought so fully or so well, but to help you to realise the meaning, try to express in ordinary speech the following:

1. Four score and seven years ago our fathers brought forth on this continent a new nation conceived in liberty and dedicated to the proposition that all men are created equal.
2. . . . whether that nation can long endure.
3. It is altogether fitting and proper that we should do this.

4. The brave men, living and dead, who struggled here have consecrated it far above our poor power to add or detract.

5. The world will little note nor long remember what we say here.

6. It is rather for us to be here dedicated to the great task remaining before us.

7. . . . they gave the last full measure of devotion.

You may like to learn by heart some or all of this speech.

II. *Answer the following:*

1. Describe the situation of the town of Frederick or draw a picture of it.

2. Explain: "green-walled by the hills of Maryland".

3. What is meant by "horse and foot"?

4. Why was Barbara Frietchie "bravest of all in Frederick Town"? How old was she?

5. Explain: "it shivered the window".

6. What effect had Barbara Frietchie's words on Jackson?

III. *Paraphrase:*

 (*a*) Forty flags . . .
  . . . not one (lines 13–16).
 (*b*) "Shoot, . . .
  . . ." she said (lines 35, 36).
 (*c*) "Who touches . . .
  . . ." he said (lines 41, 42).

IV. *Tell in your own words the story of the poem.*

V. *You may like to learn by heart some or all of this poem.*

LESSON 28

Good-bye

SCENE: *The* PRIESTLEYS' *sitting-room*

Characters—MR. AND MRS. PRIESTLEY

MR. PRIESTLEY: Well, here we are at the end of a year's work and I'm afraid this is where we say good-bye to all our students. Olaf told me this morning that he is starting work very soon with a big business firm, the Weavewell Woollen Company.[1]

MRS. PRIESTLEY: I feel sure he will do very well in business. He's a good steady fellow.

MR. PRIESTLEY: Yes, I've no doubts about him, and I shall watch his progress with great interest.

Jan and Pedro and Olaf are all coming here today for our final meeting.

MRS. PRIESTLEY: Oh, that will be nice. I'll bake some cakes for tea; I don't suppose they get home-made cakes at their colleges.

[1] You can meet Olaf as a business man in *English Commercial Correspondence and Practice*, by C. E. Eckersley and W. Kaufmann (Longmans).

MR. PRIESTLEY: They'll like that I'm sure—and so will Hob. But I hear the students in the study. Let's join them.

Mr. Priestley's Study

MR. PRIESTLEY: Oh, Hello Jan! It's very nice to see you again, and you, Frieda, and you, Pedro, and you, Olaf.

PEDRO: Thank you, Mr. Priestley, it's very nice to be back here again.

JAN: It certainly is; we all feel as if we had come home again.

OLAF: But, of course, there's going to be a new home for you. Frieda tells me you are going to be married soon.

JAN: Yes, in six weeks time.

OLAF: That's fine. I'm sure you will be very happy. I'm very glad you've decided to go ahead even if it does mean being hard up for a year or two.

PEDRO: It's a great pity you can't get rid of that white elephant of a factory that you own.

JAN: Yes, I wish someone would buy it, or even rent it.

PEDRO: Oh well, you may get a buyer some time. I see Hob isn't here yet. He had some bright idea about it, hadn't he?

JAN: So he said, but that was quite a long time ago,[1] and I've heard no more about it. In any case, what could he do?

---

[1] See *Essential English*, Book III, Lesson 37.

FRIEDA: I wish Lucille could have come too, then when Hob comes we should all be here.

There is a ring at the door. Mrs. Priestley goes out and comes back with a telegram in her hand.

MRS. PRIESTLEY (*to her husband*): A telegram for you, Charles.

MR. PRIESTLEY (*opening the telegram*): It's from Lucille. Just listen to this:

TELEGRAM

WONDERFUL NEWS STOP   JUST SIGNED CONTRACT WITH
METRO-LION CINEMA CORPORATION INC STOP   MY
STYLE OF BEAUTY BRACKETS   THEIR WORDS BRACKETS
OFF   EXACTLY WHAT WANTED FOR BIG NEW FILM STOP
FLYING HOLLYWOOD TOMORROW STOP   ME STAR IN
YEAR STOP   ENORMOUS SALARY STOP   FILM NAME
QUOTES LUCILLE LABELLE QUOTES OFF   OPENING LONDON
NEW YORK PARIS BERLIN ROME STOP   WILL SEND
TICKETS FOR PREMIÈRE LONDON STOP   ON TOP OF WORLD
STOP   LOVE LUCILLE

PEDRO, FRIEDA, JAN, OLAF (*together*): Well done, Lucille! Isn't it wonderful! We must make a party for the London première. An Essential English film star!

MRS. PRIESTLEY: I always knew Lucille would do something unusual.

(*Enter* HOB *excitedly.*)

HOB: Jan, he will buy it for £20,000! He's just told me.

JAN: What on earth are you talking about? Who'll buy what?

HOB: Uncle Albert will buy your factory. I told you I had an idea about it. Well, I talked to him and explained it was just the sort of place he needed. He wasn't sure about it at first but he's just got the contract to supply the whole British Army, Navy and Air Force with sausages. Moreover, every passenger in every dining-car on every train on all the British Railways is going to have the chance at every meal to get Hobdell's sausages. So a new factory, all ready-built, with four square miles of land round it for the pigs is exactly what he needs.

JAN: But I told you there is no railway line near it.

HOB: That doesn't matter. British Railways will build one.

JAN: And there isn't a good road there.

HOB: That doesn't matter either. As they are to get the sausages, the British Government will make one. Now, will you sell it to him for £20,000?

JAN: Will I? You bet I will! What do you say, Frieda?

FRIEDA: Hob, you are the fairy godmother that makes all dreams come true.

PEDRO: My congratulations, Hob! You certainly deserve them.

HOB: I've done a bit of good business for myself too. Uncle Albert is going to put me in the new factory to learn the business of making and selling Hobdell's sausages.

MR. PRIESTLEY: Well done, Hob. I'm sure you'll make

a success of that. I can see every pound of
sausages going out with a joke on the wrapping.

HOB: That's an idea! Well, Jan and Frieda, that's my
wedding present to you. You know it's a funny
thing that when a fellow hasn't anything in the
world to worry about he goes and gets married.
However, I wish you all good wishes, and, as the
fairy godmother in the theatre says on these
occasions as the curtain falls, "Bless you, my
children."

EXERCISES

1. *Write Lucille's telegram in the form of a letter.*
2. *A short story called, "The Fairy Godmother".*
3. *A composition: "What I would do if I had £20,000".*

GOOD-BYE

PRONOUNCING VOCABULARY

The vocabulary contains those words used in Book IV which had not occurred in Books I, II and III of *Essential English*.

abolish [əˈbɔliʃ]
absolute [ˈæbsəluːt]
achieve [əˈtʃiːv]
advocate (n.)
　　　　[ˈædvəkit]
advocate (v.)
　　　　[ˈædvəkeit]
affection [əˈfekʃn]
agony [ˈægəni]
ahead [əˈhed]
alike [əˈlaik]
amusement
　　　[əˈmjuːzmənt]
appeal [əˈpiːl]
applaud [əˈplɔːd]
approach [əˈproutʃ]
approval [əˈpruːvl]
arch [ɑːtʃ]
archery [ˈɑːtʃəri]
area [ˈɛəriə]
argue [ˈɑːgjuː]
arise [əˈraiz]
arrive [əˈraiv]
article [ˈɑːtikl]
assistant [əˈsistnt]
assure [əˈʃuə]
attractive
　　　[əˈtræktiv]
automatically
　　　[ɔːtəˈmætikli]
awkward [ˈɔːkwəd]
axe [æks]

badge [bædʒ]
banquet [ˈbæŋkwit]
bark [bɑːk]
barracks [ˈbærəks]
barrel [ˈbærəl]
base [beis]
beneath [biˈniːθ]
bitter [ˈbitə]
bless [bles]
blizzard [ˈblizəd]
block [blɔk]
blossom [ˈblɔsəm]
border [ˈbɔːdə]
born [bɔːn]
brave [breiv]
breach [briːtʃ]
broom [bruːm]
burial [ˈberiəl]

cafeteria
　　　[kæfiˈtiəriə]
caretaker [ˈkɛəteikə]
cast [kɑːst]
character [ˈkæriktə]
charity [ˈtʃæriti]
cheap [tʃiːp]
cherish [ˈtʃeriʃ]
clay [klei]
coarse [kɔːs]
collapse [kəˈlæps]
compliment
　　　[ˈkɔmplimənt]

complimentary
　　　[kɔmpliˈmentri]
conduct (n.)
　　　　[ˈkɔndəkt]
conduct (v.)
　　　　[kənˈdʌkt]
conscience [ˈkɔnʃəns]
consent [kənˈsent]
contract (n.)
　　　　[ˈkɔntrækt]
contract (v.)
　　　　[kənˈtrækt]
corporal [ˈkɔːpərəl]
couple [ˈkʌpl]
crack [kræk]
crawl [krɔːl]
creature [ˈkriːtʃə]
credit [ˈkredit]
crime [kraim]
cruise [kruːz]
crush [krʌʃ]
crust [krʌst]
cry [krai]
curl [kəːl]
curve [kəːv]
cynical [ˈsinikl]

darling [ˈdɑːliŋ]
debt [det]
deceive [diˈsiːv]
deep [diːp]
defy [diˈfai]

301

delicious [di'liʃəs]
deliver [di'livə]
demand [di'ma:nd]
democratic [demə'krætik]
desertion [di'zə:ʃn]
deserve [di'zə:v]
desire [di'zaiə]
despise [dis'paiz]
destination [desti'neiʃn]
device [di'vais]
dip [dip]
disaster [di'za:stə]
disease [di'zi:z]
dismiss [dis'mis]
distance ['distəns]
dive [daiv]
double ['dʌbl]
drain [drein]
drown [draun]
drug [drʌg]
dull [dʌl]
dumb [dʌm]

eagle ['i:gl]
economy [i'kɔnəmi]
edge [edʒ]
edition [i'diʃn]
editor ['editə]
efficient [i'fiʃnt]
elaborate [i'læbərit]
elbow ['elbou]
eldest ['eldist]
electricity [ilek'trisiti]
emotional [i'mouʃənl]

employ [im'plɔi]
encourage
endure [in'kʌridʒ]
[in'djuə]
ensure [in'ʃuə]
enterprise ['entəpraiz]
entertain [entə'tein]
enthusiasm [in'θju:ziæzm]
establishment [is'tæbliʃmənt]
eternal [i'tə:nl]
exact [ig'zækt]
exaggerate [ig'zædʒəreit]
exchange[iks'tʃeindʒ]
expense [ik'spens]
explode [iks'ploud]
explore [iks'plɔ:]
extraordinary [iks'trɔ:dinri]
extreme [iks'tri:m]

fate [feit]
favour ['feivə]
fee [fi:]
fence [fens]
fever ['fi:və]
fishing-rod ['fiʃiŋrɔd]
flatter ['flætə]
flee [fli:]
flow [flou]
forthcoming [fɔ:'θkʌmiŋ]
fortitude ['fɔ:titju:d]
founder ['faundə]

fuel ['fjuəl]
funeral ['fju:nrl]
furious ['fjuəriəs]
furnish ['fə:niʃ]

gallant ['gælənt]
genius ['dʒi:niəs]
glacier ['glæsjə]
glimpse [glimps]
godmother ['gɔdmʌðə]
goose [gu:s]
gradual ['grædjuəl]
gratitude ['grætitju:d]
greedy ['gri:di]
grotesque [grou'tesk]
ground [graund]
grumble ['grʌmbl]

hardship ['ha:dʃip]
harness ['ha:nis]
harsh [ha:ʃ]
harvest ['ha:vist]
hatch [hætʃ]
hedge [hedʒ]
hike [haik]
hire [haiə]
hook [huk]
horizontal [hɔri'zɔntl]
host [houst]
humble ['hʌmbl]
hurricane ['hʌrikən]
hut [hʌt]

immortal [i'mɔ:tl]
infant ['infənt]

injury ['indʒəri]

inquire (enquire)
  [in'kwaiə]

inspiration
  [inspi'reiʃn]

inspire [in'spaiə]

instalments
  [in'stɔ:lmənts]

invalid ['invəli:d]

involve [in'vɔlv]

issue ['isju:]

journal ['dʒə:nl]

kitchen ['kitʃin]

knit [nit]

labour ['leibə]

lack [læk]

lad [læd]

lead (v.) [li:d]

lean (adj.) [li:n]

lettuce ['letis]

liberty ['libəti]

licence ['laisəns]

limit ['limit]

lining ['lainiŋ]

lonely ['lounli]

loose [lu:s]

lounge [laundʒ]

lump [lʌmp]

luxury ['lʌkʃəri]

mad [mæd]

magic ['mædʒik]

malice ['mælis]

manufacture
  ['mænju'fæktʃə]

mean [mi:n]

mental ['mentl]

military ['militri]

model ['mɔdl]

moor [muə]

motto ['mɔtou]

mould [mould]

muscle ['mʌsl]

mustard ['mʌstəd]

neglect [ni'glekt]

nervous ['nə:vəs]

nice [nais]

nightingale
  ['naitiŋgeil]

nose [nouz]

oblige [ə'blaidʒ]

original [ə'ridʒinl]

orphan ['ɔ:fn]

oven ['ʌvən]

overwhelmed
  [ouvə'welmd]

panelled ['pænld]

panic ['pænik]

patch [pætʃ]

pathos ['peiθɔs]

patient ['peiʃnt]

pavement
  ['peivmənt]

penalty ['penəlti]

performance
  [pə'fɔ:məns]

picturesque
  [piktʃə'resk]

pile [pail]

plaster ['plɑ:stə]

plum [plʌm]

policy ['pɔlisi]

pony ['pouni]

post [poust]

poultry ['poultri]

poverty ['pɔvəti]

president
  ['prezidnt]

private ['praivit]

privilege ['privilidʒ]

problem ['prɔbləm]

proceedings
  [prə'si:diŋs]

produce (n.)
  ['prɔdju:s]

produce (v.)
  [prə'dju:s]

profit ['prɔfit]

proportion
  [prə'pɔ:ʃn]

prosperous
  ['prɔspərəs]

protest (n.)
  ['proutest]

protest (v.)
  [prə'test]

puncture ['pʌŋktʃə]

rat [ræt]

recent ['ri:sənt]

reception
  [ri'sepʃn]

reconcile ['rekənsail]

reform [ri'fɔ:m]

refuse (n.) ['refju:s]

regain [ri'gein]

register ['redʒistə]

regulations [regju:'leiʃnz]

reinforcements [ri:in'fɔ:smənts]

rent [rent]

reserve [ri'zə:v]

resolute ['rezəlu:t]

responsible [ri'spɔnsibl]

revive [ri'vaiv]

reward [ri'wɔ:d]

rogue [roug]

root [ru:t]

row (n.) [rou]

rude [ru:d]

sacred ['seikrid]

saddle ['sædl]

salary ['sæləri]

sale [seil]

scene [si:n]

scone [skɔn]

scorn [skɔ:n]

scoundrel ['skaundrl]

scrape [skreip]

scream [skri:m]

screen [skri:n]

seldom ['seldəm]

sentiment ['sentimənt]

sentry ['sentri]

serpent ['sə:pənt]

shabby ['ʃæbi]

shadow ['ʃædou]

shower ['ʃauə]

shrewd [ʃru:d]

shy [ʃai]

sick [sik]

sidelight ['saidlait]

slaughter ['slɔ:tə]

sledge [sledʒ]

slide [slaid]

slump [slʌmp]

smart [smɑ:t]

soak [souk]

solemn ['sɔləm]

sonnet ['sɔnit]

sprain [sprein]

spray [sprei]

stable ['steibl]

stagger ['stægə]

stain [stein]

stale [steil]

steadfast ['stedfəst]

stern [stə:n]

stile [stail]

sting [stiŋ]

stool [stu:l]

storey ['stɔ:ri]

storm [stɔ:m]

stout [staut]

strain [strein]

straw [strɔ:]

stride [straid]

strip [strip]

strive [straiv]

stuff [stʌf]

suburban [sə'bə:bn]

suck [sʌk]

superintendent [s(j)u:pərin'tendənt]

supreme [s(j)u:'pri:m]

survivor [sə'vaivə]

suspect (v.) [səs'pekt]

sweat [swet]

sweep [swi:p]

switch [switʃ]

sympathise ['simpəθaiz]

talent ['tælənt]

tape recorder ['teip rikɔ:də]

task [tɑ:sk]

temper ['tempə]

tempt [tempt]

thaw [θɔ:]

throw [θrou]

thus [ðʌs]

tolerance ['tɔlərəns]

torch [tɔ:tʃ]

toss [tɔs]

tour [tuə]

translate [trɑ:ns'leit]

tray [trei]

treason ['tri:zn]

treasure ['treʒə]

treat [tri:t]

trial ['traiəl]

triumph ['traiəmf]

tunnel ['tʌnl]

tweed [twi:d]

tyrant ['taiərnt]

tyre ['taiə]

underrate ['ʌndə'reit]

uniform ['ju:nifɔ:m]

vacant ['veiknt] vote [vout] wit [wit]

vast [vɑːst] within [wi'ðin]

ventilation warn [wɔːn] workhouse

    [venti'leiʃn] weapon ['wepən]   ['wəːkhaus]

vertical ['vəːtikl] whereabouts wound [wuːnd]

vitality [vai'tæliti]   ['wɛərəbauts] wrapping ['ræpiŋ]

vivid ['vivid] whereas [wɛər'æz]

volunteer [vɔlən'tiə] winding ['waindiŋ] yell [jel]

PRONUNCIATION GUIDE TO PROPER NAMES

THIS list gives the pronunciation of the names used in this book that might present difficulty.

Agonistes [æɡə'nistiːz] Holborn ['houbən]

Areopagitica [æriɔpə'dʒitikə] Irene [ai'riːni]

Austen ['ɔstin] Jacobite ['dʒækəbait]

Berkeley ['bɑːkli] Jan [jæn]

Brontë ['brɔnti] Leigh [liː]

Bunyan ['bʌnjən] Lincoln ['liŋkən]

Cambridge ['keimbridʒ] Lochiel [lɔ'xiːl]

Carlisle [kɑː'lail] London ['lʌndən]

Cavalier ['kævəliə] Macaulay [mə'kɔːli]

Chatham ['tʃætəm] Mackintosh ['mækintɔʃ]

Crewe ['kruː] Maclean [mə'klein]

Crimea [krai'miə] Micawber [mi'kɔːbə]

Culloden [kə'lɔdn] Naseby ['neisbi]

Defoe [də'fou] Ophelia [ou'fiːljə]

Derby ['dɑːbi] Priestley ['priːstli]

Devizes [di'vaiziz] Roger ['rɔdʒə]

Edinburgh ['edinbərə] Satan ['seitən]

Frieda ['friːdə] Shrewsbury ['ʃruːzbəri]

Gadshill ['gædzhil] Stirling ['stəːliŋ]

Galileo [gæli'leiou] Stuart ['stjuət]

Gettysburg ['getizbəːg] Tewkesbury ['tjuːksbəri]

Giles [dʒailz] Thames [temz]

Guinea ['gini] Warwick ['wɔrik]

Hereford ['herifəd] Worcester ['wustə]

MAP OF PLACES MENTIONED IN *Essential English* BOOK IV

UNIVERSITY OF CAMBRIDGE

LOCAL EXAMINATIONS

Lower Certificate in English

ENGLISH COMPOSITION AND LANGUAGE

(Two hours and a half)

Three *questions are to be answered:* **one** *from* A, **one** *from* B, *and* **all four** *parts of question* 7 *in* C.

Care must be given to spelling, punctuation, and paragraphing, and you must obey the instructions about the length of your answers to A *and* B.

A.

Write a letter of between 80 and 100 words in length on **one** of the following subjects; you should make the beginning and ending like those of an ordinary letter:

1. Explain to a friend living in another country the meaning of one of your national proverbs and give one example of its application:

2. A cousin with whom you have arranged to go on holiday in December writes to tell you that his (or her) leave is postponed until January. Answer the letter, telling him (or her) what new arrangements you are able to make for the holiday.

3. Give instructions to a friend on the care of an animal or bird which you have left in your friend's charge during your absence from home.

B.

Write a composition on **one** of the following subjects; the length should be between 250 and 350 words:

4. Describe your impressions of some market or bazaar with which you are familiar.

5. If you had the choice, would you prefer to live in an ancient or in a modern town ? Give reasons for your preference.

6. An English friend has recently been spending a holiday in your country. Write an account of the ways in which you entertained him (or her) at your home or on sight-seeing expeditions, taking care to mention your friend's reactions to these experiences.

C.

7. Read carefully the following passage and answer the questions (i), (ii), (iii), and (iv).

In the early days of British railways, travelling by train was a novel and adventurous experience, and, for third-class passengers at any rate, attended by considerable discomfort. First-class passengers were provided with closed compartments, and some who could afford the extra expense would travel in their own private coaches placed upon railway 5 wagons. But their less fortunate fellow-travellers were packed into open carriages, where they were exposed to the inclemencies of the weather and to the smoke and cinders from the engine. Judged by modern standards, journeys were slow and tedious.

Intending passengers, having completed what would now be regarded as needless formalities to obtain their tickets, viewed the moment of departure with a mixture of dread and excitement. When the time came for boarding the train, the hearts of some failed them and they would refuse to proceed. Others faced the dangers and unknown terrors of the railroad with a feeling of reckless daring. Once on their way, passengers had little to do but look at the scenery and think of the risks they were taking. When a viaduct was crossed, they trembled at the thought of being so high above ground; and when the train plunged into a tunnel, they imagined possible consequences varying from a severe cold to a living burial. Occasionally, a train coming from the opposite direction would be passed, to the astonishment and often the alarm of the passengers. But this did not happen very often, as trains were few and far between. This infrequency lessened the chance of accident, for there was no system of signals, and thus safety was secured at the cost of inconvenience. When at last they safely reached their destination, the passengers dispersed, pleased with the novelty of the journey, but relieved at escaping the perils which it involved.

(i) Choose **six** of the following words or phrases, and give for each another word or phrase of similar meaning to that in which the word is used in the passage:

attended by considerable discomfort (line 3);

tedious (line 9);   needless formalities (line 11);
moment of departure (lines 11 and 12);   boarding the train (line 13);
astonishment (line 21);   few and far between (line 22);
destination (line 25);   dispersed (line 25).

(ii) Choose **five** of the following words, and give for each another word or phrase opposite in meaning to that in which the word is used in the passage:

adventurous (line 2);   refuse (line 14);   reckless (line 15);
severe (line 19);   occasionally (line 20);   lessened (line 23);
safety (line 24);   novelty (line 26).

(iii) Give short answers to **four** of the following questions, using one complete sentence for each answer:

    (*a*) What discomforts had third-class passengers to endure?
    (*b*) In what respect were first-class passengers more fortunate?
    (*c*) Why did some passengers give up their intention to travel?
    (*d*) How did passengers occupy themselves on the journey?
    (*e*) What were the passengers afraid would happen to them when the train entered a tunnel?
    (*f*) Why were accidents comparatively few?

(iv) Explain simply in your own words the reasons for the *dread* and *excitement* of travellers at the thought of a journey by rail. Do not use more than 80 words.

INDEX

The figures in heavy type are for exercises.

309